Floating City

Hustlers, Strivers, Dealers, Call Girls and Other Lives in Illicit New York

SUDHIR VENKATESH

ALLEN LANE
an imprint of
PENGUIN BOOKS

ALLEN LANE

Published by the Penguin Group
Penguin Books Ltd, 80 Strand, London WC2R ORL, England
Penguin Group (USA) Inc., 375 Hudson Street, New York, New York 10014, USA
Penguin Group (Canada), 90 Eglinton Avenue East, Suite 700, Toronto, Ontario, Canada M4P 2Y3
(a division of Pearson Penguin Canada Inc.)
Penguin Ireland, 25 St Stephen's Green, Dublin 2, Ireland (a division of Penguin Books Ltd)
Penguin Group (Australia), 707 Collins Street, Melbourne, Victoria 3008, Australia
(a division of Pearson Australia Group Pty Ltd)
Penguin Books India Pvt Ltd, 11 Community Centre, Panchsheel Park, New Delhi – 110 017, India
Penguin Group (NZ), 67 Apollo Drive, Rosedale, Auckland 0632, New Zealand
(a division of Pearson New Zealand Ltd)
Penguin Books (South Africa) (Pty) Ltd, Block D, Rosebank Office Park,
181 Jan Smuts Avenue, Parktown North, Gauteng 2193, South Africa

Penguin Books Ltd, Registered Offices: 80 Strand, London WC2R ORL, England

www.penguin.com

First published in the United States of America by The Penguin Press,
a member of Penguin Group (USA) LLC 2013
First published in Great Britain by Allen Lane 2013
001

Copyright © Sudhir Venkatesh, 2013

The moral right of the author has been asserted

Printed in Great Britain by Clays Ltd, St Ives plc

A CIP catalogue record for this book is available from the British Library

ISBN: 978–0–241–00275–9

www.greenpenguin.co.uk

To Amanda, a forever love

CONTENTS

FLOATING CITY

CHAPTER 1

WHEN WORLDS COLLIDE

I arrived at the gallery early, nervous and excited. Shine was coming into my world.

For five years, ever since arriving in New York City in 1997, I had been trying to understand the city's underground economy, the little-known world of shadows where people hid income, broke laws, and found an endless number of creative ways to make a buck. The technical term for my vocation is "ethnographer," which is a fancy word for a sociologist who spends a great deal of time watching people in their everyday situations—hanging out, to be precise, as opposed to using a survey or asking questions like a journalist. I was committed to the idea that time itself made a difference. Time to see the things that people might ordinarily hide, to hear them say the things they might ordinarily be ashamed of, to give them the sense of safety they need to reveal the things they fear, to build up bonds of trust. Ten years with Chicago's crack gang became the subject of my previous book, *Gang Leader for a Day.*

Now the challenge was the same: I needed a way *in*.

That was Shine. An accomplished Harlem crack dealer when I first met him, he'd been trying to expand into new markets as the crack business slowed. That meant going to Midtown and Wall Street, the Village and the Upper East Side. As I followed his adventures across society's boundaries, I met a huge variety of people making a living outside the margins of the legal world—prostitutes, pimps, madams, adult filmmakers, immigrant wranglers, and a thousand varieties of middlemen taking their little piece of the action. Sometimes this became a formal study, as when I got a grant to research street markets in Harlem or interviewed more than 150 prostitutes as part of a collaboration with the Urban Justice Center, and sometimes I came away with little more than a tantalizing sense that things connected in ways I could not yet see. But the most fascinating and moving development of all was when Shine began meeting people I knew in my normal life—when the crossing of boundaries went from "interesting subject" to painful reality.

The party was already jumping when I arrived. Inside the big white loft, lumber and scrap metal and giant wrecking balls seemed to be strewn about aimlessly. It looked like an abandoned construction site, not art, although it's possible that a decade of researching crime and poverty had made me a bad audience for this sort of thing.

Across the room, I saw Shine's cousin Evalina. I had known her for a few years. In my study of illegal economies, Evalina always seemed to pop up in surprising places. Short but voluptuous and always full of zesty energy, she had worked for Shine in high school, then ran away to the West Coast to find herself. After getting arrested for car theft and shoplifting, she finally came back to New York, where Shine let her sell cocaine again on the condition that she go back to school. Eventually she'd found her way to photography and then sculpture. She had a piece in tonight's show. I was beginning to think it might not be a bad idea to start following her adventures too.

"Isn't this exciting?" she said, coming up to me. "Don't you love all this crazy stuff?"

"Uh, yeah, exciting," I said. "Congratulations on getting into the show."

She smiled and seemed very happy, but I couldn't help thinking that she was trying a little bit too hard. Like me, she stood out in this sea of white faces. I knew from Shine that she was smitten with the art world of Soho and Chelsea and someday hoped to own a gallery of her own. In the meantime he was letting her keep 30 percent of every sale that she could make downtown. Evalina loved being able to accommodate her fabulous new friends, but she wasn't always so smart about getting their money up front. This was, in fact, one of the principal reasons Shine was coming to the gallery tonight. If he was going to survive in this new territory, he told me, he was going to have to find a way to make these damn artists pay up.

There he was now, standing in the doorway in his jeans, hoodie, and white high-top sneakers. He paused to scan the horizon, as any salesman would. He looked confident, tall, handsome—and completely out of place.

With three people of color in the room, this was now officially the most "integrated" gathering I'd ever seen in Soho.

Shine hesitated for a moment. Maybe it was a moment's doubt; I can't be sure. Then he strolled up to a clump of wrecking balls that floated in midair courtesy of invisible strings. Painted a sickly green and black, they were big enough for a large man to hide behind.

I slid up next to him. "Some strange stuff."

"Really? You think so?"

I rolled my eyes.

He thought for a moment, looking at the huge floating balls. "I think they're cool."

In the last five years, I had seen him nurse his bruised knuckles after a beatdown, care for a troubled relative, convince young men to take on the risks of the crack trade, and everything in between. Few things he could do would surprise me. But this surprised me. Was he putting me on? "Really? You think *that* thing is cool?"

He nodded. "Could be a disease or just some soap bubbles—

you know, like the kind you used to blow when you were a little kid."

Smiling, he warmed to the idea. "It could make you happy, or it could kill you. Yeah, this shit's cool. This dude gets it."

I felt a little bit annoyed. The big Harlem drug kingpin also had to be the master of this alien place? But I stifled the feeling. I had been at Shine's side when he began to make his first forays out of Harlem down to the bars of Wall Street and Soho. I knew how much courage it took, how much careful strategic analysis, how much *vision*. I had known a lot of drug dealers and none had ever been so eager to cross boundaries. If you looked at it in a certain way, Shine was an ambitious young American chasing a dream and fighting hard to overcome a mountain of obstacles. Instead of being annoyed, I should have been making notes about his adaptive genius.

Shine was not the only urban explorer I was watching, however. From various perches in the underground economy and among the wealthy young, I could see the forces of globalization and urban development transforming every New York neighborhood. In Hell's Kitchen, Rudy Giuliani's ambitious cleanup had brought in tourist dollars and whirlwind gentrification. In Midtown, multinational corporations were building new headquarters. On Wall Street, the financial services sector was booming with an energy that seemed almost manic. All over the city, middle- and upper-class people were beginning a historic migration back from the suburbs. All of this was visible to the naked eye and much celebrated in the media. But people in the underground were on the move too, and these equally enormous changes seemed to be happening without comment or notice. The waves of gentrification sent thousands of underclass strivers in search of their own new markets and new places to work. From South Asian porn store managers and Nigerian taxi drivers in Hell's Kitchen to ambitious Latina street prostitutes on the Lower East Side and even high-end call girls on the Upper East Side, the rapid change roiling this global city was creating new winners and new losers as far as the eye could see.

The turbulence hinted of the economic bubble and crash to come, but much of it seemed hard to pin down. The vast invisible continent of America's subterranean economy was shifting in a way that seemed to portend some great change, and the outcome was anybody's guess.

In this context, Shine's encounter with modern art felt like a sign. I was no longer in a Midwestern city where boundaries and borders of both social groups and neighborhoods were durable, unlikely to change no matter what forces threatened them. Chicago celebrated itself for being a "city of neighborhoods," which meant that it was also a place of systematic social and racial segregation. This had good points and bad points. Everyone had their hood and people took pride in both protecting their turf and becoming involved. Even the underground economy was local. Whether it was for babysitting, drugs, or a loan, most people in Chicago did their under-the-table deals with neighbors. It was almost inconceivable for one of my ghetto crews to cross paths with my economic peers in Hyde Park or the University of Chicago. A popular local catchphrase said it all: "Don't make no waves, don't back no losers." I had assumed that was how all cities worked. But now the stability of Chicago was behind me, at a time when the stability of the rest of America seemed increasingly shaky too. Maybe New York was pointing at America's future.

But where was it pointing, exactly?

A new world of permeable borders beckoned. The idea of *bricolage* kept coming to me, the art of combining fragments of existing things to make a new order. Maybe I was beginning to see the outlines of a new pattern myself, a fresh take on how the criminal underworld interacts with the mainstream world to make the world of the future.

At that moment, with Shine and I still standing in front of the giant green-and-black balls, I heard a woman's voice call out from the middle of the room. "Hey! Sudhir!"

It was Analise, a woman I knew from the elite subculture of wealthy young New Yorkers, many recent graduates of Harvard and Yale, who were taking over their parents' charitable foundations. She was brunette tonight, slender and lovely in that elegant offhand way that seems to come naturally to rich young women.

For a moment, my brain shut down. Once, when I was doing an interview with a street prostitute in a seedy bar in Hell's Kitchen, a pair of my students wandered in the door. An awkward hello followed before I could ditch them and get back to the interview. Another time, during a study of sex workers in strip bars, I saw a couple of former students, one working as a stripper and the other as a bartender. For me, there was no shame in those encounters. Hanging out in bars and strip clubs is my job.

But this was Analise, America's daughter.

Here I should explain. Everyone comes to his work with a given perspective, and mine begins with that Indian-American kid growing up in California. I was fascinated with everything American, from the grandchildren of Southern black slaves who'd ended up in Chicago projects to the South Asian immigrant cab drivers making it in New York the way the Italians and Irish had done before them. Born to a family that could trace its roots back to the Pilgrims, Analise was as American as they come. She was one of the fortune-kissed beautiful people born to private foundations and charity balls, to horses and private schools, to summers in Maine and skiing in Switzerland. Each time I saw her, she always seemed like a new person, full of mad adventures and intense emotions. If she also had the disconcerting habit of treating bartenders and taxicab drivers like her personal valets, it was hard to dislike her for it—her elitism had no malice. It was innate. That's what fascinated me.

Now I was worried. In the previous six months I had seen Analise at a party and another gallery opening, and both times she had taken me aside and talked to me with the manic enthusiasm and frequent sniffles I had come to associate with heavy cocaine users. That was bad enough, something I hoped would not last forever. But tonight I was in the company of one of Harlem's leading cocaine dealers, and I really didn't want to be responsible for handing America's daughter the perfect drug connection.

I took a quick look around, didn't see Shine anywhere near, felt relief. Analise was coming over to me, smiling and spilling a drink in her hand.

"Wow, didn't expect to see you here," she said. "You know the Carter One?"

"The who?"

They were twins, she said, Carter One and Carter Two. Carter One was her friend Mindy. "Their family owns the building." She waved a hand to take in the show. "Cool, no?"

Just at that moment, Shine came around an artwork. "Sorry, man. I didn't see you," he said.

I stood there for what felt like an hour. *Should I introduce them?* I wondered.

Analise figured it out before I could muster myself. She held out her hand. "You're Sudhir's friend? I'm Analise."

"Shine," he said.

They grinned at each other as if something very amusing was happening. Shine had heard me talk about how fascinated I was by the world of privileged white kids, and though I'd never mentioned Shine specifically, Analise knew I was interested in the lives of high-level drug traffickers who were adjusting to changes in the market for crack cocaine. Although I still hadn't committed to a formal study, I had been exploring the idea of drawing a contrast between the neighborhood gangs who sold drugs in Chicago and the independents like Shine who moved around New York. Now she seemed to be studying him with avid interest, following his eyes to a large nostalgic photograph of a house and backyard. I hoped she wouldn't ask him to talk about black people or how it "felt" to grow up as a thug. Analise wasn't usually that insensitive—on the contrary, she had a basic kindness that I found touching—but with her eyes so bugged out and her energy crackling, my mind was racing ahead to the worst possibilities.

"That picture is awful, don't you think?" Analise said, turning her body away from me and toward Shine.

"He should have taken it from the inside," Shine said.

She seemed surprised. "Why do you say that?"

"Because of the title. *What I Saw.*"

She chuckled. "Yeah, but it still sucks."

"I didn't say it was good."

They began looking at the art together, stopping at a large furry doll. "That's sexy."

"I'd buy her," Shine affirmed. I saw cheap fur glued to a beanbag. What they saw, I had no idea.

Already, they were a conspiracy of two. I felt about as useful as a plant in the corner.

Turning her attention to some pink puffballs by the same artist, Analise laughed. "She hasn't gotten laid in a while."

"I think she's just unhappy," Shine said.

I felt compelled to object. What supported their instant mutual conclusion that the artist was a woman? As far as I could see, nothing beyond clichéd assumptions about the color pink. "How do you know it's a girl?" I demanded.

"Of course it's a girl," Analise said.

"It's no dude," Shine agreed.

Their confidence defeated me. How had they formed such a rapid alliance? Were they performing for me?

Before they could move to the next masterpiece, Evalina appeared. "You guys made it!" She reached out and gave Shine a big kiss and squeezed my hand, then turned to Analise. "Oh, hi. We saw each other in the hallway."

Analise nodded a routine hello and then caught herself, doing a big double take. "Oh, yes," she said. "You're Taylor's friend."

As their eyes met, a look passed between them and Evalina nodded silent confirmation to the question in Analise's eyes: yes, she was *that* friend. A connection had been made.

But Analise would want to go to the source. Now the only question was, how long would it take her to figure out who was supplying Evalina?

I made an excuse and headed for the bar, letting the three of them wander off together. I was feeling more and more uneasy. I wasn't actively facilitating Shine's drug trafficking, and God knows I had no ability to control Analise. But as I watched them drift from sculpture to sculpture, chatting away with sudden intimacy, I scoured my memory. Had I ever said anything to Analise that would make Shine feel I had betrayed his trust? Had there been anything that would make Analise feel she'd been an unwitting object of study? Worse, had I put my thumb on the scale and distorted reality? Or was this chance meeting the reality I should document? After all, we were standing in an art gallery bought with trust fund dollars by Upper East Side blue bloods (with the help of thousands of dollars from the city's burgeoning art development fund), displaying creative works by black and white hipsters with varying degrees of art education and social background, attended by a mix of Wall Street tyros and nightclub kids and trustafarians and even a few aspiring buppies from Harlem who had just come in, a place that just happened to serve as the perfect new market for a pair of crack dealers trying to reinvent themselves by heading south of Ninety-sixth Street. What more did I need?

Half an hour later, Shine came over to the bar. We were invited to Analise's party tomorrow night, he said.

"Got some new business? A new client perhaps?" I asked.

I'd meant it to come out like a detached sociological inquiry, but even I heard the tone of judgment in my voice.

Shine just looked at me, then shook his head slowly to display his lack of concern for whatever qualms or jealousy I might be feel-ing. He was a businessman and that was that. He never apologized for it. "Got to, man. You know that."

We shook hands good-bye. He patted my back absentmindedly and crossed to the door. Though he was a large man, something stoic and contained gave him a compact look.

Just before he reached for the door, he found Evalina in the crowd and gave her a nod. In a decade of studying the drug trade, I had seen the exact same gesture at least two hundred times. Shine never carried drugs himself. Soon, the nod said, he would send a courier to drop off a package.

I scanned the room myself and found Analise in the crowd. She was watching Shine too.

I spent the next day back at the university. Though I would usually spend my time at my desk reading journals or preparing for a class, I sometimes ventured to an editing room to pursue my latest experiment, documentary filmmaking. I was finishing up a film about the last days of a Chicago housing project before the city tore it down.

But even as I worked in my office and the editing suite, I was distracted by the previous evening's events. I didn't know how to feel about the whole thing. On one level, I should be happy that

Shine and Analise had crossed paths. What a documentary that would make! Or I could start collecting data for an unusually provocative study. But I hadn't met Analise as a sociologist meets interview subjects. I'd met her at a wine tasting at Harvard when I felt completely out of my element and she reached out to me and helped me feel at home. I was hesitant to put her under the microscope. I felt more as if I should protect her. If I went to her party with Shine, at least I could monitor his interactions with Analise and add a whiff of normative expectations. She was unlikely to ask him if he could provide her with cocaine in my presence.

But Shine called at the last minute to tell me he was going to be late, so I should just meet him there.

I showed up around eleven. Analise had rented a Chelsea gallery and decorated it with six-foot mirrors leaning up against the wall, white tablecloths with a faint hint of violet embroidery, a few antique chairs, wine flutes with gold leaf, and art deco champagne coupes from the 1930s. The women were smartly dressed, the men fashionably scruffy. Everyone was shouting; everyone had a drink in hand.

Through the crowd I caught a glimpse of Evalina, her solid little frame vacuum-packed into a black dress. Standing at her side was Brittany, an exceptionally beautiful young woman who had been one of Analise's classmates in college. A glamorous shipwreck, Brittany had recently decided to capitalize on her good looks by letting wealthy men take her out to dinner at New York's most famous restaurants. At least she could eat well, she said. But stepping so close to the invisible line must have set her mind to work. The last time I'd seen her, at a party on the Upper East Side, she amused herself by asking me about men's desires: Do you like perfume? Lingerie? What kind of lingerie? Role playing? What kind of role playing? Should I learn to talk about sports?

Please don't learn to talk about sports, I told her.

Now she was waving a cigarette at me and pointing at the back door. I made my way through the crowd and down a small metal stairway and found Evalina and Brittany standing with the smokers on a small patio. A small vial of coke appeared and Brittany dropped a few white flakes on her gold shoes. "I'm such a spaz," she said.

Analise came down the stairs and tottered up to us on alpine heels. "Oh, my God—I've been running around like a crazy person," she said, pulling a cigarette out of her tiny nightclub purse.

Without a word, Brittany handed her the vial of cocaine.

"Thank you, Lord."

For me, it was an uncomfortable moment. Although Analise had not been especially secretive about getting high in the past, we had both chosen to pretend that nothing unusual was happening. Either she assumed I was too straight or she wanted to keep our relationship in a zone of normalcy.

Analise handed the vial back to Brittany. "Are we getting together tomorrow?" she asked.

"Can't. Going up to Boston. Don't forget, you have to call the hotel."

"Damn it. I'm sorry. This party sucked everything else out of my brain."

Lighting fresh cigarettes, they talked logistics about some kind of social event: trains, taxis, timetables. My mind drifted to Shine. This was supposed to be a working night for me, not a social affair, wasn't it? Where was he? Was he coming? Had he delegated tonight's drug deals to Evalina and forgotten to tell me?

There was also a slim but real possibility that Shine had taken Analise home last night and given *her* the drugs to bring tonight. I could see the headline now: "Upscale Drug Ring Linked to Columbia Professor."

I didn't want to think about that.

When I returned to the conversation, I had missed too much.

"He's how old?" Brittany asked.

"Not that old," Analise answered.

"Dinner? Or just—?"

"No, dinner."

"I'm tired of dinner."

"So just drink. That should help."

What were they talking about? It didn't sound good. Analise noticed my curiosity and held forth the vial. "You want some?"

"*No*," I said, sharply—too sharply.

Analise gave me a curious look and I just shook my head, already turning to walk away. This was out of my hands now. I could call and try to convince him not to sell drugs to Analise, but I was pretty sure I knew what he would say. "She's over twenty-one." That was his usual answer in situations like that. So I just said good-bye and walked outside. The night air was cold, sharp with the approaching winter. There were no cabs. The nearest subway was fifteen minutes away.

I started walking.

Even then, all I could see was an awkward situation. Whatever hopes I might have had about documenting the collision of worlds began to blow away in that cold autumn wind. I'd have to find another way to chart the connections the global city forged among disparate social types.

But the next night, the third night running, Analise called and said she was in trouble and didn't want to go home—her boyfriend had beat her up. Could she come spend the night in my spare room?

I said yes without hesitation. Then I wondered why she'd called me instead of Brittany or another girlfriend.

Half an hour later she was on my doorstep with an overnight bag. This time she wore no makeup, not even lipstick, and no adornments except a few loose bracelets on her arm. Her shoes squeaked on my floor as she passed through my front door. She looked small and vulnerable, wet from the rain.

We stood a few feet apart. This was the first time we'd seen each other outside of a public social gathering, I realized. We usually managed to sneak to a quiet corner for a private conversation, but we had never been *alone* before. Neither of us knew exactly how to greet each other.

Without thinking about it, I moved forward and gave her a hug. I could hear her struggling to hold back tears.

"Thank you," she said.

I suggested we get her to a hospital.

"I'm fine. He just grabbed me a lot."

What about going to the police?

"*Definitely* not."

What she wanted, she said, was a drink. She didn't drink, but right now she wanted a drink.

Maybe that's not such a good idea, I thought. But I held my tongue. I mixed two vodka tonics and put one in her hand. As soon as she took the first sip, she began talking.

"J.B. stole my money! I never, ever thought he would do *that*. I mean, almost anything else I would believe, but not *that*."

J.B. was short for "Junebug," her nickname for the wealthy young blue blood, heir to a family fortune, she had been dating since college. As far as I was able to see, he was an amiable young man with a single distinction: he absolutely loved flaunting his wad, throwing it at bartenders in thick sandwiches and slipping folds of twenties through the windows of taxis. Once he rented an art gallery for a party and pasted hundreds of twenty- and fifty-dollar bills on the walls. I remember thinking this seemed rather gauche behavior for someone from the hereditary elite, but then I was born into an ethnic caste of Indian Brahmans (the "Alladi") that had its own distinct dialect. They tended to think everything was gauche.

"But the guy is a millionaire!" I said. "A *multi*millionaire. How much did he take?"

"About thirty thousand dollars—this time. I think he stole fifty thousand before that. Maybe more, I'm not sure."

She had been hiding the money in her apartment and didn't notice it missing until now, she said. When she confronted him, he said she was stupid for leaving so much money lying around, so he was going to invest it in something with a higher rate of return.

This raised a number of immediate questions in my mind:

a) Where did she get all that money?

b) Why didn't she put it in a bank?

c) Why didn't she *count* it?

d) Where was it now?

I was afraid to ask. The vodka now seemed like a very good idea.

Six months earlier, Analise had confided to me that she'd angered her parents by refusing to be a good socialite and get married and pursue a life of fashion and charity. She preferred traveling in India and looking at art. She'd even told them she was thinking of starting some kind of business of her own, which was most assuredly not proper behavior for a young woman of leisure. They'd threatened to cut her out of the family estate. That night, by the third vodka tonic, she revealed her deepest fear about this possibly impending disinheritance, which was that it might destroy her relationship with Junebug. Or, as she put it: "Who the fuck wants to marry a poor piece of shit!"

At the time, it was hard to imagine a mind-set that equated failure to collect a hereditary fortune with being unmarriageable. But that night in my apartment, the more she cried, the less I felt I had any standard to judge.

I ventured a technical question. "What kind of investment?"

"He said he needed to get some work done on some new projects."

This was J.B.'s weakness. He took pride in discovering new talent. He would find directors fresh out of NYU and tell them he'd finance their genius movie idea. They'd spend weeks drawing up elaborate plans for cast and crew and platform media releases. Alas, his trust fund never quite matched his needs. When his parents refused to offset the difference, J.B. concocted a scheme with his parents' chauffeur to fake an injury and collect on the payment. When that fell through, he stole from Analise.

As Analise told this story, all I could think was that Junebug the heir was really just another black marketer scamming away in the underground economy, no different from the West African hotel clerks who touted illegal fun to tourists or the Latina prostitutes standing on Midtown street corners. His entire filmmaking operation was off the books and financed with money he'd siphoned from his trust funds using shady methods right at the edge of the law. How funny would it be if I did a study comparing J.B.'s film business to Shine's drug business? My mind drifted to a conversation I'd had with a faculty member at the University of Chicago right at the beginning of my academic career. "I want to study the suburbs," I'd said. He looked at me as if he'd seen a bug. "They're white and middle class," he'd said. "What's there to study?"

But Analise was in no condition to see the humor. "I knew from the start he was ripping me off," she was saying. "But I always thought he'd fess up, you know? Just hit rock bottom and promise to pay it back. But there was always more coke, and more drinking, and more fighting."

I said I was sorry, and realized I meant it.

"Now I'll be all alone," she said.

She reached for the box of Kleenex on the table. "Sudhir, I want to tell you something. I don't really trust a lot of people with this . . ."

At that moment, I felt a tingle up my neck. Analise wanted to confess, to share, to make me see her in the round and recognize her hidden qualities. I had been at this exact point so many times before. Waiting for moments like this is my job, basically. They are a wonderful gift of trust from one person to another. All I had to do was receive her message in the calm, detached, professional way I usually did. But after a decade of listening to Chicago's underworld and nearly half that time in New York, I still found it hard to listen to these confessions, and this one felt especially hard. I wasn't prepared for this from someone successful, someone who didn't need to be crossing into the underworld—someone I *knew*.

She didn't seem to notice my dismay at all. "There are a lot of people whose money he took," she continued. "I wish it was just mine, but he has other people's money."

That sent me reeling in another direction. Other people's money? This answered Question A but raised a few more:

e) What other people?

f) Why did she have their money?

g) What were they likely to do when they found out their money was gone?

A lot more of the alphabet was still to come, I feared.

Analise ducked her head, looking shy for a moment. "Do you remember what I told you about Brittany?"

I assumed she meant about her dating rich men. Or maybe something with drugs, which would make more sense to me—I had trouble seeing Brittany as anybody's courtesan.

"Yes, of course," I said. "I hope she's having more success—or maybe not!"

"Well, I guess I should've told you more about her."

"Like I said, you don't have to—"

"I manage her."

I went silent as I considered various possible interpretations of the word "manage." The previous night's conversation about Boston came back and I remembered Brittany saying she was tired of dinner. And I remembered what Analise had said back.

"And a bunch of other girls," Analise added.

"Wow. Okay," I said. I felt a crazy impulse to just get up and leave the room, until I remembered I was in my own home. "That's great!"

Trying to act casual, I practically shouted the words.

"It's not fucking great," Analise said. "Please don't treat me like an idiot."

"No, I mean—not *great* but just, you know, great for you if that's, you know—"

She cut into my babble with force. "I make *good* money. Money that J.B. fucking stole. And I keep some of their cash because they don't feel safe keeping it at home. Which J.B. also stole."

With that, the whole story came out. She didn't get started managing women like Brittany through planning or ambition, she said. It's just that everyone else was so incompetent. Brittany would offer to pay for the hotel room—at the St. Regis! Her friends were worse. They'd pay for town cars, they'd pay for dinner, even supply a little free cocaine. The men were totally taking advantage of them. In no time at all, Analise had doubled their earnings. It was organizational skills like everything else, scheduling and getting people paid, simple stuff really. But success attracted other clients and one day Analise woke up and realized she was running a business, just as she'd told her parents she would. And a fairly substantial one. "I'm good at it," she said with a shrug. "What can I say?"

I didn't know how to respond. I was still in a state of shock.

"I feel like I'm helping people," she added.

Those exact words I had heard many times before. Criminals always try to frame their actions in some high-minded way. Sex workers tell me they are "therapists" offering a quasi-medical service. Drug dealers say they are taking money away from the bad elements in their community. And even though all my training and personal inclinations discouraged judgment, it was disturbing to hear the same words—the same rationalization exactly—from Analise. I couldn't resist the response that blurted out. "That's what they all say."

She seemed surprised that I'd challenged her so bluntly. She thought about it for a moment, then shrugged. "I guess I like the thrill of it," she admitted.

Finally, I felt my professional side start to stir. If we were going to go down this road, she was going to have to take me a little more seriously. "Listen, you know I study this stuff," I began, using my best college professor voice. "I don't judge the others, and I won't judge you."

She nodded.

"But you're a—"

I didn't want to say "pimp" or "madam." I paused to gather my thoughts.

"You're a *broker*. That's different."

"You say 'different' in a judgmental way. You just said you weren't going to judge me."

"I mean different like more dangerous. I don't think you have any idea what you're getting into, or how vulnerable you are." I knew I was hemming and hawing and that judgment was underneath it. Most of the time, I just took in whatever craziness people told me about their lives. But I had seen terrible things happen in this world. Over and over, I'd seen people who were basically good acting savagely in the name of money and fear and respect. I kept coming back to the difference in our relationship. Maybe Analise was something short of a true friend, but she wasn't a research subject either. Should I take out my notebook or conduct an intervention? I didn't know.

"What I'm doing is not like what Brittany is doing," she said. "If I was doing that, forget it. My friends, my reputation, my whole world would be over. But this is different. I'm just a manager."

What psychological mechanism, I wondered, persuades an intelligent, sophisticated person to believe in superhero powers of invisibility and invincibility? I was both fascinated and outraged. "This whole *world* is dangerous! You think you can keep it a secret? You really think Brittany isn't telling anyone?"

She thought for a moment, then shrugged sheepishly. "Well, maybe. But I'll deny deny deny."

Was she really stumbling into this so thoughtlessly? Should I keep listening to these foolish rationalizations? Or should I be the good friend who shocks her back into clear-eyed thought? After all, I was a student of this world. I knew more than I ever wanted to know about its pitfalls and tragedies. The least I could do was give her some idea of the trouble she was getting into.

"Can I tell you the number one thing the 'brokers' I know worry about? It's not the police."

She shrugged her shoulders.

"It's the image. The idea that they use drugs and violence to maintain their hold over confused young girls who were probably sexually abused by uncles and fathers. That's what makes it okay to send them to jail for a long time. I mean, weren't you sharing cocaine with Brittany last night? Imagine how that would sound in court."

"That's fucking crazy!" Analise yelled, throwing herself back on the couch so hard she spilled her vodka. "You've seen Brittany! Like I have to force drugs on her so she'll obey my evil wishes."

"I don't think that 'like I have to force drugs on her' is going to be an effective defense in court," I said.

Calmer now, I went into professional sociologist mode. The need to put Analise's activities into an analytic frame took over. "How many women do you manage?"

From my voice, you'd think I had a clipboard and a number 2 pencil.

Analise's eyes widened. She wasn't expecting specific questions. But I have found that specific and even minutely detailed questions actually relax people, grounding their confessions in scientific objectivity.

"Five," she answered. "Sometimes six or seven. But five on a regular basis."

"Okay, five," I said. Pondering the other people I knew in her line of work and all the activities I had entered into little boxes and charts over the last few years, I began running the numbers in my head. "So you're pulling in, I'd say, at least five thousand dollars per week. At least. But I figure that probably five weeks won't be profitable because you'll be on vacation or whatever, so I'd say you'll earn about a hundred thousand dollars a year on this. And you're probably laundering it through Max, yes?"

Max was her family lawyer. I knew him from some foundation work. Her expression showed me I had scored a direct hit.

"So you're evading currency laws and tax laws and banking six figures and you're telling me you've never even nudged any one of your five young employees to work extra or keep working or—what was it you told Brittany yesterday? 'So just drink'?"

"That's an awful thing to say," Analise said.

"I'm sorry, but you're a 'broker.' That's what brokers do."

"That really hurts, Sudhir."

"Think about it, Analise. Have you had that conversation yet, the one where one of the women says she wants to stop? You'd lose twenty thousand dollars a year. Are you sure you won't try to talk her into sticking it out just a little bit longer? 'Just one more time'? What if Junebug says he'll leave you if you don't give him money to buy an amazing script he found?"

The vodka was making me belligerent. She ducked her head and I continued.

"I *know* this shit, Analise. One night something bad happens in some fucked-up hotel and they come crying to you and you talk them down. You calm them. You may even call the dude and calm *him* because you don't want him to be a threat and you're the perfect broker-manager-psychiatrist who thinks of everything and covers all the bases. And you feel great! Because you did it! You came through! They needed you and you got the job done! And you got paid! And maybe you even got the client to pay you extra to keep things out of the press, because, well . . . that's just how *good* you *are*."

By then, Analise was crying. When I noticed, I felt awful. The poor thing just got beat up by her boyfriend and here I was haranguing her. "I'm sorry," I said. "That was really uncalled-for."

"You're right," she said. "I'm a pimp."

"No! I got carried away. You took me by surprise."

"But I *like* this job," she said. "I like helping these girls. I *am* helping them."

Suddenly she lifted her head up and started to laugh. "And okay, no, I am not Mother Teresa. I do like the thrill of it. I do. I like *crime*."

The truth was, Analise probably *was* helping them. In the high-paid world of New York prostitution, I had learned, the majority of "brokers" were women who "age out" by moving from selling their bodies to managing or "helping" others who did. And all the ones I had met were, like Analise, white and fairly well educated. They played a variety of roles, from consigliere to confidante. The best helped their women find doctors and lawyers and helped them manage their money—for a fee, of course—by laundering it and setting up legitimate bank accounts. They offered counsel in times of trouble and got them out of jail with a call to a friendly cop. Eventually, some even helped them exit the sex trade for marriage or a comfortable retirement. As much as I could have sat there describing this underground sorority, I mostly wanted Analise to see the dark side too.

But this was a good place to stop. I suggested she get some sleep.

She looked up at me with a shy expression. "Will you keep on talking to me about this stuff? Not tonight, but sometime. It feels good to talk about it, and nobody else understands."

This made me feel very strange. Again, listening to intimate confessions is my job. Trust is an emotion I've spent a lifetime learning to encourage. But on this night something was off. In my teaching and writing, I would often repeat with confidence a statement that now strikes me as downright reckless: *The poor live in the same world as you and me, and it's the job of the sociologist to demonstrate these relationships.* Now Analise was teaching me an uncomfortable truth. In real life, I did seem to feel more comfortable studying people of a lower economic and educational level. I hated admitting it. It hurt to admit it. But it was true. I had been trained to fit people into boxes, to draw lines between drug dealer and sex worker and rich kid and socialite. In fact, the entire premise of academic sociology is that each individual has his own little world and economy that can be studied and charted out, so the smart thing to do, in order to document social roles, is find people who are *not* changing.

My own background was hobbling me too. Like it or not, as a "Chicago sociologist" I had internalized the idea that the Chicago style of urban living was universal: that people stayed in neighborhoods segregated by race and class, blacks with blacks and whites with whites, poor separated from rich, and their children living in the same way, the patterns passed down through generations. Now *that* was a setting handmade for a sociologist. All an eager, aspiring young ethnographer had to do was hang out long enough for the locals to let you into their lives. Shine had been telling me since our very first meeting to get a car and drive around the city and get a feeling for the immensity of it—the huge variety of communities and peoples and neighborhoods—but I'd dismissed it as the usual boilerplate advice people give tourists. The truth was, despite all my own concerns about the transition from Chicago and my tentative steps into the rich variety of worlds contained in the city of New York, broad and shallow was just not my style. I really did believe in immersion. Find a place, hang out, get to know the people, and keep coming back. But Shine kept pushing me. "You need to move around more, you understand? I keep telling you, but you don't listen." Now I was realizing that Shine and Analise were teaching me the same thing. So were many of the other New Yorkers I had met and studied. They were all pointing me away from the idea of static, unchanging lives to the themes of movement and change. Instead of drawing boundaries, they were crossing them. Instead of looking for places to anchor their work, they were constantly pulling their anchors up and putting them down elsewhere, wherever a new opportunity arose. My challenge was similar. New York was different and it needed its own kind of sociology. It required new concepts beyond *neighborhood* and a new method of immersion that wasn't fixed in place. These people were on the move. That was the defining fact about them, and their true community seemed to be the sum of all the relationships they were forging, the many social ties that they formed as they crossed the terrain of the city. So losing the notion of geographic areas as primordial urban units of socialization was my first step.

But what did it mean to frame "community" as a network? Especially in the underground economy, a dangerous place by definition, where patterns of life were fragile and elusive? And these New Yorkers were moving not just in physical space; they were also reaching beyond their preordained lot in life. Capturing this might mean setting aside other equally tried-and-true sociological principles, such as *Where we come from defines who we are* or *Education is the key predictor of success.* Those truisms weren't going to explain why a crack dealer was going to art shows or why the daughter of a wealthy financier was moonlighting as a madam. I was watching entrepreneurship in its truest and fullest sense, risk taking for both material gain and personal transformation. Since New York's underground economy gave its residents a chance to reinvent themselves across worlds—since it was the chance encounter across predictable boundaries that could bring people like Shine and Analise more dollars or stature—I needed a sociology built less on neighborhoods and more on the networks anthropologist Clifford Geertz called "webs of significance." By watching the underground economy's hidden strivers, I could record a form of social mobility that had little to do with college degrees or handshakes at corporate boardrooms. And though the pursuits of the underground were the timeless essence of New York, money and success, they also spoke to what the city was becoming in the twenty-first century: global in feel and increasingly fast paced, its people endlessly shuttling across familiar social landscapes and tribal boundaries as they wove new patterns in the world. This was the future being made, and I was there to document it.

My excitement began to rise.

At the same time, so did a queasy feeling. None of these ideas felt solid or certain or quantifiable on a spreadsheet in any way. They felt like quickened breaths, much like the ones I took when Analise told me about her new profession. I wasn't in formal research mode and certainly couldn't explain any of this in a way that would be comprehensible to most of my colleagues. I hadn't yet done any of the things a good researcher should do: design a careful study, be a skeptic, find more data, and keep questioning until some version of truth arose. But the feeling alone was already raising fundamental questions about how I did my work and what it was good for. Suddenly, unexpectedly, I was compelled to question the framework that had given so much meaning to my life, the lines I had drawn around myself. I couldn't sit. I had to move. I had to follow where things took me.

I left Analise sitting on the guest room bed, a bit forlorn and a bit drunk, a beautiful, lost girl who had somehow become an enthusiastic criminal. I walked back down the hall and stood in the doorway to the living room. The vodka glasses were still on the table. I was woozy too, drunker than I'd thought. A drifting feeling washed over me, maybe the oldest feeling I knew: the fear of being unmoored and unattached and lost. I had no idea what to do next.

This unsettling doubt was the flash that finally lit up the pattern in the rich chaos of the last five years. Five years of prostitutes, drug dealers, madams, johns, porn clerks, and cops finally began to make sense, or at least hint at the possibility of making sense. The first pages of this book had just been written, and now all I had to do was learn how to read them—to understand this story, and my own.

CHAPTER 2

NEW YORK, NEW YORK

N ow spin the wheel back to those first tentative steps. A new century was looming, bright and shining with possibility. I was settling into New York City, starting my exciting new job at Columbia University as a young professor striking out for the first time. I couldn't wait to set up a new apartment, get to know my new colleagues and students, and develop some new research projects.

A few warning signs appeared. My wife and I felt conflicted about leaving Chicago. I started to feel guilty about moving us out of the comfortable home we had created in the Midwest.

Columbia wasn't the easiest place to start my career, but it was the best place. The university had a reputation for treating young faculty poorly. Rarely did they grant tenure, and when they did, junior professors were still thought of as expendable labor. Most of my friends and advisers urged me not to take the job. But I turned down the other offers that came my way—including one from the downtown competitor, NYU—because I was hungry and I felt I needed the stature and challenge of an Ivy League badge. The pressure cooker of the University of Chicago taught me that I needed a high-stakes environment to motivate me.

The department was going through a period of transition. In a bitter struggle between two competing visions of sociology, Herbert Gans represented the discipline's original aim. A public intellectual who wrote for a wide audience, he carried the mantle of the great old Columbia sociologists, like Robert Merton and C. Wright

Mills, who combined vivid storytelling with thoughtful explorations of great national issues.

But a genuine respect for this tradition sat uneasily next to the growing belief that sociology should be a science. Gans's contemporaries, like Harrison White (a trained physicist) and his enigmatic and ambitious student Peter Bearman, were formalists who fought for a much narrower, lab-coat view of the discipline, focusing on objective research and academic sobriety. This had been the trend since the 1960s, when young sociologists decided to fight for their legitimacy as scientists by drawing a contrast with the swashbuckling anthropologists and new journalists. Opinions hardened to the point where many scholars had a knee-jerk definition of academic quality—if too many people can read your work, it must not be very good. But if you could quantify your research and make it sufficiently unreadable, then you were onto something. Translated into my life, the warning was simple: "Write *only* for sociologists, because a popular book might jeopardize your chances for tenure."

I was caught in the middle, searching for my own way. Truth be told, I shared the same view of sociology as Bearman and the scientists: only through careful, systematic observation and analysis could we really learn about the world. I didn't want to give that up. In my own career, I had gained a great deal of credibility by being objective and attentive to detail. Being seen as a scientist opened up doors and helped me to avoid the "activist" label used to dismiss researchers who become advocates for various methods of social change. I spent as much time with White and Bearman as I could, learning as much as I could about their approach.

At the same time, I knew I was hired because my research spoke to social issues like race, inequality, and the fate of our cities, subjects that fell squarely into Columbia's legacy of encouraging the public intellectual tradition. In this regard, I had already been schooled by working with Professor William Julius Wilson in Chicago. As my graduate adviser, Wilson always insisted that the scientific method alone was incapable of swaying the opinion of policy makers or the public. You also had to write well. You had to tell a story. Wilson would do it with epochal books like *The Declining Significance of Race* and *The Truly Disadvantaged,* in which his vivid and passionate writing reached beyond the academic community and changed the way his generation looked at poverty. I wanted to reach out to a larger audience too, to touch hearts and minds of people who were riding the train to work as well as those sitting in offices making public policy.

With this in mind, I had spent many hours in the university archives in Chicago researching the history of the field. I discovered that the two contrasting visions were, in fact, the original tension that caused its birth. One of the founding fathers was Robert Park, a journalist by training. He argued for a sociology that could inform the public. He incorporated the criticisms of the scholars who were pushing for a more scientific, empirical approach, recognizing the dangers, inherent in journalism, of anecdotal portraits that proved nothing of broader significance. In the piles of archival notes I noticed that one scholar had scribbled, "Rigor and Relevance." That summed it up for me: truthful, scientifically valid insights that are comprehensible and that speak to timely social issues. I tried to achieve these two objectives with my first book for the general public, *Gang Leader for a Day.* Its success meant that a few more people understood the complicated struggles for America's urban poor, from their complex strategies for putting food on the table to fending off the local drug lord. More truth and fewer clichés meant better social policy and, ultimately, better lives for the people I studied. That was the theory, anyway.

But the two visions were like warring bulls. If you went too deep into storytelling, you were labeled a journalist. If you went too far into hard-nosed, number-crunching science, you were doomed to the bookshelves of specialists. When I arrived at Columbia, I couldn't find a middle ground. Although my colleagues were supportive and encouraging, everyone gave me the same intimidating advice: publish in the leading journals (which were all dominated by scientists) or you won't receive tenure. It seemed that I would have to pursue wider relevance at my own risk.

For me, it was a devil's bargain. As an ethnographer, I was confronted with a problem that went far beyond literary style. My specialty was selecting from the chaos and splendor of the given world one small part that could stand for the whole: the perfect research topic, the world in a grain of sand. But the approach of the lab coats was statistical. They favored long questionnaires, computer analysis, lots of numbers from the United States Census. They'd laugh at me if I focused on one small part of the city. And I couldn't even argue that they were completely wrong. I wasn't a journalist studying individuals. What I found *had* to be applicable to a bigger population. I would have to say something about the entire city—*all New Yorkers*! And right then, I could barely find the subway.

S*tart with what's comfortable,* I told myself, *and hope it takes you somewhere.* Since my work on Chicago crack dealers was my academic foundation, it made sense to start from there. My entry point came via Michael Clark, a major player in the Midwest drug scene. I had known him for years and written about him without upsetting him too much. Back in 1997, he had offered me the help of a cousin in New York called Shine. "He'll hook you up," he promised. Then he took my notebook into his hands and wrote down a phone number.

I didn't call Shine right away. I wanted to discover the city on my own, and calling Shine felt like a crutch. But after stumbling around Harlem trying to strike up conversations with drug dealers and sex workers without much success, I got out the notebook and dialed the number.

Shine lived less than a mile from my new apartment, it turned out, but he was down in Harlem and I was up in Morningside Heights. Coming to New York, I had expected a replay of my experience at the University of Chicago, where arriving students were given maps divided into safe and unsafe neighborhoods and warned repeatedly about which ones to avoid—all the black neighborhoods, basically. And to some extent, the tiny incline of Morningside Park, one block long and barely steep enough to be called a hill, did create an invisible barrier between the worlds of Columbia University and Harlem.

But here was my first lesson, unnoticed at the time, in the ways in which New York is not Chicago. The friendly neighborhood bar I had just discovered was also Shine's friendly neighborhood bar. A warm and unpretentious place where most of the customers worked for small local businesses, it was a pleasant contrast to the university environment and certainly better than the noisy off-campus places jammed with students. I'd leave the West End to the ghosts of Jack Kerouac and Allen Ginsberg. I just felt more comfortable among working people.

Shine laughed when I told him the name of the bar. "Hell, I'll be there tonight watching the game," he said. "Drop on by."

When I headed over after work, walking fast in the brisk winter air, I wondered how I could have overlooked a major ghetto drug dealer among the ordinary working people. But when I saw him, I immediately saw why. Shine was a large man, fit and athletic, with a quiet, watchful presence, but his dark blue pants and dark shirt made him look like a U.S. postal worker taking a break after the day's shift. In a room of uniformed men, nearly all black and Latino, he blended right in.

I ordered a drink from the bar and carried it to his booth, sitting down across from him.

For a moment, we didn't speak—just sat, surprisingly comfortable, taking each other in.

"How's Michael?" Shine finally asked, his white teeth making a crisp contrast against his red lips and black skin as he smiled. "How's he living?"

"Good, good," I muttered. "He's settling down."

"That nigger's been settling down since he came into this world," Shine said.

"Yeah, but if you're that good . . ."

You don't even need to try, the old line was. Ghetto wisdom. I didn't have to finish the thought because Shine knew just what I meant, and he knew that I knew that he knew. Social codes like this are how people signal their allegiances, and I had learned them well during my long immersion in Chicago's drug culture.

"He's good with people," Shine continued, speaking with respect. "Knows how to get them moving. Nigger practically turned around his neighborhood, that's what I heard."

By this, Shine meant that Michael had taken such effective dictatorial control of his drug block that he'd made it both safe (which made his neighbors cooperative) and extremely profitable, all while staying out of jail. In response, I tried to stay positive without endorsing his crimes.

"Yeah, he's successful—and his kid, Jackie, she's going to take over the world. She's five. What an amazing little kid."

Trying to fill in the silence between small talk, I added, "New York's not as friendly as Chicago."

Shine looked skeptical. "You like friendly people?"

"Sure. Of course. Who doesn't?"

"This ain't Chicago, my brother," Shine said. "You can't get far with friendly out here."

But then he frowned and looked at me more closely, pondering the mystery of my character for a long, silent moment. Finally, he came to a conclusion. He nodded and lifted his glass to take a gulp of ice. "I can see how you got along with niggers," he said. "You don't seem all that scary, so they can't see you coming. That's how you get 'em to tell you all our secrets, ain't it?"

The way he said it, laughing and crunching the ice between his teeth, it came out like the sly compliment of one hustler to another. I couldn't help feeling a momentary pleasure.

"So what next? What's your plan?" Shine said. "You want to move into the projects here?"

This had been on my mind since the day I'd arrived in the city, of course. *What next? What should I study?* The thing I'd noticed right away was the same thing everybody notices, the special energy of the place. Chicago's beauty was wrapped up in its Midwestern sameness, the predictable rhythms of its people, the solid embrace of caste and clan. In contrast, New York seemed like chaos barely held together. I wanted to do something that tapped into that somehow. Even if I could put all the office politics aside, another study of crack gangs trapped in the projects didn't seem the most promising pursuit.

"So this will be the last time I see you," Shine said.

"Maybe," I answered.

We stayed very solemn for a moment, then cracked up laughing. Relaxing another notch, we drifted into a conversation about Michael and the other Chicago characters we had in common, which became the story of how I'd wandered into the projects one day and got taken hostage by Michael's gang. "Next thing I know, I'm moving in—and seven years go flying by."

Shine kept his head down, a diamond glittering in his ear. "Michael said you were writing a book," he said.

In my experience, there was one good way to explain an enterprise like mine to someone like Shine. "Everybody's got to hustle," I said.

Shine nodded solemnly at the tabletop. "Everyone hustles," he agreed. "Especially around here."

So we understood each other. We were good. I went back to my current obsession. "The city seems too big, too hard to get my hands around. I'm not sure where to start. I'm not sure where to hang out. How do I even know where the significant locations are going to be?"

Shine was about to get up to refresh his drink, but the bartender made a motion to stay put; he would bring a drink over. Shine settled back into his chair with a sigh. He could see that I was frustrated. Setting up a pattern that would last for many years, he responded with matter-of-factness. "Just keep on keepin' on, that's what my auntie says."

"Yeah, but keep on keeping on *where*?"

He laughed. "That's exactly what *I* said."

For a moment he was quiet. The noise of the bar rose up around us and pushed us closer together. Shine leaned forward and shook his head. "Shit, I've been doing the same thing for years. I'm getting itchy, man. I keep asking myself, What next? What's the next thing I can get into and *do* something with? So I was talking to my auntie and she says that—'Just keep on keeping *on*, nephew'—and I sit there thinking to myself, What the *fuck* is this woman talking about? Has she even heard the concerns I am expressing? The whole *point* is *where to go*."

"So where are you going?"

"Hell, I have no idea."

We sat back, absorbing the similarity of our problems. Both of us stuck between past and future, both looking for a way forward. The solution would seem obvious later, but not in that moment— just that oddly fraternal feeling, the sense that we were joined in a common struggle to find our way here in the city of New York. I had left Chicago just as the subjects of my first book were aging out of the drug world. Most ended up in jail or dead. Now Shine and I were asking the same question:

Is there a second act?

. . .

This was when Shine first told me to start by getting a car and driving around the city. It just seemed so banal and obvious I didn't take him seriously.

"You need to float," he said, adding a "bro" like punctuation.

"Float?"

Shine pointed to the bartender. "Like that dude. He used to be a comedian, then he drove a truck. He worked on a farm, he played baseball. Now he's here."

"Where does the car come in?"

He tucked his head a notch and narrowed his eyes. Was I too stupid to understand a metaphor?

"I get it," I said.

His eyes moved to the clock above the bar, then to the window. The foot traffic on the street was starting to thicken, a trickle toward the deluge of five o'clock. He began the patting-the-pockets ritual that precedes departure.

"Don't let me keep you," I said.

"Yeah, I got some business to deal with. People getting off work, they want what they need." He stood up. "You got my number. Call me."

He reached over to the bar and threw some bills on the counter, pointing to my drink to let the bartender know that he had paid for both. He had a blue New York Yankees cap in his hand, which he put on his head gently and with great care, then gave me a nod and walked out the door.

I spent the next two years in Harlem, mostly with Shine and his friends. I was lucky enough to win a research grant to study the history of black street markets, which helped me understand the history and culture of the place but also gave me a chance to build the trust I needed to launch a study of more contemporary markets—even with Shine's backing, people weren't going to let me watch their criminal activities right away. Talking to the "old heads" about the history of the community would help to settle everyone's nerves. And truth be told, that's the way a good Chicago sociologist would proceed. Becoming intimate with one neighborhood just naturally seemed like a good foundation.

As I expected, everyone from small-time street vendors to car thieves to loan sharks had a story about the past they wanted to share. And as they grew comfortable with me, they started introducing me to the people busily working in the alleyways. It was slow cooking, but the time seemed to be well spent. I learned that the underground economy was still a primary source of sustenance for Harlemites who could not find jobs or who were mentally or physically unable to work full-time, which put a different perspective on all the headlines about unemployment. Their off-the-books wages were at least as good as most minimum-wage work, the only other realistic option. And their earnings flowed through the neighborhood, raising everyone's standard of living. But I also saw the painful price they paid, from living in constant fear of the law to living almost entirely in a world of cash with little savings and no credit. Frequent exposure to street and domestic violence didn't help, especially when they were afraid to go to the police. And they weren't exactly building up a useful résumé for future employment.

But all of these people did their business on the same few blocks, day after day, just like the men and women I'd observed in Chicago. Walking around with Shine and taking my own solitary journeys on the streets near the university, I could easily tell that people from other areas of the city came into Harlem to buy goods and services off the books, from pirated videos and crafts on the street to car repair and sexual services. Yet these were all invisible to me. I knew that many Harlem residents left the neighborhood to do off-the-books work in other parts of New York. Some were nannies, like Shine's mother, who took the bus to the homes of wealthy families. Janitors and housekeepers worked odd jobs in Midtown corporate offices. Craftspeople and artists and street vendors sold their wares on sidewalks all around the city. Shine himself served clients all over the five boroughs.

So I felt productive but uneasy. I was gathering stories of Harlem's underworld and I certainly had a wide range of black marketers to follow and observe. I even spoke to my university about launching a formal study of both modern-day and older underground markets in New York. But I was afraid it was too much like my work in Chicago and that I was missing all the ways that the underground markets of Harlem connected to the larger city. I knew I needed a different approach to really do something original.

In the academic world, as it happened, the latest craze in urban sociology involved a new way of thinking about today's cities. Urbanists like Saskia Sassen and David Harvey had written poignant studies about New York's rebirth as a global metropolis more intimately linked with Tokyo and London than with Newark or Philadelphia. These great service economy centers transcended regional economies, unlike the old "twentieth century" cities (such as Buffalo or Cleveland) that lived and died by the resources around them. Global cities were dominated by finance, real estate, entertainment, and media, while their aging counterparts had to feed on the crumbs of manufacturing and heavy industry. As a result, New York and London were filled with cosmopolitan jet-setters while most of Cleveland's and Buffalo's citizens were making do in their aging neighborhoods.

This new narrative rang loudly in and out of the academy. Mayors and business leaders from São Paulo to Mexico City to Bangkok dreamed of replacing their sooty heavy industries with sleek modern technology companies that would ensure their place in the emerging global networks. How could they attract the global headquarters of major multinationals, as Britain did? Or could they use art and architecture as a vehicle to attract global investment, like Spain? Could New York's dominance of finance be challenged?

I personally liked the focus on global flows and the power of this perspective. Traditional sociology, beginning at the dawn of the twentieth century, had portrayed cities as many different gardens knitted together. In this so-called "ecological" view, your neighborhood determined your eventual job, your educational path, whom you might marry, and even your chance of being victimized by crime. Segregation wasn't necessarily so bad, because an urban economy still brought people together and a gentle, paternalistic government could feed resources equitably back to each garden. It was also a neat and tidy way of intellectually managing the chaotic bustle of cities brimming over with immigrants, freed slaves, native populations, and all manner of transients. But the new breed of sociologists studying globalization argued that faraway places were closely intertwined despite their physical distance, causing a disruption in the old ecology or perhaps even a new ecology altogether, and this idea was starting to make intuitive sense to me after just a few months in New York. Black neighborhoods were turning white, Greenpoint was going from Polish to Latino, Mexican day laborers were living side by side with young white artists, and suburban whites were now moving back to cities in droves. A minority since the early 1970s, whites now made up 77 percent of all Manhattan apartment buyers, and the homes they purchased were often rehabbed rental units that once housed minorities and the working poor. The city was gentrifying at a pace that had not been seen in decades. The laborers were relegated to the outer boroughs.

And with gentrification, New York was becoming a city of sharp contrasts. As Sassen wrote pointedly, 90 percent of the highest-paid professionals arriving in the new New York City were white and

their conspicuous consumption and service needs were spawn-
ing entire industries, which were mostly staffed by minorities
coming from distant homes. The global city was becoming a
divided city, fragmented in all sorts of ways that were just starting
to become clear.

For me, the challenge was to import this abstract theory into
my own brand of ethnography. How could this flotsam and jetsam
be captured by a hunker-down sociologist who liked to pitch a tent
and watch people do their thing? There was also the problem of
subject. The arguments about the underground economy were
mostly based on speculation and little concrete information. In the
academy as well as the media, all the talk of "global cities" tended
to be centered on the glamorous life of elites who played in skyscrapers. My colleagues in the art and literature departments all
but worshiped the new breed of international polyglot artists, the
British rappers who mixed tracks with Bronx DJs, Hong Kong
filmmakers who cast Western actors, even the fusion chefs who
mixed classic French cuisine with Chinese flavors. These people
seemed to define modern life. And economists were starting to tell
us about the great wealth accumulating in these cities and the unexpected effects it could have—a real estate investment group in
Hamburg could derail a land use project in Denver simply by playing with fancy debt instruments, which made the global elite relevant to anyone who wanted to affect policy.

But something was missing in all of these portraits. New York
and London each contained eight million people, Tokyo had thir-
teen million, and only a small percentage worked in finance, real
estate, arts, and other major industries. If cities like New York were
really taking on a unique place in the global socioeconomic system,
the lives of those outside the skyscrapers also had to be taken into
consideration. And the conventional wisdom assumed that this
wonderful New York gumbo was produced by the city's *mainstream*
economy, which left out the underground supports I was already

seeing in Harlem. What if I focused on the subterranean ways people made their living? Wouldn't that strike a unique chord—especially since most scholars studied the underground economy purely in terms of deviance? In Chicago, I had seen crack gangs and local citizens work together in ways that wove invisible connective threads deep into their communities, and I knew the underground had potential to reveal unsuspected truths about the way society really works outside the speeches of politicians and the self-serving pronouncements of the financial community. If immigrant nannies worked off the books for the yuppies who bought the high-priced condos, if low-income black drug dealers served white hedge fund traders, wasn't it possible that the whole vast global city was actually knit together by the invisible threads of the *underground* economy? Wasn't it possible that staring up at the glamorous skyscrapers made you blind to the true picture?

Since a sociologist studies relationships, my daunting task would be to find and chart the connections among the high and low. But here I was at a distinct disadvantage. I wasn't producing surveys of ten thousand New Yorkers; I didn't work with census data for multiple cities. My last book told the story of Chicago's ghettos by focusing on one gang and one community. A genuine criticism could be made that it was difficult to generalize from the two hundred low-income black gang members I observed to the twenty-five thousand that filled Chicago's streets, many of whom were neither black nor low income. My department colleagues were the first to make me aware of the need for scientific precision, pushing me gently but forcefully to deal with what social scientists call the "generalizability problem." In the last few decades under pressure from the lab-coat side of the discipline, the scholars who study large numbers of individuals have had great fun discounting studies with small n's—small numbers of people in the sample, which effectively limits the relevance of the work for the wider population. Especially at the new Columbia, size mattered.

So what made me confident that my research had any relevance for the wider world?

Again, the specter of journalism raised its ugly head. If I tried to narrate the new New York with nothing but stories of ambitious street vendors or drug gangs in Harlem, most sociologists would laugh. The groups simply represented too few residents to be meaningful. This left two choices. I could abandon the big picture and focus on finding something unique that had escaped the scientists using "big data." This could mean uncovering a strange lifestyle or hard-to-access group, perhaps a disappearing culture or some other unusual case that begged for explanation. Alternatively, I could try to expand my focus by including not just low-income black populations but a much wider range of New Yorkers of varying classes, ethnicities, and backgrounds.

I had already taken the first path, having produced research on poor slums, drug-running gangs, and marginal groups. Now I wanted to find as many different New Yorkers involved in the underground economy as I could. I would have to fill up as many boxes as possible: poor, rich, middle class, men, women, Latino . . .

But this approach only raised further problems. First, my expertise was precisely on those who were shut out of society: the gentrified, the displaced, the unemployed. These marginal figures were usually the *victims* of great social changes. Or worse, they were the criminals, the traffickers in sex and contraband who were generally seen as victimizers. While I would have to include a much broader cast of characters and types, there still remained the possibility the conventional wisdom might be right. There was a risk of overstating or romanticizing the influence of these networks of people. Also, there was no map to this territory. No one really knew exactly who was making money illegally because they were, by definition, hidden from public view. Even if I had a hundred different characters and types in my study, critics could complain about another hundred who'd escaped my net. Would I ever really be able to say that my sample truly represented the diversity of illegal commerce in the city?

For the moment, I didn't need to answer these concerns—I only had to be aware of them. But I couldn't put them off forever.

To start a study, I always focus on the two things a sociologist needs in his toolbox: a) a few guiding concepts, and b) a strategy for getting evidence.

For strategy, I couldn't shake Shine's idea of "floating." It wasn't scientifically precise, but it did remind me to step out of my Chicago shoes and acknowledge that people moved in a different way in New York. As they moved around the city, they were likely to forge ties to new people in unpredictable ways. So I decided to follow people as they led me to *other* people. I would keep track of all these connections and branch out into as many new worlds as I could. And if none of it seemed to make any sense, I would try to be patient and wait for a pattern to emerge.

With the concept of permeable boundaries and a strategy for gathering information, it was time to start figuring out how to get all these people to talk to me. Asking hedge fund traders or real estate brokers to talk to a scientist about their connections to the economic underground might not be easy, but it had to be easier than getting hoodlums to talk about their crimes.

My first lead came from a police officer named Michael Collins, the friend of a policeman I knew in Chicago. When you're studying the black market, it's always a good idea to let the cops know what you're doing, so I introduced myself to him as soon as I landed in New York. We discovered we shared a love of history and became friendly. One night, just when I was starting to wonder where my work in Harlem was going, he made an offhand comment that surprised me.

"The days of street prostitution are over."

Over? Really? And what had things been like before?

Collins filled me in on the 1980s and 1990s, when prostitutes in little more than garter belts and bras flagged down cars on Tenth Avenue, when entire blocks were Wild West zones filled with all manner of crime.

"So where are the prostitutes going?" I asked. "The Internet?"

Some, he said. But there was a weird thing lately. Cops who were picking up women at bars and hotels for just regular stuff—the usual random reasons like disorderly conduct or drugs in public view—were finding hundreds or thousands of dollars on them. "They're not hookers," he said, "but they have all this *money*. There's something new going on." Part of this was because of city policy, he explained. The increasing police presence and decreasing tolerance for various street nuisances—from open-air prostitution to squeegee men—were motivated by a desire to protect the gentrifiers and tourists coming into Midtown. He didn't understand where the street workers went or what kind of women were coming into the hotels and bars, but I wanted to. This seemed exactly like the boundary crossing, the connection making—the floating—that I should be studying.

To get at this story, I decided that I couldn't act alone. I'd waste months as I had done in Harlem trying to build trust. So I linked up with the Sex Workers' Project at the Urban Justice Center, an advocacy group that provides legal services to sex workers. One of my students and I decided to work on their new project examining the rise of so-called "indoor" sex work. The match seemed beneficial for both parties: I could gain entrée into the sex trade and they would get the free services of a trained ethnographer.

My first attempt was cold-calling escort agencies to find some of the new sex workers. Only three out of twenty-five agency managers returned my call. The first hung up as soon as I said what I wanted. The second yelled at me, "Nice try, Mr. Police Officer!"

The third caller waved me away, but advised that I look at strip clubs. "That's where a lot of these women are starting to hang out. Because most of the women who do this, they're more like mistresses than hookers. They hang out in these bars and pick up these high-priced dates."

I thought about it. From what I read in the media, strip clubs were becoming more than just seedy places where hustlers and pimps hung out. Some of them were as costly as the fanciest night-clubs. High-end professionals went to them and spent lots of money. And since it was safe to assume that the dancers didn't declare all their tips and that their nightly wages were paid under the table, these were hybrid spaces that mixed legitimate and underground economic activity. Plus there'd be cigarette girls and back-room poker games and lavatory attendants. All of this clicked with my concept about permeable borders.

My explorations of the strip clubs of New York started with a midlevel place in Tribeca. The clientele was economically mixed and tourists were at a minimum. I went in and sat like any other customer, trying to blend in while glancing around periodically to take in the larger picture, but I guess I asked too many questions or failed to ogle the dancers with sufficient conviction because, on my third visit, a tall African-American guard approached me. He looked to be about six foot four, 250 pounds, built like a professional football player. Twice I had seen him throw out drunks who'd touched the strippers.

"How's your night going?" he asked, his face expressionless.

I smiled at him, trying my best to be friendly and disarming. "I thought you guys weren't supposed to talk to people."

"I talk to people when they're doing something I need to know about," he answered, giving me a stare that said, more eloquently than any words, that I was one of those people.

Honesty was the best policy, I decided. I told him that I was a sociologist from Columbia and had purely scientific—

"Come with me," he said, grabbing my arm.

"That's really not necessary," I said.

"You can explain to the manager."

All the way across the floor, he squeezed my arm hard enough to leave bruises. We reached a dark staircase and he pushed me up one flight, then pressed me against the wall with his massive palm while his other hand rapped on a metal door. A small square window slid open and shut; then the door opened. Inside sat three extras from a John Cassavetes movie: a young woman in lingerie and two middle-aged men with gaunt faces and greased black hair combed back over their heads. One of the men had a calculator in his hand; the other played with a small rubber band. Both had unbuttoned shirts and silver chains in their chest hair. Both shot me bored looks as the half-naked girl continued with what she was saying.

"The best thing about me, I don't flake out like some girls. I'm *dependable*."

"I wouldn't even know what that means, sweetheart," said the man with the calculator.

"I'll be here," she continued. "I'll show up when I say I'm gonna show up—and I'll be ready to do my thing."

Unimpressed, the man with the rubber band looked at the security guard, then at me. "Who's this guy?"

The guard tightened his grip on my arm. "He's been snooping around."

"Was he alone?" the man with the rubber band asked.

"I think so. There was another guy at the bar."

"I'm alone," I said, starting my usual introduction about sociology and the study of the underground economy.

The man at the desk ignored me and just stared at the guard, who lowered his head in shame.

"My bad. I'll go find the other guy."

He walked out of the office.

"What the fuck was that?" the man with the calculator said.

"Stupid fucking nigger," said the man with the rubber band. Then he looked me over again and sighed. "Say again?"

"I'm a sociologist," I explained. "I'm doing a study of sex work in New York, and how people make money in clubs."

The man with the calculator laughed. The man with the rubber band shook his head. "What is it with you people?" He turned to his partner. "Must be, what, the fourth guy wants to study us? This year?"

"Sounds about right," the other one said.

"Look, a little advice," the man with the calculator said. "None of these girls want your free condoms and nobody needs an AIDS test. Why don't you go looking for people under bridges or somewhere who really need the fucking help?"

Clearly, he was a bit shaky on the concept of sociology. "I'm not a social worker," I said.

"You don't want to help?" said the man with the rubber band.

"Why don't you want to help?" said the woman in lingerie.

All three pairs of eyes focused on me.

This always seems to confuse people. I think what I do is ultimately helpful, that gathering good information will help destroy stereotypes about the poor and lead to a more accurate diagnosis of our society's problems. But I also believe that in order to gather that information accurately, I have to put aside emotions like pity or affection. "I think it's important just to know what people do for a living," I said. "To *really* know. How much they make, how hard it is, why they do it, who they are, things like that. Then other people take all that data and decide what to do about it."

"How hard is it?" the woman in lingerie repeated. "It's hard, baby! I'll fill your ear with that."

The man with the calculator turned his palms up. "Yo, sweetheart."

She went silent, looking away.

Turning back in my direction, the man leaned forward in a way that said he was ready to sum up our encounter. "Look, I can't have you around here. I don't really understand what you're up to and I really don't have the time. So I'm going to ask that you leave. I'm assuming you won't be back here, right?"

"Well, what if I just talk with her?" I blurted out. "Just one conversation. That's it, and then I'm out of here."

"Why not?" the woman said. "It'll be fun."

"Okay. Fine. I don't run your life. But not here. You can meet him outside."

"Thank you," I said, appreciatively. "Let me write down my name and number for you. I'm legit. I don't want any trouble, really."

"Just get the fuck out of my office."

I rose, said a polite good-bye, and made my way through the dimly lit hallway and out onto the street, excited about the chance to interview the aspiring dancer. She would be my first shot at gaining a foothold in this intriguing economic sector.

I waited outside the club for two hours. She never showed up.

I tried to contain my disappointment. Years can go by before a researcher is fully accepted into any sort of group, especially one in which criminal subcultures are lurking, but the clock was ticking at Columbia. I had to research and publish enough material to make a case for tenure before too much more time passed. The strip clubs—legal establishments where illegal activity occurred—were the perfect solution. I could try upscale bars or nightclubs, but the challenges would probably be the same. The Urban Justice Center was helpful, but they were overwhelmed providing services to sex workers and didn't have time to make introductions for me.

What I needed was a guide, a Virgil who could teach me and vouch for me. I needed a *broker*.

I thought about the first time I met Analise. I had just arrived at Harvard on a fellowship from the Society of Fellows, a sixty-year-old organization that had no requirements other than attending dinners with famous writers and scientists at a grand mahogany table once owned by Oliver Wendell Holmes. Of the two dozen or so Junior Fellows in residence each year, a few would volunteer to help plan meals and pair food with bottles from the society's private wine cellar. In a particularly inept attempt to fit in, I agreed to take on this task. The problem was, I knew nothing about wine. I paired red wine with fish and chose modern California wines rather than the twenty-year-old French Burgundies that lined the cellar. My companions were not pleased. Vomit was mentioned several times.

I decided to hold a tasting so I could take notes and improve my selections. But when the guests began arriving in their loafers and barn jackets—accompanied by dates who seemed to be multiple incarnations of the same strawberry blond—disaster struck again. I tapped a glass with a knife and said, "Welcome! Tonight we begin with a 1982 Château Lee—"

With my mouth open, I realized I had no idea how to pronounce this French word. Then Analise leaned over and whispered, "Lee-oh-*nay*."

Afterward, she took me aside. "These are white wine glasses," she said.

"That's all I could find," I said.

"This is the Society of Fellows," she said. "You should have the right stemware."

Stemware? I slumped. "It looks like I'm going to be a real disaster as wine steward. I had no idea it was so technical."

She gave me a warm smile. "It's not that hard once you know a few basic things." With that, she commenced a quick-and-dirty introduction in the basics of wine. Soon she was asking me about India and telling me about her visits there as a teenager and college student. Her parents had thought of it as a punishment, sending her there to "think things over," but she'd loved it.

"I feel so much smarter when I come back because I just don't give a shit about what anybody else thinks. That's the answer, Sudhir—just don't give a shit. Same with wine. There's no right or wrong, really. It's about knowing what you like." Then she gave me a merry wink, my first true welcome to the inner sanctums of America's elite. "You just have to start drinking—a *lot*," she said.

I laughed. After that, everything was easier.

Years later, away from eating clubs and ensconced in New York strip clubs, I found myself needing another Analise who could serve as my consigliere. But now the stakes were higher than scorn and a few rolling eyes from my colleagues. There were only so many times bouncers and security guards would gently escort me into the back room for a conversation. In my work with gangs, I discovered quickly that leaders would speak to me if I signaled that their peers were taking part. Maybe they thought I'd divulge their competitors' secrets, but I knew that they mostly wanted me to affirm how much smarter, richer, more talented, and more violent they were relative to their competitors. Even if I never did that— and I rarely did—their jealousy was enough to make them willing participants. I was hoping that strip club managers would eventually join my study out of the same need for competition, but that happy occasion was years away at best. For now, I just needed them to let me in the door long enough to hear my offer.

Over the next few months, by dint of persistent effort, I did manage to convince eight or ten women to talk to me at least briefly. They told me about the fees they paid the clubs, the costs of renting the back rooms, the risks of being harassed or even beaten up for failing to pay. They told me that sometimes when they were in tight spots they had to take loans from the club manager, and also spoke of helpful managers who protected them from abusive johns. But were the experiences these women described common or idiosyncratic? Was there a set of close ties like in the Chicago projects, where the gangs looked like the enemy within but were in fact intimately tied to their neighbors? How did the clubs compare to the Internet? To the back pages of the alternative weeklies? And how did all the players and levels tie together? I would have to get a lot more *n*'s before I could call it serious research. And I still needed a consigliere to help me put a frame around it.

Then it happened. I found my strip club Analise and the new world finally began to open for me.

His name was Mortimer Conover. I met him in a bar in Hell's Kitchen, where he stood out because he was an old-school sport who always wore a jacket and tie and pocket square. He must have been in his mid-seventies, but his passion for the ladies of the evening was undiminished.

"I can travel the whole world in one night," Mortimer liked to say. "I can go to Russia and Missouri and Mexico and the Dominican Republic and never leave the neighborhood."

Mortimer held down the corner booth of a bar on Ninth Avenue, the same place he'd been patronizing for the last twenty years. Completely nondescript, with a sign that read "Bar" hanging over a wooden door, it was the sort of place you could walk by and not even realize it was there. Inside it was nothing but a line of booths and bar stools, which bore a vague resemblance to a watering trough in a feedlot. Mortimer sat in the back opining on politics, sports, great Irish politicians, and the mysteries of female psychology.

He followed predictable patterns. First an old-fashioned. Then a glass of water. Then multiple glasses of red wine. Periodically he would walk out back and light his pipe. When he started slurring his words, he would switch to tea. Between drinks, he would slip in a few moments with a lady friend.

Of his past, Mortimer said little. He had been "in business," he said. His crippled right hand had been injured in "the war," though he would never specify which war. His son, John, was a construction foreman who lived in Elizabeth, New Jersey. His grandchildren were all in high school and he carried the photos in his wallet to prove it. His heartbreak was his daughter-in-law. "I'm a sexual predator, according to her," Mortimer explained one night, his voice wistful and bruised.

Eventually, Mortimer told me the story. When he was already in his sixties and retired from his job, he'd approached a woman in a strip club with an offer of money for sex. She turned out to be an undercover police officer. A furor ensued. His son nearly refused to pick him up from jail, and his daughter-in-law, a devout Christian, cut him off completely. No more invitations to Thanksgiving dinner, no more weekends with the children.

Mortimer kept me company on many nights as I waited around for a sex worker to grant me an interview, but I never noticed any health issues. That changed the night he collapsed on the floor of the bar. One minute he was holding court as usual and the next he flopped down writhing in obvious pain. His lady friend rushed to the bar phone and speared out the numbers for 911 with her long fake nails. A heart attack, everyone figured.

It was a stroke. When Mortimer came back to the bar a month later, his left hand was a claw like his right hand and he couldn't even grab his drinking glass. His eyesight had weakened, and now he wore thick black eyeglasses. He limped and needed help walking or climbing stairs. When I helped him to the bathroom or into the garden to smoke his pipe, his hand shook ferociously.

Everyone in the bar seemed to adjust naturally to his new state. The bartender put a straw in his drink and even found some straws that held up in hot tea. Mortimer now felt nervous carrying cash

around, so the bar manager kept a running tab for each of
the women he slept with and Mortimer paid once at the end of the
week. There was always a gypsy cab to drive him home, a service
that included a personal escort upstairs to his apartment. Several of
the sex workers made sure his fridge was filled with sandwiches
and his bathroom had toilet paper. And to save him from exhausting trips home, the porn shop next door made up a little room in
the back where Mortimer could enjoy his ladies of the night.

This fascinated me. This underground world had adapted to
protect its own, creating an impromptu community of sorts. Gradually I realized this was the same thing I had seen among drug
dealers and prostitutes, often in response to an outside threat.
These types of communities weren't locally based or geographically
segregated, like the ones in Chicago, but were latent everywhere in
an intricate web of social relations and ready to emerge in response
to specific events and situations. Put more simply, had there been
no Mortimer who needed help, the "Mortimer community" would
never have surfaced.

Not only that, but further questioning revealed that most of the
ladies hadn't had sex with Mortimer in years. Usually they would
just take their clothes off and let him fondle them while he told
tales of past loves. I would find out later that this turns out to be
surprisingly common, which suggests that many prostitutes may
deserve their claim to being lay therapists. As one sardonic Russian
prostitute would tell me about a rich client, "Most of the time, I tell
him why he shouldn't leave his wife."

Even as I saw a group of people coalesce around Mortimer, I
was hesitant to call it a community. It wasn't a community in the
sense of some suburban cul-de-sacs or a church group in which
people have placed a label on their common bond. Mortimer's
friends were helpful to one another, but their ties were not rooted
in religion, ethnicity, neighborhood, or even a common stigma like

race or sexual identity. When asked, Mortimer's supporters said they were simply doing what you'd do for a friend who needs help. "There's another guy like this down the street," they would say, or "You should see this guy across town who's doing so much worse." And this was not the only bar where the prostitutes and johns passed their time together. There seemed to be many such informal networks, ad hoc communities built upon mutual interest and affection. And these people came together by crossing all sorts of boundaries, like race and class, that sociologists usually think of as keeping people apart. Mortimer was a white man living off retirement income; the women helping him were lower-income Latinos and blacks. In the same way, the bar was filled with Irish cops and corporate white-collar workers, but there were always a dozen or so North African immigrants who congregated each evening in the corner. In this little bar, this little world, they were all tied together for better and worse. Half the patrons owed money to the other half—mostly for sex—but they also lent money to each other and fixed each other's cars, bet on sports events and sold each other electronic equipment. As people spent more time in the bar, in fact, they were almost expected to take part in these ventures. Reciprocity became a means of signaling that one was local, to be trusted, and such trust would become the basis for receiving the kind of treatment that Mortimer was now getting.

For me, this could pose problems. There were only so many times I could say, "I'm just here as Mortimer's friend. I have no interest in lending you five hundred dollars for your surefire illegal moneymaking scheme." But Shine's words kept returning to me. These were *floating* communities. I knew from earlier research that you could always count on things to go wrong in underground trading, and surely these communities were as precarious and fickle as any of the bonds formed in the black market. Floating may have signaled some kind of fluidity, but it certainly didn't mean floating free. I'd seen people get kicked out of the bar or lose the trust necessary to be a commercial partner. Typically, someone will try to profit from their relationships, conflicts will ensue, people will take sides, and the little world splinters. How long would Mortimer's network survive?

But I had seen enough to want more. If I could find the right places—if I could follow the right people—I might see something that was invisible to most of the world.

Tonight Shine was behind the wheel of his black German sedan, cruising south down Malcolm X Boulevard on a mission he would not reveal. Shine's way of hiding his life from me behind the calm demeanor of a power player was frustrating, especially since I told him I wasn't studying him. Maybe part of it was as simple as learning to trust me, but his style reminded me of the gang leaders I knew in Chicago: they loved to boast and give the impression of success. Most who said they were high earners couldn't even afford to live on their own, as Steven Levitt and I documented in the study made famous by *Freakonomics*. I was dying to ask Shine to talk straight about these subjects, but it didn't seem to be the best time to bring this up.

With one hand on the wheel, Shine steered an arc from 110th Street onto the country road that cut right down through Central Park. We skimmed past joggers and bicyclists, close enough that I could have touched them with an extended hand. A few shouted at us to slow down. But Shine was intent on the same old sermon—I had to bounce, I had to float, I had to jump and hop and bob and weave. He made it sound exhausting and mandatory, like a vast and endless gym class.

Now he was physically dragging me along. The cold night air swept over the convertible's windshield and into our faces. My eyes wouldn't stop tearing and everyone seemed to be staring at us, wondering why the hell we were driving with the top down on such a chilly night.

"This is New York!" Shine continued. "We're like humming-birds, man. We go flower to flower. Didn't they teach you that in Chicago?"

"No," I said. "They taught me to sit your ass down and don't ask no questions."

He laughed like that was the funniest thing he'd ever heard. "Shit! You really did get schooled by black folk!"

Perhaps to emphasize his point, he started running through red lights. You'd think that a drug dealer would be careful in public, but apparently prudence clashes with the manly virtues required by the drug trade.

This was the first time Shine and I had been together outside Harlem, I realized. I sure hoped he knew what he was doing.

Up ahead, the road emerged from the park into the brownstone rows of the West Side. I felt the impulse to escape, to get in a cab and go somewhere quiet and safe.

He made a quick turn on Fifty-seventh Street and headed west into Hell's Kitchen. Once dominated by the tough Irish street gangs memorialized in the Sean Penn movie *State of Grace*, it had joined the vast number of New York neighborhoods that couldn't seem to make up their minds about what they wanted to be. Gen-trification was slowly blooming along Ninth Avenue in the form of frat guy nightclubs and endless ethnic restaurants, but these bits of trendiness were sandwiched in between mini red-light districts, where porn shops and seedy bars seemed to fill entire blocks. Along Tenth and Eleventh Avenues, where factories and warehouses were interspersed with turn-of-the-century brick apartment buildings, the signature sound was the steady beeping of trucks as they backed into loading docks. Yuppie couples with expensive strollers coex-isted with big Puerto Rican families and urban hipsters. Cheap hotels and adult video parlors sat next to gleaming new condos and renovated brownstones. In this sense, Hell's Kitchen had become a sort of postmodern neighborhood, stuck between genres—just like the world music my more artsy academic colleagues admired.

Once again, all this would have been a rare sight in Chicago. Gentrification and urban development took place there, to be sure. Indeed, the national program of "urban renewal" was first developed in Chicago in an effort to reclaim seedy areas. But Chicago mayors typically sent bulldozers into down-and-out neighborhoods and then resold the land for private development—sports stadiums, universities, highways. It was a rapid-fire form of social bleaching. Gentrification in New York was like an IV drip. As old buildings came down, property changed hands, creating new neighborhoods in a more organic way. As a result, transitional communities cropped up where ethnics and social classes mixed with one another, sometimes harmoniously and sometimes less so. This was now happening in Chelsea, where the number of artists and gay families was growing every day. It was happening all over Brooklyn, where hipsters were tearing down the aluminum siding put up by working-class Poles and Italians and reinventing the neighborhoods for a new century. I wondered how the original residents adapted when they discovered that their borders were so permeable.

Shine pulled up in front of a porn shop. The plastic sign read "Ninth Avenue Family Video." A woman waved at us through the store window.

"Angela," Shine said. "She's cool. You'll like her."

We walked in and Angela gave Shine a big hug. She started speaking in Spanish, joking with Shine that his hair was turning gray. Still caught in her embrace, Shine reached over the counter to shake the clerk's hand. "Jun, my brother, what's happening?"

Jun was a small, gentle-looking South Asian man in a blue plaid shirt. He had wispy black hair that scraggled about his head as if it was lost. "Not much, not much," he said.

Shine introduced me. I reached my hand across the counter.

"Manjun," he responded, grasping my hand in both of his. "It is my honor to meet you."

Angela took my hand next, her eyes so soft and comforting she could have been taking in a long-lost relative. I immediately felt relaxed.

But Shine was already standing near the doorway to the back room. "Come on back here for a minute, Angela," he said.

She gave me another melting smile and turned away.

"Jun, come too," Shine said. "I need to talk with both of you. Sudhir, just watch the cash register for a few minutes."

"What if people want something?"

"Just take their money," Shine said.

I stepped behind the counter, feeling nervous and ridiculous. I had no idea how to open up the register.

The floor behind the counter was raised so the clerks could see better down the aisles—four aisles, eight walls, probably a thousand videotapes and DVDs on each wall. I'd never been surrounded by so much pornography. And I had no idea what I was doing here. Who was this Indian clerk and why was he in business with this amiable Latina woman? What did they have to do with Shine? What did they have to do with me?

"Yo—you guys got *Prison Girls Five?*"

A heavyset Latino man was calling up from aisle two, not even bothering to cross to the counter.

"Um, let me check," I said.

I could see Shine speaking with Angela and Manjun in the far corner. They were all nodding their heads and interrupting one another, but I could only catch snatches of the conversation. Judging by the hand gestures, they were upset about something and feeling overwhelmed by life. Whatever it was, they seemed to be taking forever.

"I got to see those chicks in chains, bro. The Indian guy said you were getting it in."

What would a real clerk say? Thinking of how I'd been treated by clerks in other situations, I aimed for the sweet spot between boredom and misanthropy. "Just what's on the shelf," I said.

Two more patrons walked in. One asked if the store bought "used shit" from customers. "You have to come back when the manager is here," I said. "Maybe twenty minutes?"

Finally, Manjun returned and traded places with me in the narrow space behind the counter. From the back of the store, Shine beckoned me. I walked down aisle two past a gauntlet of porn. In front of a metal shelf labeled "Foreign," Shine and Angela waited like hosts on a receiving line.

"Angela said she and Manjun will help you," Shine said. "Get her phone number. Or just come back and talk with Jun anytime. Sound good?"

"Sure," I said tentatively, unsure where these introductions were going.

Angela gave me one more warm, motherly smile. Later, I would learn that Angela was not actually an employee of the store but a sex worker. This did not seem to affect her relationship with Manjun, however. The two of them worked together like partners. Manjun managed the store and earned extra income by allowing Angela and her friends to use the back room for their private dealings, with Shine providing drugs as necessary to Angela's friends and clients—a floating community if ever there was one. Angela was the glue that held it all together.

But right now, as I would soon learn, I was catching them just as demand for their services was disappearing due to the wider gentrification of the neighborhood. As strollers replaced strolling johns, the importance of their community would become significant in another way: as a way to see one another through the hardships to come.

"I'm not sure what Shine told you, but I'm a college professor,"

I began. "I'm working with an advocacy group in the city. I'm trying to study the world of—"

"I know, sweetie. I know," Angela said, taking my arm and
leading me toward the front of the store. "He told me you wanted
to meet different kinds of people. I get it. But first— Well, since
we're going to help you, we're in kind of a . . . Maybe you could
help us a little? We're in a kind of *situación difícil.*"

Uh-oh. What had Shine promised them?

"Do you mind grabbing a few of those boxes and stocking the
shelves? It's easy. The boxes are labeled and you just need to put
things where they belong. Jun usually has a guy who comes around
to help and he didn't show up today."

Not knowing what else to do, I grabbed a box, opened it, and
peeled away the blue plastic wrapping that held together each bundle
of DVDs. I couldn't get over the adolescent sense that I was doing
something wrong, but the sheer abundance of all the penises and
breasts seemed to neutralize the effect. Box of porn in hand, I studied
the shelves. Each section was clearly labeled with handwritten signs:
"Gay," "Extreme," "For Women," "New Adult," "Bondage," "New
Releases," "Foreign." There was a sign for "Language" that stumped
me for a moment. Did that mean foreign language or dirty language?

At the cash register, Shine, Manjun, and Angela were laughing
about something. Shine knocked fists with Manjun and cast a look
my way, grinning at the sight of me with a box of porn in hand.
Then he hugged Angela and headed for the door, tossing me one
last bit of advice:

"Have fun!"

Shine didn't return for weeks. He and I both knew that I needed
to get out of Harlem. My wheels were spinning and I'd been
losing faith that I would see all that New York had to hide from the

law. I could tell that he'd grown tired of me complaining that I was not getting anywhere in my research. But the ride he gave me to Hell's Kitchen and to Manjun's store was exactly the boost I needed. Even this brief departure from Harlem helped me to focus my attention on the ways that different worlds came together underground. Just like Mortimer's bar, Manjun's store wove together a heady mix: Angela was Latino, but many of the sex workers who came in were Asian and Eastern European. If they couldn't afford a hotel room, they brought their clients—often white and working or middle class—to the video parlor. Day by day, the sex workers grew comfortable enough to discuss their dates with me in the room. Their repeat customers spanned the ethnic and class spectrum; a Midtown lawyer and a city bus driver were equally likely to shake Manjun's hand, pick up a DVD, and, if the mood was right, ask about a sex worker who might be free for a few hours. Cops dropped by nightly. Manjun always had free coffee and tea for them, though some came in for a little window shopping as well.

On many occasions, I saw acts of help and camaraderie like the ones I'd seen around Mortimer. Manjun's store had become a communication node like Mortimer's bar, where people came to advertise information and hear the latest news. When cops heard from Manjun that an abused woman was lying in a hotel, they sent over a social worker—a task police found much easier back in the days when prostitutes and social workers met one another on the streets. For cash under the table, doctors came to Manjun's store to service undocumented laborers who lacked insurance—two babies were delivered right there in the storeroom. Disputes were settled, small-business ventures were launched, women met men they could marry to acquire a resident alien card. On it went. Trading begat trading, all of which demanded reciprocity. Hang around long enough, and you were pulled into these exchanges. Fortunately, the longer I stayed, the more these locals began to associate me with Manjun. Eavesdropping on conversations was a lot easier when people saw me as the nonthreatening Indian who stocked shelves, and the presumption of my low status also freed me up from having to enter into their schemes.

Gradually, between Mortimer and Manjun, I met people from a wide range of backgrounds who came together in this little underworld in a way that I had not seen in the Midwest. In the sex trade alone, I had seen empathetic doctors who sold pharma off the books, landlords who rented rooms by the month, loan sharks who laundered money, and fake-ID sellers who found visas for immigrant women. Each was rooted in a different community, but each spread roots far and wide across the city. I still had to figure out ways to observe people on the move—the invisible roots spreading, not the stately tree. I finally felt I had seen enough to be a contributor to a project with the Urban Justice Center, and even started to entertain the possibility of my own independent study down the road.

But I had already seen enough to temper any romanticism about the new New York. Yes, people were making connections and crossing boundaries. In fact, nearly everyone I met wanted to tell me how vast and interconnected the underground really was. Unfortunately, many of their stories turned out to be little more than boasts about underclass solidarity. It only took a little prodding to uncover darker tales of theft, physical abuse, deportation, and immigrants losing thousands of hard-earned dollars on off-the-books financial ventures gone awry. A few astute urbanists had tempered the celebration of global cities with warnings about how they would affect the underclass, pushing them into part-time jobs or the underground economy amid growing resentment against South Asians, Middle Easterners, and Muslims of various stripes. Some warned that Manhattan was becoming a "theme park." Others pointed to city politicians who threw taxpayer dollars at high-profile financial service firms, a slap in the face to average New Yorkers who needed money for subways and schools.

More and more, I was seeing that life in this underworld couldn't have been more different from the Chicago projects where I'd last roamed. There, trust was an outcome of the likelihood of seeing the same neighbors day in and day out. Your enemy could be your business partner tomorrow and your romantic partner a year from now. Forgive and forget was practically a lease requirement. But when you entered new worlds with unfamiliar faces, how did the systems of trust and patterns of association *work*? Predictability was vital in the underground, where people were always looking over their shoulders for the next predator, and the furious pace of New York only increased the anxiety. Just months after bringing his family to the United States, for example, Manjun was already beginning to see the Midtown sex trade crumble and his income from Angela and her friends disappear along with it. What did the global acceleration of people, resources, money, and opportunities do to the durability of social relationships? There must be new forms of danger to go with the new forms of opportunity, and I had to understand the hazards in order to understand the solutions.

Another thing that caught my attention in those early days was the flip side of failure and danger. Some people seemed to have been in the game for a long while—Shine and Angela, for example. They must have had a particular kind of competence that gave them the power to move across boundaries in more effective ways. What was the basis of that competence? That was the essential question that could lead to changes in government policy and new methods of helping this beleaguered community. But once again, I couldn't help but think of the Chicago model. There, a roaming gangster's best move was to befriend the local thug, cop, or community leader who could help him out of a jam. When Shine drove his car out of Harlem, who were his allies? Or were the assets softer here, like the capacity to talk your way out of trouble or into some juicy new scheme? Everyone who knew Shine talked about his quiet, charismatic, persuasive nature. He was a "player," they said. Perhaps his soft asset was a kind of proficiency across local languages and value structures, translating local idioms just like a UN diplomat working across international borders.

I had many questions, but still no answers. To add to the difficulty, the city itself was changing all around me. As Mayor Giuliani's second term ended, the city government had underwritten large-scale makeovers of seedier areas. Neighborhoods like Chelsea and the Lower East Side went through their spectacular rebirth as hip destinations for the young and artsy. Wall Street and Midtown saw an explosion in corporate relocations, and the middle and upper classes flocked back to the city along with the businesses that served them. Personally, I was still more comfortable sitting in a Chicago park where gangs have occupied the same corner for three generations, continuity that gave a historical context to what I was seeing. New York was making it hard for me to get too comfortable sitting in any one place. Without even looking for it, I was starting to experience the tension and dynamism my subjects lived with every day. Manjun's store may not be around much longer—*I had to float.*

CHAPTER 3

THE SHIFTING GROUND BENEATH YOUR FEET

In the autumn of 2002, after my first few months of coming to the porn store, Manjun invited me out into the neighborhood. "Let us go make a walk and visit." For a moment I felt as if I were back in Chicago, where my interview subjects often led me through their neighborhoods to teach me about their lives.

As Manjun walked, he held his head high with his hands interlaced behind his back in the Indian fashion, his balding head reflecting the neon lights above. "Mr. Sudhir," he began, "you told me you are here with me because you want to see differently, yes?"

He was referring to a much interrupted conversation we had been conducting in the odd moments when there were no customers in his store. He knew I was anxious to get deeper into the underground economy in New York, and that one porn store in Hell's Kitchen could only be a piece of the story.

"Yes," I answered. "Very much."

He sensed my impatience.

"Mr. Sudhir, look and tell me what do you see?"

I looked around. I saw sex stores, bodegas, a diner, a Chinese takeout place, a few people standing around smoking cigarettes and drinking liquor from bottles in brown paper bags. Across the street, two Hispanic women shivered on the sidewalk as they met the gaze of passing drivers. "The usual scene," I said.

"This is the most spiritual place in the city," he said. "No doubt. No doubt."

He dragged me up to a tall black man standing outside an adult video store. "Shoomi!" he cried. "How is your evening?"

The man responded with African formality. "Manjun, my friend. I am very well tonight. Please tell me, what is happening in your life? How is your family?"

Manjun said everyone was very well. "I want you to meet my very good friend. A *professor*! He teaches at the prestigious Columbia Collegiate University of New York. He is expert in human civilization. And *mathematics*."

Like a good South Asian, Manjun always managed to reference my "mathematics" degree.

"He wants to look at the below-the-belly world," Manjun explained. "The world of new people like us. He thinks we have no god."

Manjun was joking, but I had to register outrage. "I didn't say that!" I turned to Shoomi, spreading my hands to show that I was a reasonable man, unlike certain other people on the sidewalk. "I study the black market, which some people call the *under*belly of society. Meaning the margins of society. The way Manjun says it, it sounds dirty."

Shoomi put his hand on my shoulder affectionately. "Mr. Professor, don't get lost in the garbage. That is my message to you. The garbage will only distract you. You have to look at the people."

"Yes, the people," Manjun said.

"Still, there is a *lot* of garbage," I said with a laugh.

Shoomi looked at me with pity. "Mr. Professor, I have been here five years. I have finally brought over to this country my wife and three daughters from Nigeria. The first week, I took my daughters on the train and I bring them here. I tell them, this is where I work. I work at this store, I work in this area. It is filled with many different kind of people. Lots of garbage. But the people are like you.

They are searching. We are all searching. That is what I told my daughters."

Manjun suggested that I couldn't see the god because I didn't believe in God myself.

"Perhaps that is true," Shoomi answered. "Americans are losing their faith. But are you American? You sound American, but don't act American."

This was something I heard a lot from foreigners. I had too much patience to be American, they said. I was willing to let things unfold instead of trying to make them happen. I was never sure whether to be flattered or insulted. And explaining it always seemed like an endless pit of complication. "I was raised here," I began, "but I was born in India and—"

"You are Indian then," Shoomi said. "You are not born here."

"Just like us!" Manjun cried.

With that Shoomi began naming the people he considered members of our improvised tribe, a litany that reminded me of the "begats" in the Bible. "Kurana at the gas station. Works all the time, prays all the time! Hindu. The newspaper stand is Ahmed— Muslim like me. Over there, getting on his bike, my good amigo José. Catholic. That police officer, very good man, also Catholic."

"What about your friend Santosh?" Manjun said. "He prays a lot!"

"And your friend who works on weekends," Shoomi said. "He is an imam, no?"

Of course, nobody wants to be lumped into an oppressed group. They wanted to be sure I saw them as more than a social problem. They were still coming up with names when a small brown man rolled up to us on a battered old bicycle, an empty thermal pizza box tied to the back.

"Carlos, my friend. What is happening in your life?" Shoomi said.

Carlos had a big smile on his face. His eyes were jet black and full of excitement. He pointed a thumb backward toward his chest. "*Soy un padre*," he said.

"Your baby came?" Shoomi translated. "Yes! Very good! Congratulations, Carlos!"

Carlos took out his wallet and produced a small picture of the mother, child, and some family members. "Very *pequeño*," he said, looking for the English words.

"Very nice, Carlos. I send you from my heart all the prayers for great blessings for your child."

But Manjun seemed concerned. "Are they coming here?"

Shoomi pointed at the photo and flapped his hands to mime a plane flying to the United States. "They come here?" he asked. He pointed to the sidewalk. "*Aquí?*"

Carlos looked sad. Shaking his head, he put the photo back in his wallet and said good-bye. As he rode off, I saw him wipe his eyes with the back of his hand.

"You see?" Shoomi said to me.

W alking around Manjun's neighborhood helped me to make some quick counts. Within three blocks, there were nine porn stores like his. Some sold adult DVDs alongside music CDs and popular movies; others offered peep shows behind the adult video aisles. There were also live shows with female dancers. Many of these businesses operated illegally, which brought a steadily increasing level of risk. Ever since Mayor Giuliani launched his "quality of life" campaign to make the city more attractive to tourists and the returning suburbanites, the police had been cracking down on "nuisances" that ranged from squeegee men who cleaned car windshields at traffic lights to adult entertainment venues like Manjun's store. The squeegee men had mostly disappeared from view, and some of the store owners had moved to the industrial waterfronts of Queens and the Bronx. But most just toned down the signage, moved the dirty stuff to the back of the store, and waited to see how hard things would get.

A week after our first walk around the neighborhood, Manjun introduced me to two homeless men who were masters of panhandling, squeegee work, recycling, petty theft, and shoplifting. Another time it was a South Asian kiosk vendor with a clever sideline in stolen passports and temporary work visas. Then the pastor of a church on Fifty-first Street who was famous for getting illegals day care and nanny jobs. He wanted me to see the goodness in his little corner of the world. But his innate desire to look on the bright side made me skeptical.

There were too many heartwarming tales. I had to have my own independent way of finding these stories, and I needed to see things for myself. For a sociologist, half the job is trying to see the holes in your theory. I needed more prostitutes, more pimps, more madams, more under-the-table employment brokers, more counterfeiters who dealt in fake social security cards—not just the Manjun-approved ones. I especially needed to find more illegal immigrants and learn how the underground economy helped keep them alive.

One day I told Shine about my frustration. I meant nothing by it. We were just talking and I was complaining in an ordinary way, as you would about any work problem. I told him that no one really had done a study on the complicated lives of people who toiled underground and it could really help my career. I may have admitted that I was starting to fear that Chicago was the only place I could be a successful academic. Okay, maybe I was whining.

The very next time I arrived at the store, Shine was standing at the counter laughing with Manjun. I had just begun to say hello when a customer came up with a mangled copy of a DVD. "Got a better copy of this?"

"I'll look in back," I said.

Shine was amused. "They can't tell you apart, my brother. Your brown ass looks just as porn clerk as me and Jun."

Manjun laughed too. "He find his true calling! Maybe he take my place!"

When I was digging through the boxes in the back room, Manjun left Shine at the cash register and came up to me. "I hear you want to meet some more people. You don't think I am helping you enough?"

"No, no, no," I said. "You're helping me *so* much. I just think you want me to see the good things and good people here, and I'm researching, you know, the below-the-belly world."

Manjun nodded and said to me bluntly, "Mr. Professor, I find what you need. Just know, please, that life changes. Sometimes it changes very fast. Look, I help you, okay? But anything you want, you should tell me now. Tomorrow, I don't know. You understand?"

"Not really," I said.

Manjun was sweating, I noticed. And he had been wearing the same clothes for the last few weeks, which was unusual, because he was a fastidious man, attentive to his hygiene. He sat down on the cot and waved me away when I asked what was wrong.

I walked toward the front of the store and confronted Shine. "What did you say to him? He looks like he's having a heart attack!"

"Look, do you want my help or not?' Shine responded impatiently. "You wanted to find people like Jun, right? Jun said he'll find them. So what's the problem?"

"I don't want you to pressure him."

Shine gave me a smile that said I didn't know how the world worked.

"You must be getting something out of this," I said.

This may not have been the nicest thing to say. But it was frustrating dealing with all of Shine's secrecy, and since we couldn't talk openly about things, I often turned to sarcasm to express my concerns. And I may have been extra suspicious because my experience in Chicago taught me that secrets could be dangerous. In one case, some local gang leaders used my research to find new underground traders to extort. But at the same time, trying to expand my list of contacts in order to gauge the feasibility of a study didn't seem too risky. I just didn't want to end up helping Shine expand his own business at my expense.

Now he was even more amused. "And what if I am getting something out of this, my brother? What if I am? We ain't in church, are we?"

In the underground, he was telling me, everyone is a user and everyone is a resource. I was no different.

Looking back, I have to admit he gave me fair warning.

From the back room of the porn shop, I was beginning to map the ways that the local underground economy spread into the world beyond. My first priority was to interview enough women working indoors to finish my collaboration with the Urban Justice Center. Angela's help was crucial here. I spoke to dozens of street-walkers right in the back of the store. Sometimes the women took me around the neighborhood and pointed out the doctor that gave them off-the-books health care, the bartender who stored their money safely, the hair salons that gave them reduced rates. The information came quickly and I wrote it down as fast as I could.

Sex brings people together, literally but also socially. It seemed to weave its threads all through this hidden world, bringing the community together in a thousand different ways. South Asians clerked and managed the video stores. West African men stood outside dance clubs to recruit johns. The wives of those West Africans provided day care to mothers who sold sexual services. Mexicans and Central Americans toiled clandestinely inside the video parlors and clubs as cleaners and laborers. And since the sex workers I was meeting came from every corner of the world—from

Europe and Africa and Australia, from China and Singapore and Brazil—you could say the invisible thread of sex was weaving the whole world together. Certainly they were as global a phenomenon as a multinational executive on his corporate jet.

Angela's role in the life of Manjun's shop seemed to perfectly demonstrate my thesis. The illegal money she brought in helped keep the legal business alive, and the legal business gave her a refuge for conducting her illegal business. There was no clear line between underground and aboveground. With her peers, I tried to trace the same connections through monetary transactions. How much did they earn? Where did they save and launder their money? Did they have credit cards or did they use loan sharks? With each answer, I was able to tease out a surprisingly elaborate infrastructure that ranged from Manjun's store to the strip bars and peep shows, to the bars, hotels, and health clinics. I began to see that these women weren't supporting drug habits—the conventional and suspiciously convenient view of prostitutes—but more likely families, neighborhoods, businesses. And most of the women also had other part-time gigs, often legal, that wove them into the community in another way.

But the underground economy didn't stop at sex and drugs, of course. Day laborers told me they earned only minimum wage for cleaning bodegas and washing dishes. Most worked sixty to seventy hours per week at multiple jobs. Each job brought them an average of three hundred dollars a week and lasted about nine to twelve months. They piled together in astonishingly cramped apartments, most of which violated every possible city zoning code. The security guards at the porn shops brought home about five dollars an hour, but their hours varied, so they also drove taxis and gypsy cabs. Homeless persons panhandled, shined shoes, and—when they could get away with it—washed car windshields at the more lively intersections. They made about a hundred dollars in any given week and they were routinely arrested for vagrancy, loitering, shoplifting, and other petty criminal acts.

On and on I went, gathering data and identifying broad economic patterns. But good sociology is always a mixture of close focus and long shot. You dial in and pull back, dial in and pull back, a delicate dance over the data gaps. And as I pulled back, it became quite clear that, for many immigrants and underclass Americans in the area, the story of living in the global metropolis wasn't at all glamorous. It was one of worsening outcomes and increasing vulnerability. This was most visible in the decline of street prostitution, for example. Women who might have brought home three hundred or four hundred dollars a night before told me they were barely making a hundred dollars a night and fought with one another over the lone john walking the streets. They were all depressed, and without a clear sense of what the future held.

I felt the need to learn more about their vulnerability as well as the associations, like those of Mortimer and his friends, that helped them make ends meet. Since my work with the Urban Justice Center had given me expertise in the sexual underground, and since the sale of sex was so integral to this world as well, it made sense to keep sex work as a point of focus. I decided to look into the infrastructure that supported the sex workers to see what kinds of social networks wrapped around the sex trade to make the economy function. And to address the generalizability problem, I needed to broaden my reach. In 2003, I decided to focus on Manjun and three other South Asian–born store clerks who worked in the neighborhood. Two were from Bangladesh, one from India, and one from Pakistan—populations I had never studied. The challenge was figuring out how to win their trust.

For the first few months, I met them on a casual basis, usually with Manjun during his after-work meals and tea breaks. Eventually I began to tell them about my anxieties about understanding

New York, because I find that sharing my own personal anxieties is a useful means of building a relationship. I told them that I'd love to launch an in-depth study of the changes taking place around them. I told them I needed to find people who really trusted me, people who would allow me to enter their lives for long periods, before I could really start a long-term study. I was about to get into the subject of sex when one of them interrupted me with a knowing wink. "You should see what goes on in my store."

This was Santosh, the oldest and the most successful of the four. At fifty-three, he was part owner of a thriving business and the patriarch of a large family that included his wife, his mother, several brothers and their families, two sons, and a daughter-in-law who was expecting the baby who would make him a grandfather. But the success of his American life was completely rooted in the underground economy of sex.

He told me his story as he stood behind the counter of his store, stuffing years of epic immigrant drama into the snatched moments between sales. He arrived in 1993 and started off driving a cab. On a good night, he made one hundred dollars. After a year, he realized he could make a little more on slow nights by leaving his meter off and driving men around in search of prostitutes. Sometimes he'd walk away and let them use the backseat. In time, he developed a knowledge of bathhouses in Midtown and brothel brownstones up in central and Spanish Harlem where sex workers waited behind every door. In a ten-mile radius, he could find his customers a partner of any race, nationality, or sexual persuasion they desired. Each john gave him ten or twenty dollars to find a brothel or bathhouse, sex workers tipped him what they could afford at the end of the week, and the brothel owners paid ten dollars per client. He told his wife he was "consulting" for some businesses, which freed him up to drive the taxi nearly every night, and before long his illegal earnings were as high as two thousand dollars a month—more than he made for cab driving.

One day, a friend suggested he invest in a video store. He bought 15 percent of the store and started working there as a night clerk. But the bathhouse operators and sex workers wanted to keep working with him as well, so he made extra revenue by telling his customers and cab drivers where to find a brothel, bathhouse, or private sex club. All of this earned enough for him to bring his brothers and mother to the United States, but they all thought he was still a software consultant.

"What if they come into this store and find you behind the desk?" I asked him.

He smiled. "If they find me here, then it is *they* who have to do the explaining to me!"

Azad was another clerk who came to my aid. An immigrant from Pakistan, he now worked at a kiosk that sold newspapers and snacks. On the long afternoons when business was slow, he told me that his first job in America had been at a newspaper stand in Chelsea, a legal enterprise although he was paid off the books and therefore made very little money. After a few months, a prostitute who lived in the public housing development across the street offered to pay him ten dollars if he could refer any customers, and that same afternoon a customer asked if he knew which building that blond hooker lived in. Was he going to throw money away?

Soon Azad provided this service for the woman's friends too. Sometimes he held cash for them or stepped out of the kiosk to let them change their clothes. He earned about a hundred fifty dollars per week—more than half what he made selling newspapers—which he saved so he could bring his family over. Eventually he found a better job as a clerk in a Midtown bodega, but his experienced eye fell on the street prostitutes and he soon discovered they had similar needs. Teaming up with another bodega clerk, Rajesh, he created a network of local store owners and clerks and delivery-

men, along with johns, drug dealers, and black marketers. The key
was the kiosk vendors. Tourists at a local hotel might ask a bellhop
where they could find prostitutes or drugs. The bellhop would tell
a kiosk vendor, who would call Azad and Rajesh, who would alert
a drug dealer or prostitute. Or a deliveryman from a local restaurant would hear of some available cocaine and check in with Azad
and Rajesh, who would put the word out among the kiosk vendors,
who would put the word out to all the bellhops and clerks in their
network.

For his part, Manjun stumbled directly into his life of crime.
The porn shop was the very first job he landed on arrival and the
shop workers had already had in place a deal with local sex workers,
which was why the back room had a bed. Women could entertain
their clients for a fee of twenty dollars an hour, which was much less
than the hot-sheets hotels charged. Sometimes they came in just to
rest, so the fee was lower. And sometimes, a prostitute or petty
criminal would want to hide from the police for a few hours; they'd
pay fifty dollars an hour. Manjun resisted at first, but he needed
five thousand dollars to bring over his wife and infant son, and the
extra money could save him years of waiting. It did save years—he
was able to send the five thousand dollars in just six months, spar-
ing her the difficult life of a single mother in Bangladesh.

But all this was invisible to the mainstream culture, and this
invisibility would soon have consequences. As Mayor Giuliani
began his cleanup of the Times Square area, nobody in power gave
any thought to the thousands of "support" people whose survival
would be affected when the economic driver of sex was removed
from the scene. And the optimistic view that these workers would
be forced toward more legitimate work turned out to be puritanical
hypocrisy—it was *crime itself* that gave these men an entrée into
the straight world. In time, Santosh began selling laptops of dubi-
ous origin, Rajesh started offering small short-term loans, and
Azad operated an increasingly successful sideline as a job referral

service for undocumented immigrants. Whenever otherwise legitimate employers found themselves in need of some quick off-the-books labor—and they often did, even the hedge fund titans and investment banks down on Wall Street—Azad made it happen for them with one phone call.

All of Manjun's friends had been robbed at gunpoint. None of them had health insurance or unemployment insurance or 401(k) contributions, and the taxes deducted from their paychecks went into the ether because none of them had real social security numbers. I heard the same story again and again from Central American dishwashers, West African security guards, and Mexican laborers. They lived day to day, always looking over their shoulder, hiding their crimes from the police and their success from thieves. And sometimes, as I would soon see, they lost the battle.

As the months passed, a grim mood fell across Ninth Avenue Family Video. On the very same block, a man stabbed another man in a drunken fight, a woman was found shot to death, and a drug dealer shot a man who had come from the suburbs to buy crack—a white man. That brought the police out in force. I avoided the streets myself, afraid of being the subject of a random answers-the-description stop-and-frisk.

One particular night stands out in my memory. Even from the back of the store, I could feel the cold coming through the front door every time a customer walked in. The crash of the door slamming back into its frame made the small chime seem not just unnecessary but purposely annoying. Manjun was constantly in motion, fussing with things and sighing heavily. Almost every hour he brought me a fresh cup of tea.

Manjun's son kept me company. Joshi was ten now, and he had grown up in the porn store. He was playing with his Ping-Pong paddle and a small rubber ball, slapping the ball with relentless focus against the one small patch of wall that wasn't covered by X-rated DVDs. Wall, floor, paddle. Wall, floor, paddle. Wall, floor, paddle.

Sitting with him felt comfortable. With his brown skin and quiet, introspective skill at amusing himself while the adults were busy, he seemed like a younger version of myself.

We heard a voice at the door and Joshi put the paddle down and slipped away. It was Angela, come to check her voice mail and drink a hot cup of coffee. She held four fingers up and stuck her tongue out to signal exhaustion and relief, meaning she'd had four dates so far that night and would very much like to flop down in front of a TV. "I can't do this much longer," she whispered.

I liked Angela a lot. From the first night, she was open and honest, admitting right away that she was a sex worker. But she was unlike most of the other immigrant and low-income streetwalkers I had studied in New York and Chicago. She had ambition and the courage to cross borders. She came to Manjun's store because she wanted to escape from her usual traveling grounds in the East Side projects to a better neighborhood where she could meet a wealthier clientele.

That night, I could see in her face the toll of accommodating so many men. It was painful to see. She was only thirty-four but always looked so tired that she appeared to be nearly a decade older. And business had been getting steadily worse since the Giuliani reforms. For the last few months, Angela was averaging just one client per night. Sometimes not even one.

Gradually, she told me her story. She'd come to the United States as a young girl, but death and mental illness had taken her parents and left her alone on the Lower East Side. She was just a teenager, hungry and undocumented, and ended up trading sex for food. She worked Avenues B and C for a decade, then moved to Hell's Kitchen to try the Midtown tourist trade. She'd been jailed many times, though she always said that "an arrest is just a chance to make a friend on the police." This optimism, this insistence on seeing the seeds of future opportunity in every setback, defined her character. It probably explained much of her desire to branch out of the projects. And despite her difficult life, she was always kind and patient.

"Three of my own and one black," she told me that night. Each transaction had been fifty dollars, all in the bathroom of a bar on Eleventh Avenue. Two of the men lived in Harlem, one on the Lower East Side, and one in Hell's Kitchen. Accidentally, the last man had given her a bruise on her arm during his climax. "At least they took hand jobs," she said.

But she was okay to keep working, she said.

I could tell Angela wanted a moment alone. Maybe she needed a drink or some pills. It wasn't my business to judge. I left her in the back room and joined Manjun and Joshi in the front. Five minutes later she left with a wave and a smile, and I offered to put Joshi to bed.

His small cot was pressed against the far wall, lengthwise to the twin bed that Angela and her friends used. After many nights alone, he had his own routine. First he opened a small bag of clothes in the corner and took out his pajamas. After changing into them, he made a quick visit to the bathroom to brush his teeth, then ran to the front of the store to kiss his father good night. He returned rubbing his eyes and climbed aboard the creaky cot. He pulled the blanket over his head and whispered to his toy soldier for a moment or two before falling asleep.

I sat in the chair watching him, trying not to fall asleep myself while I waited for the next prostitute to come with some data. There were only a few patrons in the aisles, a couple of drunken college boys and an amorous couple. In the convex mirrors hanging from the ceiling, I saw hands and bodies reflected in strange proportions. Outside, an older man looked in and hesitated, nervous to enter. Everyone looked clammy and preserved under the fluorescent lights.

Finally, the last interview was finished. But Manjun didn't want me to go. "Twenty more minutes I am done too. Come with me— eat Sula's special midnight dinner."

Manjun's wife, Sula, cooked in an Indian restaurant, so I was tempted. But it was too late, I said. I had to get some sleep.

The expression on Manjun's face went from eager to desperate. "I'm in trouble, Mr. Sudhir," he confessed. An inventory of the store had shown stock missing, so the boss wanted Manjun and the other clerks to take a cut in their paychecks to make up for it. But the money he earned from the back room was dwindling, with less and less sex business every month. Even worse, a few weeks earlier a man had walked into the video store and ordered Manjun to empty the cash register. Manjun gave him four hundred dollars in small bills. Then the thief dragged him to the back room and de- manded the "other money," meaning the rental payments from the sex workers, which Manjun kept in a small locker. It was twelve hundred dollars in all, a devastating loss. He'd been saving the money for his many needs, from Joshi's school clothes to Sula's doctor bills, but it also represented the future: a possible trip to Bangladesh, a down payment on a business venture, a sign of ac- complishment to keep him going when he felt depressed. Most of all, perhaps, it represented the promise that he would only have to resort to such illegal schemes temporarily. Now he would have to scale back his dreams or move even deeper into the underground.

"You must come home with me," he said. "That is the only way Sula will not yell at me!"

He softened me with a cup of hot tea, milky and sweet, with a few cloves and pods of cardamom, reminders of my Indian child- hood so sharp they rendered me unable to refuse.

The truth was, I didn't want to go home either. After ten years of marriage, my wife was talking about a separation. We were very young when we got married and our "priorities were changing," as they say. I wasn't ready to talk about any of this yet, but I didn't mind a little comfort from a South Asian family that reminded me so much of my own.

Off we went on the 7 train, rumbling deep into the heart of Queens. Manjun carried the sleeping Joshi wrapped in a blanket.

When we arrived, Sula gave a warm hello to me and a cold nod to her husband. She took Joshi in a possessive way calculated to demonstrate her irritation and disappeared into the bedroom.

Manjun sighed. Ever since Sula had started working, Joshi had had to sleep half the night at the store. They couldn't afford a babysitter. Sula hated it. And she was in some kind of mysterious pain that had been troubling her for almost six months. Neither she nor Manjun would tell me what was wrong, just that they couldn't afford a "women's doctor."

When she came back into the room, Sula started right in on Manjun. "Why must we live like this, in this country? Why have you brought me here?"

She even made me a character in their drama. "Sudhir would never fail his wife," she said. "Sudhir is a *real* man, not like you. He takes care of family!"

Joshi came to the door, his sleep disturbed by the raised voices. I offered to put him back to bed and left them to their squabble. Joshi refused my offer to read and got down on the floor and took a plastic soldier in each hand, speaking to them softly while moving them across his raised knees. The sight shot the ache of an old memory through me. So many times I did the exact same thing, hiding in my room while my mother raised her voice against my father and this "godforsaken country." So many times the shy voice that searched for the right English word turned into a piercing instrument of marital war. Whenever a silence blossomed and we saw a glimmer of relief, my mother would find a new focus for her rage.

With the raised voices of his parents beating through the door, Joshi put his soldiers on sentry duty and got into bed. Would he remember this moment for the rest of his life? Would part of him always be ten years old and anchored to the battlefield of his bedroom floor, fighting an imaginary war to distract himself from the source of pain?

A few days later, I watched Manjun come into the back room of Ninth Avenue Family Video with another cup of sweet cardamom tea. As I took the white Styrofoam cup, I noticed that his hand was shaking.

"Still nervous?"

Since the robbery and his pay cut, he seemed to be getting more anxious by the day. But he shook his head. "The chances are very slim something like that happens twice. I should be *com-fort-able.*"

The additional emphasis on the last word seemed intended to lend it the air of scientifically determined fact.

Something had been puzzling me. How did the thief know about the extra money? "Are you sure you never told the ladies?" I asked.

Manjun didn't want to talk about it. His face was resigned. I was sure one of the sex workers had discovered Manjun's cash reserve and told someone either knowingly or accidentally. But Manjun didn't like to distrust people.

"What about Officer Michael?" I asked. I had a feeling that my history-loving friend on the police force would do everything he could to help someone like Manjun.

But Manjun still hadn't reported the robbery to the police.

"It wasn't your fault," I told him.

"Maybe tomorrow," Manjun said. Then his eyes went flat, staring blindly into a wall of gay porn. "Or maybe I go home."

"Bangladesh?"

"Maybe Delhi. Anywhere. Nothing here for me now."

"How does Sula feel?"

"It is her idea."

"But what will you do? How will you make a living?"

He shrugged his shoulders, put the cup of tea on the steps, and waved a hand at the sea of erections and open mouths, shaved bodies and swollen breasts. "What do I do here, my friend? What do I do *here*?"

The mood lifted a little when Angela and her friend Kristina arrived, their night's work done. "Angela hit the jackpot," Kristina said.

That meant Angela had had three clients, two quick exchanges in a bar and one local store owner whose wife was out of the country. Kristina had only had one.

Since Angela began confiding in me, her efforts to penetrate the Midtown tourist trade had become the subject of much discussion in Manjun's store. She knew that I'd been working on my study of the indoor sex market with the Urban Justice Center, where she had received help in the past with some legal issues and lease negotiations with her landlord. Since she was one of the women who hoped to leave the streets for more lucrative venues like hotels and private calls to apartments, she began sharing her own ideas about what to study and what kind of support they really needed. Shyly, she talked about her discomfort in posh Midtown bars. She said she didn't understand how to advertise herself online but was taking lessons from some more Internet-savvy friends. "I'd really like a bank account," she told me. "I need a Visa card. And I need to find good doctors who can help me for a few bucks. Or some kind of legit side job just so the cops don't steal my money when they stop me and find all of it in my pocket. I need to be *cleaned*."

The irony in her use of "clean" made me laugh. The very same word that the media used to describe Giuliani's strategy to make Manhattan more hospitable acquired a subterranean shade coming out of Angela's mouth, raising echoes of money laundering and identity changes. But the same sentiment held true in both cases. Just as Midtown was changing from seedy to mainstream, Angela wanted to wash out the streetwalker and move to the more acceptable domain of "escort services."

Figuring out how to make this change was not easy, particularly for an immigrant woman who was not comfortable applying for jobs, who felt ashamed of her difficulty communicating in English, and whose life until that point had been limited to the Lower East Side and the various Caribbean countries where her family had lived. The several dozen women she had introduced me to, including other Latinas and European immigrants like Kristina, as well as white Americans who were transplants to the city, all shared the same passion. And the same obstacles. Without a credit history or bank account, it was hard for them to rent an apartment, apply for a job, or otherwise think of a life beyond their nightly vocation.

But they all were managing, and their improvised methods fascinated me. Kristina told me about a group of women who could find landlords willing to rent an apartment (or sometimes just a bedroom) for cash and no contract. Angela convinced several doctors on the Lower East Side to treat her friends. An ex–social worker from Greenpoint came to Manjun's shop at night to counsel women and set up appointments at health clinics and day care centers back in Brooklyn.

It was becoming clear that a community like Mortimer's did exist in this world too, but it wasn't geographically rooted to a single neighborhood. Just as Manjun's friends helped to show me the complex infrastructure of the local underground economy, Angela and her coworkers helped me see that my instincts had a solid foundation: for the modern city's sex workers, community was *networked*. The new sex trade was no longer confined to seedy neighborhoods but spread through friendships and clients all over the city. These kinds of impromptu social links across distant areas of a city had been identified as far back as the 1960s by Chicago sociologist Morris Janowitz, who called them "communities of limited liability." Back then, he had been looking at whites and suburbanites who had cars and greater mobility. Like me, he was looking through a Chicago lens that probably led him to assume that black and brown members of the underclass were more fixed in their neighborhoods. But from what I could see so far, Manjun and his friends had managed to create the same networked pattern. The question was, given how vulnerable they all seemed to be, would the networks endure? Were they a model for the future or just a fleeting adaptation?

The fact was, Angela and her friends were still barely eking out a basic living, which placed them in constant risk of a sudden catastrophic blow of bad luck. Soon I would witness the terrible stress this put on every one of their brave and creative attempts to shore up their defenses.

On a frigid Saturday night in November, when frost crazed the windows of the overheated shops, Angela and Kristina had finished up their evening's work and come to rest in Manjun's back room.

"Maybe I'm too old for this," Kristina said.

"Of course you're too old, sweetie!" Angela answered.

Kristina was from Romania, but the differences in language and background didn't seem to hamper her friendship with Angela. She pulled a small bottle of whiskey out of her bag and poured them each a slug.

Manjun appeared at the door to the back room looking apologetic. This meant it was collection time. Angela pulled out a small wad of bills, but Kristina said she didn't have enough this week.

She was broke and really sorry. Manjun waved her concern down with both hands. "You go home. Be safe," he said.

Kristina looked embarrassed. "You're very sweet, Jun."

When Manjun went back up front, Angela leaned close and whispered, "I'm not going to last here much longer."

I wasn't surprised. With one client a night, the writing was on the wall. I expected her to say she was going to return to the Lower East Side, but she wasn't giving up that easily.

"I go back home and think about things," she said. "Then I try again." She laughed. "Maybe downtown. I don't know. I don't like quitting."

"You never struck me as the quitting type," I said.

But then Angela sighed and started talking about other women who were similarly unsuccessful and who were retreating—some to other neighborhoods, some to other lines of work. The sudden shift from optimism to gloom struck me as ominous. I didn't know her well enough at that point to know how resilient she really was, but right then she sounded like a woman on the verge of real depression.

A strange, unexpected feeling came over me. In Chicago, on another research project, I'd watched the demolition of projects send thousands of families into homelessness and poverty worse than anything they had experienced before. I had seen hundreds of black men, just teenagers, arrested for selling crack, their lives scrambled forever for a few hundred dollars a week. Now I seemed to be hearing a new version of that old sad tale. Maybe it was my own frustration coming out, but I was desperately eager to understand what it would take for people to avoid these fates. I could count on one hand the number of Chicago gang members who'd stayed out of jail, saved their money, and found work in the legitimate economy. The same seemed true of these other illegal economies. At the same time, every time I picked up a copy of the *Village Voice* there seemed to be more and more advertisements from indi-

viduals and agencies offering sex for sale. Someone was making
money. If it wasn't Angela and her friends, who was it? What was
the pattern of success and failure? What was the range of outcomes?
Failure? Prison? Death? A successful integration into the new country? Return to the homeland with money in the bank? Again,
my need for generalizability made me hungry to search out all
possibilities.

Predictable but unattractive thoughts nagged at me. Those who
fared better were probably white, middle class—people who *did*
have bank accounts and credit cards and all the things Angela
couldn't access. But these thoughts were sheer prejudice, and just
as likely to be false as true. Only data could determine the real
reasons.

As Angela finished her morose monologue, we both saw Manjun sitting in the front of the store looking even more despondent
than she sounded.

"Sula's sick," she whispered. "That's why he's worried."

Feeling helpless, I sighed heavily. Angela held out her whiskey
bottle. "Let it go, *mi amor.*"

I took a quick slug and coughed, then slid down onto the cot.
Up around us a silence rose, broody as a wet November day. You'd
think that, after a decade at this, I could accept the suffering of the
people I studied. But it hurt to think that nothing I could write
would really change the lives of people like Angela and Manjun.
Sociology had been founded with grand dreams of reforming society, but now the short-term reformers were putting their hopes in
economics. Pay people to attend school, starve them to induce pro-
ductivity, use threat of lower pay if performance suffered. Even if
all of life's problems really could be answered with incentives and
numbers, I didn't want to live in a world where Manjun was just
a "wage laborer" and his suffering nothing more than a "market
externality."

A few days later, things got much worse. Christmas was

around the corner, and I was planning to visit my parents in California. I took the subway down Ninth Avenue just to drop off a gift I hoped would mean as much to Joshi as it had once meant to me—the ultimate South Asian nerd heirloom, *The World Book Encyclopedia*. I had become ridiculously fond of that little kid.

But when I walked into the store, there was a new clerk working behind the counter. "Where's Manjun?" I asked. The clerk answered me in the broken English of a brand-new immigrant. "He no work here." He had no idea where Manjun was. Or even *who* he was. He wasn't friendly about it either. I pushed my way through the store and peeked into the back room. There was no trace of Manjun's belongings, not even the meager collection of DVDs Joshi used to watch. The beds were gone too, which meant that Angela and the other prostitutes must also have moved on. A small endangered world had disappeared forever.

I rushed to see Santosh, who looked pale and exhausted. "Please, not now," he pleaded. The store was filled with customers. "I cannot give it to you now. You will meet me, later tonight."

"Give me what? Where is Manjun?"

"You haven't come for his money?" His voice trailed off and he began rubbing his head.

"Santosh, what money? Do you know where Manjun is?"

"Come back tonight, later. Things will be quiet and I will talk with you."

I looked for some of Manjun's other friends, but none were at their jobs. I called Angela and some of the sex workers who'd worked out of Manjun's store in the past, but not a single one answered her phone. I went to his home in Queens and no one answered the doorbell.

A few hours later, I returned to Santosh's video store. He was gone. He'd left early, they said.

· · ·

The next day, I managed to connect with Officer Michael. He picked me up in his car and we drove to a quiet street. "You know what it's like, Sudhir," he said. "These places, life can turn from good to bad just like that."

The thief had come back. He'd beat Manjun pretty badly, sending him to the hospital. Because of the severity of the attack, local police believed Manjun had been letting someone sell drugs from inside the store, and the thief had come looking for the stash.

I couldn't believe this. Manjun was losing money on the bed rental business because of his soft heart at a time when he really couldn't afford it. That was the kind of person he was, a good person. I couldn't believe he had ventured into the drug trade. Something was missing, some part of the story was invisible to us—and now the secretive rules of the underground were affecting me. My friend was lost because of some kind of underground conflict resolution mechanism that we couldn't see.

This is what normal people go to the police to solve—and to lawyers, small-claims courts, and all the other arms of the justice system. But in the underground, the law is typically not a helpful protector. Manjun's underworld option would have been to pay for protection, but I couldn't imagine the mild South Asian gentleman searching out those kinds of helpers. Here is where the real fragility of the underground became clear to me. It was fine for me to talk about the provisional communities that gathered around a cause like Mortimer's, but I could not avoid the darker side of this world. There was real violence here. And yet, whatever Manjun had done or not done, I honestly did not know whether I wanted to find out the truth. Unlike the big-n researchers who work the telephone and never see the nameless souls who give them forty-five uninterrupted minutes, an ethnographer is always haunted by his subjects and their tragic vulnerabilities. Insight gets more painful when you grow close to people.

A few weeks later, after returning from the holidays, I dropped by Manjun's old store again. No sign of him. I looked for Shoomi; no sign of him either. Most of the porn stores seemed to be going out of business too, replaced by wine bars and children's clothing stores. The end of the year must have meant the end of their leases too.

Santosh was gone as well. I'd heard that, using the small profit from his porn career, he'd opened a restaurant near the main subway stop in Jackson Heights, so I went up to ask him to lunch. As I entered, an older woman wearing a long red sari led out two Indian men who looked as if they had just landed at JFK, bags in hand, bleary eyed and hungry. She shouted in Santosh's direction, "Why do they all come today?"

Santosh grabbed her arm and steered her toward the back room. He returned with two small cups of tea, strong and milky sweet.

"Sometimes I miss our old place," he said. "It was nice there— mostly because I could get away from here!"

It turned out that the restaurant had been part of Santosh's mini empire for a while. The angry woman in the red sari was his wife. And the two Indians were part of yet another business Santosh had going: smuggling undocumented immigrants into the United States.

Smiling at his relentless enterprise, I asked him how much he charged for his smuggling services. "Five thousand!" he said. "And ten thousand for all settlement-related *ac-tiv-i-ties*." He said the final word slowly, with mocking precision.

"'Activities'," I said, smirking. "That's a nice word for it."

"Two weeks' comfort and station."

"Station?"

"Food, clothing, introductions."

In a matter of thirty minutes, Santosh gave me a very nice sketch of the market, including the number of brokers and the dangers. He also filled me in on the old neighborhood. Azad was still working in the black market, Rajesh had found a job as an accountant, some had children in college already. It felt like old times, which reminded me of why I was there.

"Have you heard anything of our old friend?" I asked.

He shrugged. As far as he knew, Joshi and Sula were heading off to Bangladesh; they were both doing well.

"And Manjun?"

Santosh sighed. "We sacrifice for our families."

Finally, he told me what really happened when Manjun's money was stolen. He'd been involved in drugs and "bad things" with another man who knew where he was hiding the cash, and that man was the one who'd robbed him. The "bad things" included counterfeit documents, he admitted.

"But where's Manjun now?" I asked, afraid of the answer.

Santosh raised the tea to his mouth. "We know only of his family." But he was being evasive—I could tell.

"Please," I begged.

He sighed and sipped his tea. Finally he said, "Sudhir, we find that Manjun was doing something not very pleasant."

Getting the story out of him took some time, but in the end I gathered that Manjun had been involved with some very dangerous people, and under their pressure he found himself forcing women from India to become prostitutes—to live in a brothel for a short stint in order to pay their family debts. The horror of this was what had been making him unravel back when I thought he was just worried about being robbed.

"And now?" I asked.

Santosh took a deep breath. "I don't think we will ever see him again."

This is why nobody would speak to me, he explained. "It is very important that the rest of us don't know anything—that we don't talk or say anything. Our ignorance is what can save us, and keep us in this country. And for you, I would also suggest that you not ask too many questions. That is not a safe way to be."

Saddened, I began talking about the needs of survival in a foreign land, finding a way to excuse the terrible things my friend had done. But Santosh grabbed my hand from across the table. "*Surviving is easy*," he said with a forceful voice I had never heard from him. "We are so much smarter than most of these people, so much better educated, and we work so hard and do nasty things, but they succeed without effort. And the demons visit you at night."

Understanding dawned slowly. In Santosh's view, Manjun had made a fatal error. He'd listened to his demons.

Eat from the hand of a demon, and his hand becomes your hand. How often had I seen this in the underground economy? People who generally lived good, decent lives turned to the illicit world to make a buck, and then it began to suck them in. Santosh was saying that Manjun could have made different choices, could have changed his attitude or his approach or his exposure, could have *imagined* a different future. But the demon's hand had become his hand, and it was too easy to keep on letting that hand do its dark work. At the same time, of course, Santosh recognized that as a poor brown immigrant in the United States, Manjun had few real options and had to seize the opportunities that became available to him. That was what made it so sad.

After that, Santosh and I had little more to say to each other. Talking about Manjun had drained us.

He asked that I come back in two weeks, for a small party for his grandchild. When the day arrived, I found the restaurant filled with balloons and streamers and "Happy Birthday" signs, and everyone greeted me as "Mr. Professor." When the party was over, Santosh came over to me and sighed. "It is important that you see this side too. This is the side I want you to remember. Not just the sadness. Maybe even you can remember your own time growing up—very much like this, no?"

"Yes, Santosh. Very much," I said as my eyes began tearing up.

Years later, I still turn back to Santosh's words, because it is the counsel that I have received countless times from the disenfranchised, whether single mothers in the Chicago projects or immigrants seeking out opportunities in the global city. *Don't pity us. Don't treat us like victims. We're more than our hardships.* But fine as that advice is, I was grappling with two seemingly contradictory thoughts. First was a vision of global New York as an unrestricted field of opportunity where even the low-income immigrant could climb the ladder and experience a better life, as Santosh had. The second was global New York as a ruthlessly hierarchical town with great social benefits for the victors and potentially devastating consequences for the losers. Perhaps this was how things had always been, whether for the early Italians or the great Irish migration. New York offered opportunities, but made no promises. This too was a form of globalization: white Europeans migrating in droves to America, creating bursting-at-the-seams ethnic enclaves where they could make a new home for themselves, often rooting their eventual Americanization in off-the-books marketplaces where people bartered, lent money, paid one another under the table, and so on—all excellent training in the spirit of American entrepreneurship. As they established credit, found legitimate jobs, and moved into the social mainstream, it would help them achieve great success.

But now, at the dawn of the twenty-first century, globalization had brought about a much different narrative of assimilation. Today's immigrants were more likely to be brown and black, from Africa and Asia. Since 2000, most of the immigrants who have

come to New York City have been from Mexico, Ghana and sub-
Saharan Africa, Pakistan, Bangladesh, and China. By 2005, histo-
rian Nancy Foner would find, recent immigrants made up a
startling 37 percent of the city population. If you counted their
American-born children, then the figure rose to half of all New
Yorkers. This new wave of immigrants couldn't just shorten their
names and lose their accents. Nor did they seem to be moving from
menial work to well-paying factory or government positions—
those jobs had disappeared in global cities. Instead, these immigrants were servicing the well-to-do via poorly paid service sector
work, as clerks, cab drivers, cleaners, nannies, busboys, and so on.
Most such jobs paid off the books and offered little hope of advancement or recourse when things went wrong. And unlike previous generations of low-income workers, these recent immigrants
weren't joining unions for a step up the ladder; as the new century
began in New York City, nearly one in three lived in poverty.

One problem became increasingly apparent to me. As I watched
immigrants like Angela, Manjun, Shoomi, and their peers shuttle
through the city, I noticed they always had limited relations with
people outside their social class and ethnic group. They may have
worked for an upper-class clientele, but these relationships were hierarchical. Angela talked about finding wealthy white clients and
Manjun dreamed of taking his engineering skills into a corporate
job, but the chances seemed small. It was painful to acknowledge
the reasons. They spoke poor English and they had dark skin.
Most of all, perhaps, they just didn't seem interested in the lifestyle
that is the second currency of global New York: the music and
movies and art and food that people talk about when they are enjoying relations that are not hierarchical. They seemed to be stuck
in their own ethnic worlds, their social courage weakened by the
demon's hand.

If there was any real hope for these newcomers to latch onto, it was the traditional hope immigrants put in the prospects of their children. But these too had grown more slender. As sociologist Mary Waters and her colleagues discovered, more than half of the second-generation immigrant children in New York would attend or graduate from a four-year college or university. But the pace of globalization today has become so fast and ruthless, with capital zipping from place to place at such hyperspeed, taking jobs and resources along with it, we seem to be at risk of creating a new class of the long-term disenfranchised. So many of the people I saw in Manjun's neighborhood had made the wrong bet. They didn't see the change coming, and now they had to be cleared out. That has always happened, but never so fast or so universally, or in such utter obscurity. Today's champions of globalization are so busy celebrating the wondrous wealth and the charming artifacts of food and music produced by international interchange that they have little time for the plight of the invisible underclass that helps make it happen.

Alas, my time here was up too. With Angela also on her way out, Manjun's disappearance meant the end of my tenure in Hell's Kitchen. Too many other people I knew were moving on as well. The neighborhood was now deep into the transformation that one critic called "the suburbanization of New York." Average household income had doubled from 1990 to 2000 and average rents rose correspondingly, a pace that accelerated into the new century. I decided it was time to start floating again, perhaps to renew my long-stalled effort to research the other end of the illegal income spectrum. But as the weeks passed, I couldn't stop worrying about Manjun.

One day I went back downtown to press Officer Michael for more details.

"You don't know what we know," he said flatly. "We think he might have been pressured into doing all the things he did."

Doing what? Selling drugs?

Michael wouldn't say. "We told him to get the hell out of town, or at least go hide."

But how would Manjun live? How would his family live? They had, I admitted, some issues with their papers.

"He'll be okay. Just give it time. I'm sure you'll hear from him."

But I had a sense I never would, and I never did. It was hard for me to accept, even harder because of the way Officer Michael seemed to be shrugging it off as just another ordinary event in the life of the neighborhood.

The only thing I could do was stay true to the pursuit that had brought us together. I had to keep moving out across the city, following threads and crossing boundaries to see where the underground could take me.

CHAPTER 4

MOVING ON UP

Two years after Al Qaeda's attack on the World Trade Center, immigrants to New York continued to experience heightened scrutiny even if they were legal residents of the country. The Patriot Act and related legislation gave enhanced surveillance and investigative powers to law enforcement and imposed new restrictions on the freedom of immigrants to travel into and out of the United States. Deportations had risen by 30 percent. The undocumented moved from neighborhood to neighborhood and borough to borough, seeking off-the-books work while keeping a low profile. Some ran into visa troubles, lost their jobs, and had to return home.

When I heard from Santosh or my other friends from Midtown, the stories tended to be of either the on-a-treadmill or the crashed-and-burned variety. They stood in sharp contrast to the conventional stories that depicted South Asians in the United States largely as professionals who experienced great economic stability for themselves and their children. Most didn't even manage the mini-mart life of Apu on *The Simpsons*. Santosh tried to expand his restaurant and catering services, but hard times had sent him back to his lucrative but illegal sideline as part of the "underground railroad" for undocumented immigrants. I could tell how things were going by the look on his face. If he greeted me with a smile and introduced me all around, he was having a legal period, but if he became stern and fatherly and told me to keep working hard and focus on the important things, then I knew he was into something murky. The same pattern held with Rajesh and the others, who all dipped back into the illegal economy whenever they lost jobs or ran into other trouble. Off the books, they drove cabs, washed dishes, cleaned offices, even repaired office computers. Some took seasonal work in upstate hotels run by other South Asians. With wages so low and travel restrictions so harsh, many were using video chat to watch their kids grow up in their home country.

But all of them held on to the dream. Maybe that was another reason I kept turning to Shine and Angela. They were actually doing it. In very different ways, they were systematically making a climb up the economic ladder. Not with complete success, of course. Angela's various attempts to recruit clients from Midtown had been a disaster, and she had been unable to find a stable of white corporate clients for private dates. In fact, she was now back licking her wounds on the Lower East Side. But she was still looking for new ways to get ahead. "Maybe I join one of those agencies," she joked one day. "Someone out there has to like dark meat, no?" She would soon focus on an ambitious plan to organize a group of street prostitutes to rent an apartment and run their own bordello.

For Shine, the climb meant a new drug.

I discovered his scheme one afternoon in a bar on Lenox Avenue. The spring of 2003 was coming, with joggers hitting the streets, merchants repainting their storefronts, the annual renewal finally under way. We were sitting at a bar and I was telling Shine about a project I was doing with the economist Steven Levitt, author of *Freakonomics*. Inspired by research on how wealthy Internet entrepreneurs had learned to reinvent their careers after the collapse of the dot-com bubble, we wanted to find young black men who had joined gangs about a decade earlier. How would they reinvent themselves when their criminal careers played out? "Basically," I said, "we're trying to answer a simple question nobody ever thought to ask before. What happens to gang members as they grow old?"

"Hell, you ought to study me," Shine said.

The thought had occurred to me, of course. But Shine had kept me at a distance, never letting me past his guard far enough to find out the things that mattered to a sociologist. To start with, was he really such a big underground success or was he exaggerating his achievements to come off like a big shot? After all this time, I couldn't say for sure. I knew that he drove a fancy German car and helped to support a large family, that he kept many thousands in a bank account and hid more in various nooks and stash points around Harlem until he could spend or launder it into reportable income. He certainly seemed conversant with the crack trade, so I had no real doubts where he was getting his money. Beyond that, I had no hard numbers. But I did know that the crack market was slowing down, and that he'd been trying all kinds of new things: a chop shop in the Bronx, a small pushcart business with two street vendors selling fried chicken and rice, a five-thousand-dollar investment in his uncle's small hatmaking business (black women still wore glorious hats to church, as you could see any Sunday morning all over Harlem). Now he warmed to this theme, but it all sounded fairly small time. He had another small investment in a shop where one of his aunts told fortunes with tarot cards. He was helping three neighbors start an underground business refurbishing old television sets. He even spent one colorful three-month stint trying to make it as a pimp.

"A *pimp*? Did you get a furry hat and everything?"

Shine didn't find my teasing amusing. Apparently, failure as a pimp had bruised his male ego. "I'm too easygoing. They took advantage of me. I'm too *nice* to be a pimp."

"I guess crack brings out a much friendlier crowd," I said.

He laughed. "They are when they want that smoke. Friendliest motherfuckers you ever saw."

But all his efforts had come to nothing, or at least nothing in terms of his previous income. Now Shine had a new idea, which he confessed a bit sheepishly. "I'm selling powder."

"Powder?"

"Powdered cocaine. The kind white people use."

Alas, the powdered cocaine market was proving difficult to crack, so to speak. He was having a hell of a time finding customers. This was because much of the market base for powdered cocaine is white and fairly well-off. He certainly couldn't use his usual set of street dealers, who would look and feel like Martians at a Wall Street bar. "They're too young and too stupid," he grumbled.

I couldn't believe it. "You can't possibly be telling me that you don't know anyone who buys powdered cocaine in the city of New York?"

"I know plenty of people, but coke is a weird thing. With crack, people keep coming back 'cause it doesn't last that long. They come back every *hour*. People who get the blow, they get enough for a night or maybe a weekend."

"So find one of them and sell him some," I said.

"But they've already got their own steady. I'm not a steady to nobody, and I don't want to be poaching somebody else's customers and get shot in an alley. I gotta find *new* customers. It's a tricky thing."

He had done a good deal of consumer behavior research, he said. Specifically, he'd called all the powdered cocaine dealers he knew, hung out at parties with his middle-class friends, even tried to purchase coke himself at a few bars. Shine believed that blow was mostly sold at parties and clubs or delivered directly to customers at their homes, but he didn't like phone delivery businesses and didn't seem to be attending the right kind of parties.

What he really needed was a cousin with connections in the art market—or better yet, some idiot who could introduce him to a troubled young heiress with a taste for cocaine, of course. But neither of us knew that then—Evalina was still looking for herself in California, and the night Shine and Analise would meet at the art gallery was still more than a year away. This left him with what looked like a single option: finding new customers in public spaces—upscale bars, luxury hotels, strip clubs, even parks. He had been canvassing a few of these spots with Cohan, another trafficker in his neighborhood who was losing business, but they attracted too much attention from security. Once at a hotel bar, they'd actually been thrown out.

"What did you wear?" I asked.

"Same shit I have on now," he said.

I looked him over. Two hundred and fifteen pounds of solid black man in a bright green tracksuit, a baseball hat with the Yankees logo, and a diamond-studded necklace. The Adidas on his feet were white enough for a hospital operating room.

"How did you approach people?"

He told a series of amusing stories. Thinking that white men would be drawn to black women, he said, he took a small group of sexy young women to a Wall Street bar. The mission was to flirt and sell cocaine. But the girls were nervous and got so loud and drunk, they embarrassed him. Next he brought along a pair of Dominican gun brokers who said they dealt with rich white people all the time, but Shine's coke made them paranoid and they threatened to shoot the hotel manager. Veering 180 degrees, he asked a famous black preacher to meet him at a Soho lounge on the theory that people who saw them together would trust him a little bit more and he could approach them later. But the preacher was disgusted at the ten-dollar martinis and criticized him for spending his money in the wrong neighborhood, leaving in a huff that soured Shine's whole night. Finally, he tried sending the girls back down just to pick up guys and *tell* them about this great coke dealer they knew—the ultimate low-pressure sale—but they came back and said they just flat-out hated hanging out with the rich white people. There was nothing to talk about. They felt ignored.

As he talked, I realized I had misunderstood Shine. Though he lived very close to the geographical center of Manhattan and appeared to have no hesitation about traveling to any part of the city to see friends or to shop, he was not as confident as he appeared. "I'm an entrepreneur," he liked to say, always with pride in his voice. He had no doubts about his mastery of the rules of commerce. But his courage had definite geographical boundaries. When it came to his business, he always spoke about the city as a series of distinct sectors, and Midtown was as distant as Beijing as far as cocaine sales were concerned. The phrases he used to describe it were "down there" or "out there" or even "where *they* are."

Thinking back, I realized that whenever we traveled south, he became self-conscious about his appearance. He also modified his gait, toning down the rhythmic swagger that came naturally to him up in Harlem. I knew that he had some white friends and some wealthy friends too, but that didn't seem to make a difference. Accepting white people's money also meant accepting their power to judge him.

Suddenly it hit me. For Shine, the rich white world wasn't just a new business market. It was a testing ground. It was a mountain to climb. It was as much a psychological challenge as it was an economic need.

I could relate.

"Maybe you should consider changing your look a little bit," I said.

He pretended to be struck by my genius. "Get some horn-rims and a button-down shirt? Oh, yeah! Or maybe some plaid. Yeah, I'd look pretty good in plaid!"

As I would soon discover, he'd been studying back copies of *Esquire* and *GQ*. He was way ahead of me. That wasn't the problem.

"The problem is, I'm just not comfortable hanging out in those places by myself," he said.

The next shoe didn't take long to fall.

"Why don't *you* go with me?" he said.

Shine's invitation was not exactly the kind of entrée I wanted into the upper reaches of the black market, but with few other doors opening, I couldn't really pass up the opportunity. Still, it raised all sorts of conundrums for me. One in particular, painfully familiar from my experiences with Chicago gangs: how much of an accessory was I when I merely *observed* a crime? I learned that there was no legal obligation to report someone who was looking for new drug spots. Only capital crimes like murder or child abduction required a citizen to make a report or face charges herself. I knew I was heading down a road that would make me very uncomfortable at the least.

The exact nature of our relationship was another puzzle. We weren't exactly friends, but we were definitely friendly. How should that affect my decision? Was I too close or not close enough?

Despite all this, I was dying to watch him in action, If everything he told me was true, my quest would feel much more solid—and vice versa.

Around this time another door opened, leading me into the upper reaches of New York society. I was on the board of a Lower East Side nonprofit organization, La Bodega de la Familia, that helped ex-offenders make a productive return to society after time spent in jail or prison. Through Angela, I had also become well acquainted with the Latino community that was being gentrified by white hipsters and artists. She frequently invited me to her apartment in a local housing project, which gave me the feeling of warmth I had missed since leaving Chicago's public housing families (and the promise of additional interviews with Angela's sex worker friends down the road). The Bodega board position also introduced me to some fascinating people on the opposite side of the social spectrum, specifically wealthy young New Yorkers who had begun to take an interest in their family's social causes. On travels to Cuba, Peru, Nigeria, Bangladesh, and other developing countries, they had seen lending, construction, small business, and farming all take place outside government strictures, often on the basis of little more than verbal agreements. They became fascinated by the different ways poor people around the world used informal off-the-books means to make ends meet, and wanted to encourage the same entrepreneurial spirit in U.S. ghettos. I began telling them about my adventures on the Lower East Side, hoping I might be able to nudge some of their family largesse in the direction of La Bodega.

To my surprise, during a lull in the conversation, they began talking about the black market activities in their own circle of wealthy young philanthropists. Some bought and sold fancy sports cars or raced them around the world, others financed independent films, still others gambled or invested in businesses, all of it carefully hidden from the taxman as well as from parents. Getting away with it was kind of a sport.

The irony was overwhelming. The same basic activity—hustling in the shadows of the law and getting away with it—was a sport for one group and a matter of life and death for another. What a story that would make, comparing and contrasting high and low as I wove those two threads together. It was also quite a challenge to the popular assumption that the underground is the province of the underclass. Clearly I needed to spend more time with the upper classes. But once again I didn't press, trusting in my infinitely-patient-ethnographer-on-the-wall approach. At most I dropped some hints.

Soon enough, an invitation came. Carter Williams was the heir to an insurance fortune, a privileged young black man who had zero knowledge of street culture. Michael and Betsy Winters were white, the children of a New York investment banker. They were all recent Columbia University graduates preparing to take over established family charities. Although none of them was exactly burning with a passion for philanthropy, they wanted to do an honest job of it.

They first approached me after reading some of my writings on urban poverty, asking me where I thought they could be most effective. I started by giving them a quick-and-dirty introduction to the budgets of poor people—how much a person got from welfare and food stamps, how much he spent for groceries, how much it cost to buy a monthly bus pass. Then we moved to more complex matters, like welfare policy and how to evaluate charitable programs. I also assigned them books like Jonathan Kozol's *Savage Inequalities* and Alex Kotlowitz's *There Are No Children Here*, then led them in discussions of the best way to make an impact with their donations. Listening to them talk, I kept thinking how great it would be if I could study them formally. It would be my *Coming of Age in Samoa*, with pastels—a pleasing reversal of the usual "tribal" ethnography.

One time, early in our acquaintance, I took them to Harlem for a crash course in living poor. They had all been social science majors, so I assumed they were already familiar with the basics of low-income life—a painful error, it turned out.

We took a cab to 145th Street and got out in front of a boxy old tenement with a rusted fire escape running down the front of the building. Our host was Silvia McCombs, a single mother of three. Inside, her apartment was modest and neat, filled with plaster saints and handmade objects like tea cozies and blankets. She had televisions blaring in each of the rooms, all set to Christian preachers warning about the devil.

"Silvia," I began, "we've been reading about bureaucracies. You know, welfare offices, health clinics, caseworkers who make sure you aren't making money and getting rich off welfare. These guys don't understand the 'man in the house' rule."

"I don't understand it either," said Silvia. "It's *bullshit*."

With that, she was off. Like many people who feel their hard-won expertise is always ignored, Silvia was thrilled to finally get a hearing. The "man in the house" rule was a clause (ruled unconstitutional by the Supreme Court in 1968) that canceled a woman's welfare if she had a man living in the house. It was sexist and destructive, it broke up families, and it was racist because similar kinds of government aid for other citizens (for white farming families, for example) didn't include morality clauses or behavioral restrictions. But for minorities, all sorts of humiliating and patronizing rules were invented.

When she slowed down, I explained that Michael and Betsy and Carter had a specific focus, which was figuring out how to use their money to help people get off welfare and back to work.

"That's right," Betsy said with touching enthusiasm. "My father asked my brother and me to focus on helping people get work. Because ultimately, work is really what makes us happy."

Silvia fixed Betsy with a skeptical gaze. Her eyes lingered on the Chanel bag and the expensive Burberry coat with the velvety chocolate nap. "Really? And what do *you* do? For work, I mean."

"Well, right now I'm helping to manage my father's estate," Betsy answered.

Silvia took out a pack of menthol cigarettes and a lighter with a little cozy around it that she had knitted herself, laying them out methodically as if arraying weapons for battle. She was clearly enjoying herself. "No, no, no," Silvia said, her voice growing sharp. "I mean, what do you *do*?"

"I evaluate the prospects of trying to help people better themselves. With our family's money, we believe we can have a major impact on poverty in the city. In fact, the mayor is keen on—"

"Fuck the mayor, sweetheart," Silvia said, taking a drag on her cigarette and blowing it to the side. "What do you *do*? What do you *make*? What do you *sell*? What do you *serve* to people? You understand me? What is your *job*?"

Carter broke in. "It's very simple, really. We try to figure out if you're worth helping. That's number one. Should we give *you* money? Then we want to know how much. What do you really need to help you get a job? We don't want to give too much because then there will be less for the next person. So that takes a bit of figuring out and that's how we spend our days."

"Shit, now we're getting somewhere," Silvia said. "So what do you want to know?" She put on a heavy mammy accent. "'Cause I sho would like to gets me some of that money you be having, boss."

Carter tugged at his herringbone jacket, gathering his dignity along with the fabric. "Well, how much would it take to get you to a point where you're comfortable enough to go out and get a job?"

"What do you mean, 'comfortable'?"

"The necessities. Child care, food, transportation, rent."

While Silvia pondered, Betsy jumped in. "Just a ballpark figure would get us started. Something around fifty thousand dollars?"

Silvia looked startled. "Fifty thousand dollars a year?"

Betsy faltered. "Well, I don't know. Seventy-five thousand?"

Silvia looked up at the ceiling. "Lord, you have finally heard my prayers!" she said, sarcasm dripping. Taking another drag off her cigarette, she looked over at me. "You getting a piece of this, Sudhir?"

"No, ma'am," I answered. I couldn't hide my own smirk, so I dropped my head and hoped the three students wouldn't notice.

Shaking her head in wonder and disappointment, Silvia turned back to the group. "What do you kids think I live on now? I mean, look around you. I hope this place doesn't seem dirt poor. I try to keep things tidy. Try to give my kids a decent home. I'm not embarrassed. So guess—how much do you think I live on?"

Carter looked around. "Thirty-five thousand dollars a year?"

"Thirty-five thousand dollars a year," Silvia repeated. "Thirty-five thousand dollars a year! And where am I getting all of this money?"

"From the federal government," Michael said. "That's why we as private citizens are trying to find—"

But Silvia cut him off. The game wasn't funny anymore, and her voice turned coldly factual. "Do you know what I get from welfare every month?" Silvia asked. No one answered. "About eight hundred dollars. That pays for clothes, subways, school materials, food, cleaning supplies, phone, cable. Some of it, anyway. You know what I get in food stamps?"

Once again, no one said anything.

"A hundred eighty dollars a month."

"That's it?" Michael said, surprised.

"That's it. And I get SSI for disability, 'cause I can't walk right, so that pays my rent. That's my big stroke of luck—having a disability. Lots of folks don't have that kind of good luck."

Betsy looked genuinely shocked. "You mean, you live on *nine hundred eighty dollars a month*? In New York? Who can live on that kind of money? I mean, good Lord."

"Tell me about it," Silvia said. "You gotta lock your money up in a *box* in this city. They got hands reaching out and grabbing every second of every day. They got theirs and they want to get yours too. And I spend every other minute I have trying to scrounge up a little more money, babysitting and cleaning and helping people out—all off the books, of course, so I'm committing a crime too, just to keep from losing my welfare. Just like I commit a crime if I dare to have a man stay!"

"I'm so sorry," Betsy said.

"Don't apologize, sweetheart. That's just the way it is."

I decided that this was enough for one day and nudged everyone into thank-yous and good-byes. Afterward, I was sure I would never hear from Michael, Betsy, and Carter again. All I had done was burst their bubbles. I was probably doing more harm than good. I saw my dreams of high-priced philanthropic consultancy vanish, not to mention any hope of a research project on the underground market activities of the American elite.

But months later, the three heirs returned. The meeting with Silvia had shaken them, they confessed. It showed them how isolated they had been, and shamed them for treating New York as a playground. Of course, maybe Silvia could have made a little more effort . . .

I began working with them individually, mostly offering them advice on particular matters that concerned their philanthropy: how to measure success, how long a family would need help before things might turn around, what the best way to deploy their resources was—education, health, criminal justice reform? I actually ended up taking them to Chicago, where I introduced them to many more poor families and to the institutions that served them. Mostly these were productive visits, although there were plenty of Silvias in Chicago who challenged their views.

Watching them wrestle with all this was quite touching. They were sincerely putting their entire belief systems at risk, and I had to give them credit. At a certain point, though, I remembered Silvia's hammering Betsy about what kind of work she did, and a fresh irony hit me. Neither Silvia nor Betsy was employed in any literal sense. Silvia couldn't find a job and Betsy didn't need one. They actually did have something in common!

My fantasy of a blue-blood *Coming of Age in Samoa* swept back. If I could find a way to compare and contrast these two people and the two groups they represented, maybe *that* would be a way to give a fresh look at the unexamined relationships of the high and low worlds of the global city. Betsy and Michael and Carter always said they wanted to pay me, but I shrugged it off. So next time I saw them, I made a semi-joke about this crazy idea I had for a "tribal" study of the Blue Blood Nation. They laughed and said I should come out with them whenever I wanted.

"It's a date," I said.

All that summer, Angela hid out on the Lower East Side. As another winter descended on New York City, I went down to her apartment to see how she was doing. The heat was radiating up the walls and the lights of the bridges on the East River glittered in the window, a bit of distant glamour to brighten the tenement life. Angela was putting out plates and decorations for her oldest daughter's fifteenth birthday. Her friend Vonnie was in the tiny kitchen making a clatter.

After Manjun disappeared, Angela agreed to introduce me to immigrant women in her community who were willing to let me study their lives. I met with several dozen immigrant women, half documented and half undocumented. They were nearly all single mothers, cycling between boyfriends and living with other family members to get by. Prostitution was a valuable source of income when other opportunities disappeared. Few were full-time street workers—in fact, almost half admitted selling their bodies only a few times a year. "Kids need gifts," one woman told me. The few who could read and write in English found menial jobs as cleaners, clerks, and cashiers. The jobs typically lasted a year or so, at which point they were back searching. These were the success stories. The women's peers who worked as babysitters or house cleaners were constantly in search of work, and so they turned to sex more often and for longer periods.

If my sights were set on documenting low-income New York, I had now formed a sample for a formal study. But hardly any of these women were catering to wealthier New Yorkers, so my dream of tracing the threads between high and low was still escaping me.

Then another door opened. At the birthday party, we fell into a conversation about the usual subject, prostitution. Angela said that, after leaving Manjun and Hell's Kitchen, she and Vonnie had been trying to get into one of the new escort agencies that were cropping up all over town. "They all tell me the same thing: 'Too old, look like a whore, look like a drug addict, look like an immigrant.' They tell me, 'The men want that young dark thing for their fantasies. They don't want their nanny!'"

Ouch.

They tried the Internet too. Angela showed me a listing she had posted:

Hey boy, you can't find anything better than what I got for you. Call me today. I could be your momma, whatever you want me. You won't forget me. No no no you won't!

She showed me some of the replies:

Are you coming down off drugs, or did you forget to go to the third grade?

Go back and light up that pipe, bitch.

"Were there any nice e-mails?" Vonnie asked.
"Sure," Angela said.
"Show us those."

"I don't save those," Angela said.

Vonnie nodded her head as if she understood perfectly. "That's what it's all about, baby. We think we *deserve* these shitty lives."

I winced. More than any other people in society, the poor beat themselves up when things are going badly. They believe what society tells them to believe, that their troubles are their own fault. This is one of the saddest things I have learned as a sociologist.

Angela winced too, recognizing the truth in Vonnie's words.

But the two women had also ventured down a more ambitious path, looking for an apartment in Brooklyn—not an apartment to live in, but an apartment for a group of women like themselves to use instead of alleys and cars, hot-sheet motels and the back rooms of porn stores. In a rented apartment, they could attract better clients and have greater control. A client who would settle for oral on the street would be more likely to stay for more. A man who didn't want to use a condom might feel more civilized in the comfort of a bedroom, might relax and talk and even become a regular. Most important of all, a professional atmosphere would shift the meaning of the interaction and take it out of the realm of the furtive and criminal.

The place they found was by the wharfs and the Brooklyn-Queens Expressway, an area packed with working-class men. There were also hipsters moving in all around, and they hoped to service this whiter, more middle-class clientele as well. At first it was Angela, Vonnie, and another streetwalker named Cincy, but two months went by and they were barely getting five guys a week between the three of them. Realizing they needed to change fast or go under, they made an impressive entrepreneurial move: they found the perfect person to break them out of their lower-class rut, a kind of sexual ambassador who could reach out to the other nations and classes of Brooklyn. She was that young dark thing of male fantasy, ideal for attracting the kinds of customers they couldn't attract on their own. The downside was, she was crazy wild and barely eighteen—in fact, she still lived with her parents.

Her name was Carla Consuelo.

Months later, in 2004, I arrived to the smell of frying onions and friendly chatter. This was a nightly ritual, the women of the apartment cooking and drinking a little before the evening's work began. They were drinking vodka, but they opened a bottle of red wine for me.

Father Madrigal sat across from me, smiling beneficently. Once a week, he came by to offer a prayer. He was from Angela's parish and he'd been working on her for almost a decade.

The peace was interrupted by a fist hammering on the door. "Open up, guys," a voice shouted in the hall.

Vonnie frowned and Angela sighed. The rule was simple. Two of the women entertained clients while a third sat in the tiny living room to remind the johns that they were not alone. The fourth took the night off. Angela and Vonnie were convinced that three was the magic number that made it look more like roommates.

But here was Carla, once again determined to break that one simple rule.

"Go home, Carla," Cincy said. "You're not supposed to be here."

"My money's just as good as y'alls," Carla shouted.

Angela opened the door and in stumbled Carla in her tight glittery clothes and wild black hair, a little bit drunk. She noticed Father Madrigal and blushed red, knowing he knew the rules as well as she did. "There's no men here," she said. "It's early. Anyway, it's a stupid rule."

Cincy stood next to Carla like a point guard. "But you agreed to that stupid rule," she said. "We all agreed to the stupid rule."

Carla sniffed the pot. "Beef stew," she wailed piteously.

Angela had met Carla in the bars and saw right away she was different from the others. She and Vonnie and Cincy felt uncomfortable with young white clients, embarrassed by their foreign accents, but Carla liked going to gallery openings and felt comfortable in Greenpoint and Williamsburg and the other areas where young hipsters were starting to arrive. She boasted that she was making "white friends" and she used the taunts on occasion to leverage advantages—like first rights to weekend nights at the apartment. She also understood the Internet and knew how to find young white guys in chat rooms. She particularly liked to find men who had recently moved to New York. "I like it when they tell me they never got fucked like that before," she said. The problem was, Carla was impossible to control.

"Do you think I don't want to come eat beef stew when it's *your* night?" Cincy said, her tone merciless.

The list of qualities Cincy disliked in Carla was long. She would show up for work drunk and show no caution approaching men. She was convinced she'd never get arrested. She was convinced she'd never get cut or beat up. She'd get on her knees outside the driver's-side door. She'd get in the backseat. She'd go into empty lots and alleys. She was constantly asking for trouble, and Cincy didn't want to be standing in the way when it came.

Most of the time they attributed Carla's behavior to heavy drinking, pills, and coke use—which wasn't exactly uncommon, but most women eventually realized that they needed to have their wits about them to ward off potential abusers and thieves. Drinking with the john was fine; drink more than him and you were playing with fire. It was hard for me to watch Carla, but this was all just part of ethnography: you learn about social life by watching people screw up, put themselves in danger, or otherwise act the fool. And Carla's constant rule breaking and dancing on the edge was, for me, a means of understanding the rules of the game that were often unspoken—or spoken behind my back. She was the gift that kept on giving, alas.

"Fine," Carla said. "I'll work outside. I'd rather be by myself anyway—the one person in this fucking world I can count on."

Out she went, slamming the door behind her.

A second later the door opened again and she poked her head in. "If I need to use the bathroom, you better let me in!"

Angela asked if I would help set the table and everyone else got back to what they were doing as if nothing had happened, talking about kids and vacations and upcoming clearance sales at their favorite outlet stores. Father Madrigal made his usual mild comments about repentance and reform.

At the door, I teased him. "How do you persist in such a hopeless cause?"

He looked amused. "I'm a man of faith," he said.

After he left, Vonnie took her turn at making the apartment a place of business, putting away the dishes and cleaning the bedrooms. This was part of the sofa sitter's duties. I said good-bye and made my way to a local bar to write up my notes for a few hours.

Later, I went back to see how the night had gone. The women were on break. They'd already delivered the first part of the night's earnings to a secure location (a friend's apartment) and cleaned up the bedrooms. They had about half an hour until the bars started closing and the streets filled up. Angela went in to clean the bathroom.

Vonnie was standing in the window smoking a cigarette. "Man, that bitch is drunk. Look at her stagger."

Cincy walked to the window. Down the street on the other sidewalk some woman was staggering like Frankenstein. She turned the corner and disappeared in the direction of the Brooklyn-Queens Expressway. A group of young men pointed and laughed.

"Oh, Jesus," Vonnie said.

"What?"

"That's Carla!"

Vonnie and Cincy ran out the door and down the street. I hesitated for a moment, wondering whether to wait for Angela, then followed. When I caught up to them, Vonnie was running directly down the middle of the street in two-inch heels, furiously determined. Carla had fallen to the pavement and was writhing like a wounded animal.

She *was* wounded. Vonnie and Cincy got to her at the same time, and Vonnie pulled back Carla's hair. Carla's lip was bulging and black with blood, and a gash on her neck was pulpy and red; her skirt and pantyhose were torn and bloody. She reached for Vonnie and her broken, bloody hands shook.

"Are you okay?" Vonnie said. "Can you get up?"

Carla looked like she was about to pass out. Vonnie told me to grab her waist and together we carried her out of the road.

On the sidewalk, broken glass glittered in the streetlights. We ended up laying Carla on the hood of a car. I reached for my cell phone.

"Call Father," Vonnie said. "No police."

I stood there, frustrated. What should I do? Go along with them or call the damn police like a normal person? I didn't want to get sucked into their criminal value structure and end up doing the wrong thing.

But Vonnie looked adamant.

Angela arrived screaming. "Oh, God! Are you all right, baby?"

Cincy was already talking to a friend at a local hospital. "They're on their way, sweetie," she said.

I took out my handkerchief and pressed it to the blood. It turned red immediately, which made me a little dizzy.

"Where was you, sweetie?" Vonnie said. "You have to tell

me, okay? C'mon, baby, where was you at? That's all I need to know."

Carla squirmed on the car hood, motioning with her fingers.

"Around the corner? By the car lot?"

Carla blinked.

"Which car? Which car was you in, sweetie?"

Why was she playing amateur detective? I had no idea. There was a lot of blood. The pain these women went through was so random and pointless. A couple of times a year, they could count on it. I felt so useless. All I ever did was sit there and take notes.

Carla had no answer, just a helpless look, so Vonnie nodded and bent down to fix her shoes. Vonnie's long, curly brown hair was falling in her eyes, her mascara running, her face flushed scarlet from exertion. "Sudhir," she ordered, "come with me!"

I had never seen a woman in heels run so fast. Vonnie was in her mid-thirties and smoked at least a pack of cigarettes per day, but she tore through the broken bottles and cigarette butts and sheets of tumbleweed newspaper like the Road Runner down a cartoon canyon. I was about ten yards behind her when she reached the edge of a parking lot. She pulled back a torn part of the chain-link fence and bent down to slide through. Panting, I pushed after her.

"Fuck, where is it?" Vonnie said. She was running around the lot, between parked cars. Suddenly she stopped. Between the fence and a line of cars, a small mattress was pushed into the gap. Brown wet spots on it must have been fresh blood. Vonnie knelt down in a meadow of yellowing valet parking tickets and looked under the cars.

"What are you doing?" I asked.

"Look for money, Sudhir. Her purse. And her knife."

Carla was supposed to carry a small knife for safety. She was supposed to put the money in her shoe or her bra and only keep a couple of tens in her purse for change, because johns will ask for change and then rob you. In that purse there should also be a cell phone, for emergency calls, but no ID to let a nutty john know your address. Her ID would be under the mattress or in a paper bag that looked like garbage. You had to have ID for the cops.

I saw a piece of something brown under a rock. It was the edge of her wallet. So we had her ID but no money or knife.

Vonnie found the pocketbook behind a car tire. Made of cheap plastic, it had been torn to pieces, its contents scattered—lipstick, crumpled receipts, a small mirror. Vonnie kept bending over to pick things up.

We heard a siren and headed back to the corner, where Angela and Cincy were watching as two emergency services personnel bent over Carla. Quickly, they packed her onto a stretcher and loaded her onto the ambulance.

We were left on the street. Everything felt very empty.

"It'll be okay," Vonnie said.

Angela looked at her phone. "Father Madrigal is going to the hospital," she said, sounding relieved.

At the apartment, Vonnie called a friend at a local gypsy cab service. Angela ran upstairs to get clothes for Carla. Then we made our way through the half-deserted Brooklyn streets to the Kings County Hospital emergency room.

Outside, Angela got a little hysterical. She was crying and saying this never would have happened if she hadn't tried to change Carla—that sort of thing. The others told her not to blame herself, but she couldn't stop. Finally, Cincy and I decided to stay with Angela outside while Vonnie went up to check things out. We huddled by the entrance in a blast of heat from a vent, stroking her hair.

"What do you mean, 'not exactly'?" Vonnie demanded, suddenly furious.

"I didn't give him the *address*. I just said, you know, it was down at this end of the street."

Angela looked devastated. "He knows the street?"

I couldn't help thinking about how different things could be for women in the sex trade. A regular escort service required some information from clients, a real telephone number at the very least, and the legal pretense of being an "escort" made working with the police more possible. But most of those women were white. For minorities and immigrants working on the streets or on their own, few such protections existed. The devastated expression on Angela's face came from realizing that the apartment didn't give them much safety either. I knew that the psychological toll of trying to change their lives and failing would be even heavier than just accepting their immigrant plight, and I wondered how long it would be before Angela just gave up—on the apartment, on their dreams, on everything. The problem was that there were now many others depending on her courage.

Carla looked up. "Um, do you think I could stay there? While I'm recovering, I mean?"

She was afraid to stay with her parents. They had just found out that she'd been selling her body and she was afraid of what they might do—especially her father, who could get violent.

Back at the apartment, the women debated. "That guy has our address," Vonnie said. "I know this girl. I'm sure she bragged about how nice it was."

"Word's going to get out this place ain't safe," Cincy said. "We got people who tell other people. Like, we have twenty people just from that factory over near the bridge. If one of them comes up here and that man breaks in, then it's over! He goes back and tells everyone, 'Hey, I was fucking one of them and some boyfriend came by, all jealous and shit.' Won't nobody come around here no more."

Vonnie steered the conversation back to Carla's request. "She knows the rules," Vonnie said. "And we're not breaking them because she got herself into this stupid mess. No one hangs out here unless they're making money."

Not only that, but having Carla recover at the apartment would make it impossible to bring clients there. She would have to stay with her parents, regardless of the risks.

By the end of the week, though, they were missing Carla's income. Despite all her difficulties, she was the best earner among them. And she was always good for her share of the rent and expenses. To keep her slot open, they would have to work seven days a week, and there was still laundry, shopping, cleaning, and all the rest. They would have to find somebody new, at least for a while—but who?

"Gloria?"

"Maria?"

"I like Kusha, that Russian girl. Doesn't even drink."

A knock on the door announced Father Madrigal, come to make a somber announcement. I took his hat and coat. He agreed, after much persuasion, to sit down at the table and accept a plate of pork, rice, beans, and plantains, but he didn't pick up his fork. "I want you to think seriously about what happened," he told them.

The women stopped moving and looked at him. With his elbows on the arms of his chair, he rubbed his hands over and over, gathering his thoughts between his palms.

"You came into each other's lives for a reason," he continued. "Not just for your needs, for money and shelter. You came because you were *called* to each other. I want you to think about that."

He paused. The women looked from one to another and then back at him.

"And I want you to think about your obligation to Carla," he added.

Vonnie moved her chair suddenly. She lit a cigarette and walked over to the window, shaking her head. "Father, I know where this is going, but I can't do it."

Angela, Cincy, and I sat quietly.

Father Madrigal began rubbing his hands again. "Well, I realize you are all under many pressures. You may not be able to do any-thing, and I understand why Carla can't stay here. But she was hurt badly. She is your partner and your friend. And she's in a danger-ous situation at home."

No one said anything. There was nothing anyone could say. It was all true.

There was a shelter for victims of domestic abuse, Father Mad-rigal explained. He had spoken to the manager already. But it would cost some money.

"How much, Father?" Vonnie said, looking miserable and furi-ous at the same time. *"How much?"*

This was the first time anyone had ever used a harsh tone with Father Madrigal. He looked at her, more puzzled than offended.

"I'm sorry, Father," Vonnie said softly.

Father Madrigal raised his hand. "This is hard on you. I know. But her needs will not be permanent needs. The room is $350 and the church will cover her meals."

Angela spoke quickly to take the floor from Vonnie. "Father, we'd be happy to pay. It's just that we are also struggling." She looked at Vonnie, then at Cincy, then back at Father Madrigal. "But we will find a way," she said.

Father Madrigal nodded. Without another word about it, we ate, talking of Carla's recovery and events in the neighborhood. Then Father Madrigal rose and said he would like to say a blessing.

We all lowered our heads. "Holy Father, I call on you in the name of Jesus to bless each of these women and to guide them in their struggle. Give them healing, and the love that every child of God deserves."

I heard a sniffle but didn't want to raise my head. I think it was Vonnie.

"I'll return in a few days to see how you are doing," the priest said, taking his hat and coat. "Be safe."

When his steps had faded, Cincy let out a sigh of relief and Vonnie poured herself another drink. "I don't know how we're going to do this, Angela."

Angela didn't reply. She moved the fork around her half-eaten plate of food.

Cincy said what was on everyone's mind. "We have to find somebody else."

Vonnie opened the window and lit another cigarette. "I'm worried about that man," she said softly. "I mean, right now he could be in one of the cars down there."

Angela looked up. "Please! Like we don't have enough to worry about."

"I'm worried," Vonnie said. "I am. If she really cut him . . ."

They were always nervous about their safety around white men. Wasn't the law always on their side?

A few weeks later, I dropped by again. The women had been trying some of Carla's tactics. They visited local bars in pairs so they didn't look so much like hookers. They almost never approached men directly, using Carla's contacts with bartenders and security guards.

"Some of these young boys look like they just left home," Vonnie said. "You can't come on to them like whores."

Angela laughed. "We just spend hours with them, drinking."

"They ask, 'Do you know any gang members?'"

No luck. Not one of them wanted to come back to the apartment with them. Angela sighed.

"Carla could get these boys. She's got the look they like. When they see her, it's like going to the jungle or something. It's dangerous, so they take a bite. But I look like their cleaning lady. They don't want to fuck their cleaning lady."

By the time another month had passed, they arrived at a crossroads. They had interviewed at least twenty women in their old neighborhood, but none of them had Carla's ability to cross boundaries. All were intimidated by the white hipsters. Finally they decided to try a white woman, even though Vonnie had reservations about "going white."

"A white woman might take over and start running everything," she said. "Then we'll be working for her."

But they narrowed it down to a Bulgarian who was living down near Coney Island. She was thrilled to move closer to the center of town.

Then they went to tell Carla. But she had news for them.

"I'm joining an escort service. In Manhattan."

She'd appreciated all their help, she said, and she would pay them back. They were stunned. For the first time, Angela seemed defeated. She was going to have to bring in strangers. They might help bring in the income, but could they be trusted? And what about Carla? Would Carla be okay without Angela to keep her under some sort of gentle control? But Angela couldn't answer these questions. She had to move on. The rent had to be paid. What was she going to do?

A few weeks later, I met up with Carla and got her side of the story. I had to remind myself to stay neutral. She admitted that she didn't have anything lined up yet in Manhattan, but said she was determined to try. That's what the attack had taught her. "You know what? I'm beautiful and I'm young and I can do better than getting my ass fucked by some cheap-ass guy in that cheap-ass apartment. I need to get out there and make some real money. This is my chance—maybe my only chance—and I'm going to take it."

From one world I flew to another like a shuttle through a loom. This night it was Shine again, picking me up near Columbia University in his sleek black sedan. We drove south to the heart of Midtown, parked in a paid parking lot, and went to an expensive hotel bar.

Inside, Shine and I both noticed the same thing right away. We were the only people of color in the place—among the clientele, that is. The busboys circling the tables and lounge area were Latino, and there was a black man behind the bar. Shine nodded at him and received a discreet nod in return.

We shrugged at each other as we took a seat. There was nothing to be said, so we just laughed.

The barman came up to Shine. "Good to see you again," he said.

I shook my head and chuckled. All his talk about needing a wingman and the staff already recognized him. I half expected him to say "the usual," but instead he ordered a whiskey on the rocks.

Work was getting out for the day, and the corporate crowd was starting to stroll through the doors. These weren't bankers. They were entertainment, media, publishing, a little younger and hipper but still with money. A few men had suits with no ties, but most wore cleanly pressed pants and trim-fit collared shirts. They drank to manufactured drumbeats and synthesizer melodies.

Shine was wearing a soft purplish linen shirt, untucked and spread widely over his dark blue Diesel jeans, and a smart Rolex like to stay in bars long. He thought he had a big sign on his face that said, "Drug Trafficker on the Prowl."

He wanted to walk out by himself, I knew. I couldn't figure out why, but Shine strategized about everything. So I said good-bye and stayed at the bar.

Michael shook Shine's hand, trying his best to mimic a ghetto greeting. "Thursday, right?" He leaned forward for a bro hug. I figured they were setting up another time for a more business-oriented visit. One by one, peer group by peer group, Shine was determined to make his experiment work.

I started to do some back-of-the-bar-napkin calculations. From earlier observations of drug dealers, I knew that a peer group was good for about fifteen hundred dollars per month, but only for about nine to twelve months. I never understood why a drop-off occurred after this point—perhaps the group disbanded, maybe a few stopped taking drugs, maybe a new dealer came along with a cheaper product. Since he was hiring a half dozen people to help, each costing about one thousand dollars per month, Shine would need to make at least fifteen thousand dollars per month to make his new venture sustainable. This meant ten groups, or a standing pool of fifty to seventy-five customers.

And this was just the minimum. Shine would want to expand. American to his core, he believed that bigger was always better.

Expansion was possible in two ways. He could continue recruit-ing new customers personally, a laborious and inefficient use of his valuable time and energy. Or he could recruit bartenders, security guards, and bellhops to find customers for him. That way, he con-trolled places instead of people. The places stayed the same and new people were always drifting through.

But Midtown and Wall Street businesses were not Harlem street corners. As he made friends with the bartenders and bellhops, Shine had to tread carefully. He would have no basis for trust and not much experience to guide him. We spoke often about this vulnerability, but he usually shrugged it off as "just another thing you have to deal with." I admired the positive attitude, but at what point would his optimism land him in prison?

By this time, Columbia had awarded me tenure and I was on my way to being named full professor. I owed much of this to the support of my colleagues and Peter Bearman, who had risen to department chair. I was publishing articles with Steven Levitt in prestigious academic journals and finishing a scholarly book on Chicago's underground economy, all boosting my academic bona fides. But I still felt like a one-trick pony, and all my successes were based on the research I had done in Chicago. New York still felt foreign and unknown.

The Chicago projects I had studied were starting to get torn down, and I was traveling there to follow families as they were evicted and forced to relocate. As a break from the scholarly work, I started to experiment with filming these families in an effort to make my first documentary. I was itching to tell Shine, because I hoped he might let me make a film of his escapades, but I was afraid he'd mock me for trying to rise above my station. I wanted to wait until I had something in the can, preferably with an Oscar for best documentary.

As a result, I was too busy to spend much time following Shine around the city.

Occasionally, we would meet quickly at a neighborhood bar and he would give me updates—or, rather, he would give me hints and leave me to figure out what was really going on. Even with a professional sociologist, Shine loved being a man of mystery. "One thing you learn in the game is that the faster you figure out the whole *white people thing*," he said with emphasis, "the longer you'll stay out of jail."

This was the kind of oblique statement that required decoding. "So . . . I take it things are going *well*?"

"Yeah, you know how it is," he said, motioning to the bartender for a refill.

"No! I don't know how it is!" I laughed. "You have to *tell* me."

"Put it like this—one day at a time."

I sighed. "So you're not broke and on your ass yet?"

"No. But you never know. Don't look for the future, 'cause you'll get stuck in the past. My grandma told me that."

I shook my head in defeat. "Okay, okay. Let me see if I understand. You have maybe—I'm guessing, a handful of steady clients? But not enough. You still haven't hired any good contact men, but you know you need to because no three-hundred-pound black street dealer is going to sell coke in Wall Street and not get noticed. So for now you need to keep going to these stupid hotels and bars yourself. But you hate it. On the other hand, it's still a new market full of opportunity and you haven't given up." I paused. "How am I doing?"

"Didn't say you were wrong." He laughed.

"I'd say you're at 40 percent of where you want to be. Maybe you have two bars locked down? A few bartenders? No hotels yet, because you'd be smiling right now if you did."

He smiled and I knew he was lying.

"So you're getting there, but it's slow and you're burning cash. You haven't figured out security yet. Something doesn't feel right about these places. And you definitely don't like walking around with that much on your person. Am I still on track?"

Shine didn't even look me in the eye. Now I *knew* I was nailing it.

That's how it went most of the times we met. It felt like a conversation with Deep Throat. But what I really needed, if I wanted to launch another formal study—and I always did—was for Shine to introduce me to these bartenders and bellhops so I could put some meaty details in a grant application and hire research assistants and all the rest of the formal machinery that makes hanging out with drug dealers academically respectable. Once again, I had to be patient.

While I was waiting for Shine to come through, Betsy, Michael, and Carter started inviting me to their parties. There were two kinds. The artsy parties happened down in Soho and the East Village, where their artsy friends lived. The family parties were all on the Upper East Side, where their parents lived. At both, people drank and caroused with bohemian abandon late into the night. Sometimes I felt like Jim Fowler on *Mutual of Omaha's Wild Kingdom*, gazing at strange creatures from the safety of my ethnographic pith helmet. They had their own idiosyncratic phrases that made no sense unless you knew the people and places they referenced, and they seemed entirely uninterested in bringing outsiders into their peer group except for entertainment—the role I probably filled. Perhaps I should have found this offensive, but the only emotions I felt were the distanced ones that accompany invisibility. Even in the projects, where I couldn't have been more different from the locals, I was acknowledged with warmth and nearly always offered a plate of food or a drink before anyone else—an honored guest. Here, they looked past me as if I was the help. Even after I'd met a few of them a half dozen times and they'd asked me who I was, whether I was in New York for vacation, they would forget every detail of the previous conversations, including the fact that they had taken place. Some were friendly, but others ignored me outright. Since I was as dark as any of their servants, I shouldn't have been surprised. But it still stung.

I had experienced this kind of invisibility once before, in Chicago. In the black communities in the 1990s, it was relatively easy to move about as a South Asian, because people just assumed that I was a member of some family that owned a liquor store or deli. In other words, I was relatively unthreatening. Standing around street corners or bars became routine, and people would have their conversations in my presence without feeling that I was an outside threat. Here I was more of a social curio, a vaguely subservient role that made me uncomfortable. It was hard to imagine them taking me seriously enough to let me observe them as a professional. I fantasized a job on a house-cleaning crew, arriving at one mansion after another just at the moment the owners began to exhibit socially significant behavior. At the same time, whenever I did get a chance to watch this privileged tribe from the sidelines, I felt wistful. Their parties were like one long beer commercial with tanned faces, silky hair, natural cotton fabrics, and toothy white grins. They seemed so breezy and light, so certain that nothing too real would ever weigh them down. I wondered what it was like to live inside that feeling.

I also kept wondering what kind of research project I could devise to formalize my interest. It would have to be something subtle, I knew. The poor often feel obligated to respond to the authority figures who poke and prod them, but rich people are the opposite—they don't like to be studied and have no problem shutting the door. So how could I get that door open?

On this night, I found my way across the park and into the elegant side streets with their limestone mansions. The club they'd invited me to had a door without a sign, which led down to a catacomb with multiple levels. I found Betsy, who began introducing me to everyone.

"Here's someone you should meet," Betsy said, and I turned to see a familiar face: Analise. I hadn't seen her since the days of my Harvard wine tasting, when she'd given me the gracious education on viniculture that kept me looking marginally less of a fool. She had a red tinge in her hair this time, but she still had the slender offhand grace that whispered old money. "Can you recommend a good Chianti?" she said, a conspiratorial grin on her face.

"I'm not sure there *is* a good Chianti," I answered.

Betsy looked puzzled. "So you know each other?"

We confessed that we did. Like a good host, she soon found an excuse to disappear and let us catch up on old times.

"So how are you?" Analise asked.

"Good, real good. I'm teaching here now."

"NYU?"

"Columbia."

She congratulated me, and I asked what she was doing.

"A bunch of different pointless jobs," she said. "You know, trying to find my thing."

I told her I was thinking about going to France. I mentioned that my marriage wasn't doing so well. Something about her seemed to invite those kinds of confessions. She rattled off the various jobs she'd held after college—a financial services firm "full of men who make you sick," a three-month stint at an antique furniture gallery owned by a friend of her mother's. "I had to sit there all day and smile at eighty-year-olds who came in. I ended up mostly making tea while they talked about some godforsaken event that happened a hundred years ago."

Her chirpy manner was forced, but her voice grew increasingly soft, and the softness brought more truth. She mentioned a boyfriend who was not altogether supportive. This led to a tangled story of her current impasse with her parents, who wanted her to find something meaningful to do with her life that didn't include anything she actually wanted to do, like opening an art gallery. "Too risky," they'd said. "Great, Mom," she'd said back. "Give me the list of boring safe options that kill your soul and let me choose one of those."

She mentioned going back to India, where her uncle had some

kind of school. She talked about a previous visit when her parents were having a marital drama. "I just sat and ate and worked with the kids on art stuff. It's so calm there. I feel like I go crazy here. I love going there. I get away from all this." She raised her hands and shoulders, as if to blame the skyscrapers around us for her current troubles.

I noticed that she kept looking around to see if anyone was watching us talk.

Then she said she had some new business opportunities and would like some advice. I found this strange, particularly since I had very little understanding of commerce—at least not the legal kind—but I agreed to meet her. With that, she went off to greet some friends. Not until much later did I understand that her business as a madam was the subject she was broaching. She was just getting started then, managing a couple of friends, and the new business opportunities were new girls who wanted to work with her. She was probably hoping I could give her some inside knowledge.

Betsy came back and introduced me to more people, all pleasant enough. But after a few of the usual questions—"What do you teach?" "Were you born here?" "What does your name mean?"—there was frighteningly little to talk about. I could have been the statue on the mantel. With each brief exchange, the idea of doing research on the upper class began to feel more remote. Their complete indifference made my usual ethnographic fly-on-the-wall approach seem almost humiliating, a symphony of awkward silences. How could you do serious research on people who barely bothered to listen to your questions?

Just a few weeks after Carla had left, Angela called to say they couldn't make the rent. I was stunned. I was sure she would find someone else to take Carla's place. Vonnie mentioned that

Angela had difficulty trusting the white Eastern European women she'd tried to bring aboard, and I had a sinking feeling that Angela's social fears might undermine the operation. I went over to the Brooklyn apartment to hear how this part of her story ended. When I got there, Angela and Vonnie were standing in front of the building looking at the beaten-up black pickup truck that was carting their stuff away. It was already full, and that meant another trip, which meant hours of waiting.

We went back upstairs and sat on a few boxes with a bottle of cheap red wine on the floor in front of us. We spent an hour counting monthly expenses, delinquent clients, and money owed. "Carlos needs to pay us two fifty, no?" "Ooh! Don't forget that one white dude who smelled so *bad*! He gave me three hundred just so I wouldn't tell anyone he was a crybaby!" "I think Carla made three thousand one month, no? Or was she lying?" In the end, we figured out that they'd actually come out a bit ahead. After two years of struggle and strife, courage and persistence and men who sometimes didn't smell so good, they came away with a combined total of $750. It wasn't nearly enough. So their year of hope and struggle would end with a retreat back to the Lower East Side.

They asked me what I thought, looking back, about the whole experiment. Not ready to trust my feelings, I leaned on sociology. There are always setbacks in American stories, I said, but the important thing is setting out on the journey. "You moved out. You moved here. It didn't last as long as you wanted, but—"

"We learned our lesson," Angela said. She was not in the mood for social science.

I hated to hear her say that. There could be all kinds of lessons. Some of the lessons could be ideas to do better next time. I started again to try to weave a positive tale, but Vonnie interrupted me.

"Nobody here wants to see a bunch of dumb Latina whores."

Her bitterness pierced the room. Why *hadn't* it worked? they kept wondering aloud. Their laughter and cries kept pointing to

the unassailable quality of race. Vonnie's explanation, though painful and crude, was hard to refute outright. From what I'd heard
and seen, there didn't seem to be an overwhelming demand for
Latina sex workers of their age. But they all could have exercised
better judgment and made better business decisions. They could
have thought more carefully about renting an apartment, dipping
their toes in with a few weeks' rental at one of the motels that lined
the expressways. Angela's suspicion of the white sex workers might
have hurt them too, and they also could have tried bringing on
more of the younger women like Carla from their own neighborhood and class. But they weren't looking for such narrow ratio-
nales. Their own hearts were pointing elsewhere, to something
more absolute and ineffable. Maybe it was a way of being in the
world, an ethnic style that wasn't suited to recruiting customers in
this gentrifying Brooklyn neighborhood.

Their experiences made me think more deeply about the notion
of floating. Global cities offered new social connections that could
be monetized, aboveground and below in the black market. However, the capacity to make unfamiliar connections could also turn
life into a series of ruthless commodified relationships. Capitalism
turned everything into a potentially salable object but it didn't
guarantee there would be buyers. So for those trying to sell something, the risk of failure was always present. Vonnie and Angela
showed just the right kind of entrepreneurial fervor, capitalizing on
global New York's invitation to float, to cross barriers and break
new economic ground. But New York could not promise buyers,
and anything that floats can also sink.

Vonnie broke the silence. "We weren't asking for a mansion,
Sudhir. We just wanted to get out of the fucking projects and
move upstate with our kids, maybe go back to Santo Domingo
for a visit."

I lowered my head.

But Angela, as always, forced herself to look on the bright side.

At least Carla was on her way, she reminded us. She had that thing young people had. She would make it and they could watch her and be happy.

"She better not forget who her friends are," Vonnie said. "When she comes running back . . ."

While she tried to think of an appropriate threat, Angela stopped her. "If she comes running back," she said, "we'll be there for her."

I hoped it was true.

Angela's circumstances put into relief one of the hardest decisions for any entrepreneur: when to call it quits and close up shop.

Shine was showing me another: for any employer large or small, the toughest part of life is letting workers go when sales start to slip. A formal severance meeting with the human resources manager can calm the rupture between boss and employee, helping to reduce the possibility of embezzlement or vandalism.

In the underground economy, alas, no such formal mechanisms exist. Which raises a number of questions: How do people manage teams when the activity is illegal? How do they ensure trust and confidentiality, and what do they do with an uncooperative employee? Carla and Manjun, two people who had experienced great vulnerability, stood in sharp contrast to the drug lords I knew who led their workers as if they were managing a McDonald's: people had shifts, with specified daily duties, and responsibilities to meet sales targets. If they failed, they were fired (or beaten, or docked pay).

But those in the underground who faced rapidly declining economic climates had no clear signposts to guide them. For example, Shine had been juggling his staffing levels since the end of 2001, hiring during times of steady supply and cutting back as supplies tightened. Just as Vonnie and Angela were packing up and calling it quits, Shine had made his final transition out of the street trade and was busily recruiting new employees to sell cocaine to white customers. But this meant two complicated tasks: hiring the right new workers and letting go of the street thugs.

Shine had always believed that it was risky to let an employee walk without a conversation about shared expectations. In this sense, he was a great business manager. He made it clear that his expectations included continued discretion. Any talking about him or his operation would carry significant negative repercussions. But if they kept their mouths shut, he might have work for them again one day.

The problem with this rational approach was that these were a) young men and b) young men with no alternatives and c) young men. They wanted to make their money now. And they weren't completely wrong. In fact, you could say their attitude was the result of a perfectly rational cost-benefit analysis of the underground economy in which they found themselves. It's hard to take the long-term view in a world where there might not *be* a long term.

One day, with his operations now firmly placed in the powdered cocaine market, I watched Shine lay off one of these young guys. They were talking on the stoop of Shine's brownstone when I walked up. He motioned for me to stop so the young guy couldn't see me listening to the conversation.

"You got a lot in you," Shine was saying. "You survive, you understand. You got what it takes. To survive. That's all it's about around here."

The kid looked like a teenager who had just been scolded by his teacher. "Momma's still gonna be pissed at me," he said, taking off his baseball cap and scratching his head. "She's gonna beat my ass when I tell her."

"Well, then, you need to get some more work," said Shine,

looking impatient. "If you need to pay that rent, then you better pay that rent. Find a job or something."

"Yeah, I guess," the young man kept saying, shaking his head. "I mean, she's *really* gonna be pissed."

"How much you bringing in?"

"About two hundred. Mostly just for the place. Clarisse went to jail, so, you know, I had to step up."

"I can respect that," Shine said. "You a man, you got to step up. I know it's rough, but you were good and, like I said, if I get rolling again, I'm calling you first."

"Yeah, man. I appreciate that, but I need some work. Maybe I could just work one corner for you, by myself. You know, maybe you could just front me something. We could keep it low down, you know, just me working out there."

"Man, that's on you," Shine answered. "You can get your own shit, my brother. This whole place is yours." Shine opened up his arms and puffed out his chest.

"No, man. I can't. Ain't got nothing. I'm out. I can't front nothing. I need someone to back me up."

"Okay, man, we're going back where we started. I told you that we're done. That's it. You got all the opportunity you need right now. Just get out there."

"No, man. It's not that easy. I'm just figuring that you and me, we could just do something small."

Shine started laughing. "My brother, you need to hear what I'm saying."

"No, no, no," the young man said. He stuck out his chest in a display of confidence, then glanced over at me. I was leaning against the stoop, making no attempt to hide my eavesdropping. He looked back at Shine. "Maybe we talk about this tomorrow because I really need to work."

Shine stood up, shrugging his shoulders. "That's what I'm trying to tell you, shortie. It's done. You dig?"

"Oh, man, I don't know. I say we just keep on hustling."

Shine sighed and gestured to me, asking me to come up the stairs and into the building. I walked past the young man. He didn't look like he was going to leave anytime soon. I knew the feeling. If you don't accept the news you've just heard, if you just wait long enough, perhaps it will turn out to have been a bad dream.

A few weeks later in a Harlem bar, Shine finally told me the story of the momentous transition he was going through. For the first time in almost a decade, he didn't have at least one crew member on the corner twenty-four/seven. Instead, he was hiring more women like his cousin Evalina, people who could move more comfortably in the downtown social world. He had decided to reinvent himself, to go for it without the safety valve of having just a few dealers on the street. He was pushing all the chips on powdered cocaine. On the white market. While once his client base was 90 percent black and Latino, that number would soon drop to less than 10 percent.

To me, the parallels to Vonnie and Angela seemed ominous. Could Shine really travel outside his own home base and set up shop in the white world? So many things could go wrong; so much was uncertain. Despite the criminal nature of his ambitions, I couldn't help feeling nervous for him.

The first item on his list was to assemble his new team. Finding the right people for the job wasn't easy, he said. He wasn't even sure what attributes he should be seeking. Could his employees be black? Would women or men be more appropriate? Did they need white references?

Meanwhile, his exit interviews with his existing crew began taking on an existential cast. "These young guys just run around now, acting fucking stupid," he complained. "At least with me, they learned how to do things the right way." But he was disappointed that they hadn't learned from him how to think in more sober ways. They still lacked the discipline he felt was needed for success in the world of business. "I have a duty to these guys, but they have to trust me. If they watch me survive, they can learn."

In my experience, gang leaders never think of themselves as running a ruthless criminal enterprise. They think of themselves as race heroes in a polarized America, but it's a vision of the country that seems, to me, antiquated—like something out of the 1950s or '60s. They are *always* reaching out to troubled young men who need adult male mentorship to survive, *always* doing a good deed for the neighborhood—until something ugly happens. But I had seen behind the curtain. I knew that when one of these young men didn't take getting fired in the right spirit, gang leaders like Shine didn't send them off with hugs and a motivational speech. They simply beat the pulp out of them. That's how it was done.

Shine had grown used to that world and those habits. He could put on his player face, put his arm around someone, and talk in such a way that their interests seemed aligned, but everyone knew his slick talk was backed up by force. As Al Capone said so well, "You can get more with a kind word and a gun than you can with a kind word alone." As Shine stepped away from his neighborhood, he was likely to find himself in situations where his old tricks would make things worse instead of better. He worried about the same thing, I know. What if, when pressure escalated, he acted emotionally or instinctively? The ghetto code could betray him. And what if his new hard-shoe customers refused to pay? How would he respond if his new employees stole from him? I couldn't imagine him pushing Evalina or some white club kid the way he pushed the boys in his crew.

I felt for Shine. He was going to have to develop new rules and routines and approaches—a whole new criminal style—all while

of launching a big study of the Hell's Kitchen underworld, and his enthusiasm for my idea that it was ground zero for the changes being wrought in New York. He wouldn't have just shrugged that off. He knew I'd be desperate for another way to tell the story. Maybe he was trying to tell me something.

On the paper, Michael had scribbled a phone number and a name: *Margot Kerry*.

CHAPTER 5

SEX IS A PASSPORT

Not so fast!" I cried. The bar was hot and crowded and I was feeling dizzy. The noise from the crowd rang in my ears.

But Margot Kerry burbled merrily along, telling me the secrets of her trade. A bartender has to *want* you in his bar, she said. Maybe the bartender hears of a guy looking for a date. Some bartenders received a fee per week, others per client. You bring your high-priced clients to the bar, *their* drinks always get filled first. Bartenders in Midtown got lots of requests for phone numbers, bartenders in Soho not so much. A bartender who really liked you would even kick out your competitors. A bartender would hold cash if you were afraid of being robbed. Strip club managers were another link in the chain, a source of new girls. A car dealer laundered Margot's money by reselling her brand-new car the same day she bought it, giving her clean cash back.

Clearly, she was enjoying the opportunity to demonstrate mastery of her secret world, the world I had been trying to break into for so many long months. But my pen didn't seem to be working very well.

"I like this," Margot was saying. "I never really get a chance to talk about my life without feeling ashamed. Thank you for not making me feel that way."

Margot was in her mid-thirties, flamboyant and redheaded and harried looking, the kind of person who is always lighting another cigarette and somehow makes it look glamorous. She gave off the air of having suffered and survived with all her compassion and sense of humor intact, which I found very comforting. Every five minutes her phone would ring and she would answer all the calls immediately. "I can help," she would say. "Leave it to me."

I tried to make mental notes as the sentences streamed out of her mouth. But the world began to slide away from me like a camera going out of focus. My blood sugar was dropping way too low, I realized.

Margot noticed and waved at the bartender, who quickly ushered us into a back room and helped lower me down onto an old sofa.

"Panic attack," I gasped.

This had been happening for a year. In the middle of lecturing to my class, riding a city bus, or just buying groceries, I'd feel a wave of anxiety so strong I'd nearly pass out. Where it came from, I had no idea.

Margot sat next to me, stroking my hand and saying soothing things. I have to admit I found her presence very calming. I felt that she would be completely accepting of anything I did, which was an unfamiliar feeling—a great feeling. I guess I needed it more than I realized. When I was breathing more calmly, she asked, "Anything you want to talk about? I'm pretty good with people's troubles. God knows, I've gone through nearly everything myself."

But I was too embarrassed. This whole thing was already so unprofessional.

"Girl troubles? You don't look like a 'guy trouble' sort of guy."

I hesitated. "If I tell you, do you promise we'll never talk about it again?"

"Whatever you want."

Somehow, that unleashed the floodgates. I told her about the people I was meeting and the people I needed to meet. I talked about global cities and underground networks, about invisible communities in Mortimer's bar and Manjun's store, and Lord knows what else. A friend told me to float and that's what I was doing—yesterday Harlem, Brooklyn today, and tomorrow wide open. I was beginning to see how each person I met would take me to a new place and introduce me to a new person, who would take me someplace else, known as "snowball sampling" in the sociology trade. But my snowball was steadily turning into a snow-boulder. People I cared about were getting hurt and disappearing. I was trapped on a speeding train that was going in a direction I didn't want to go. I wanted to get off the train, escape the routine, separate from my wife, move to France. "I'm not even sure what kind of sociologist I want to be," I said.

"Drink some water," Margot said.

I did as she told.

"Go back to 'separate from my wife.'"

I told her the story. It wasn't anything special, just a boy and a girl and a series of sad disagreements made all the sadder by the fact that we loved each other. Under these circumstances, obsessive fieldwork in the hood made sense to me. Anything was better than, ugh, *feeling*.

Gradually my breathing began to return to normal and I could feel relief coming to the surface.

"Deal with the things that cause you pain and start doing things that make you feel better," Margot said. "Can you try to do that?"

I straightened myself up and told her I thought this would be a good time to go home and lie down. Hopefully, we could meet another time when I was feeling a little less deranged.

Of course, my little breakdown turned out to be the best thing I could have done. That's humanity for you. Once I melted into a puddle in her presence, Margot seemed to view me as a kindred spirit. She was affectionate and supportive, the friend I didn't even know I needed. We began meeting in various upscale hotel bars, always in some private nook provided by a friendly bartender, quickly achieving a level of intimacy I had never experienced before on the job. I was used to others growing attached to me because I listened without judgment, but I never expected the table to turn.

Each meeting also yielded juicy kernels of professional insights. The bartender sometimes stopped by for a break, which gave me the chance to launch a few quick questions: How many women a night come to the bar selling sex? How do clients find out about you? If we met in a hotel bar, Margot would explain who was involved in their operation, who made it all go down so that the john and his hired friend could meet without fuss or capture. I was learning a lot, but I still had the generalizability problem to deal with: Was she a unique case? Would she connect me to other people like her in the sex trade? Were the bartenders and hotel clerks and cab drivers in her network representative of larger trends in the sex trade? If she was an exceptional case, there would be no point in even launching a formal study: none of my academic colleagues would be interested in a single person's experience, only those shared by the multitudes.

The truth was, Margot fascinated me. Raised in the working-class suburbs of New York and New Jersey, the daughter of a teacher and a construction foreman, she went to public schools with lots of other Irish Catholics, maintained a solid B-plus average, and was active in her church. After high school, she married a bond salesman and moved to Manhattan, where she worked part-time in a law firm and went to college at night. The plan was to get a law degree and become a solid and productive member of the middle class.

Such a classic all-American life. The best kind of childhood, blessed with solid values and a sense of security unimaginable to much of the world. And yet it all unraveled in an instant when she caught her husband in an affair. Divorce and heavy drinking followed, and one night, broke and needing a place to stay after a fight with her parents, she convinced herself that she wanted to sleep with an old friend who had always wanted her. Really she did it for a place to sleep. And thereby crossed an invisible line.

In the bar where she told this story, I watched her face as she explained the next step. She didn't seem sad, just determined to lay it out there. "A few nights later, I was in Stanton's Bar down near Wall Street," she said, teasing the ice cubes in her drink with a straw. "I was taking shots of whiskey with a bunch of traders who knew my husband, and one of those bastards flashed two hundred dollars in my face. He said it was mine if I gave him a blow job in the bathroom."

Her husband would feel humiliated if it got back to him. And she could fill her old friend's refrigerator. And she was already sleeping with one guy for a place to stay, so what difference did it make? So she took the bastard's hand and led him to the bathroom.

A week later, another one of her husband's friends offered her five hundred dollars.

After that, she kept looking for a regular job. But the easy money was too easy. She found some good bars and learned how to spot the men with free-spending ways and struck up friendships with women who were working the same bars. Most of them were just like her, college educated with some work history as paralegals or clerks. They started loaning one another clothes, recommending doctors, trading information.

Early on, she got them working in pairs. "There's a particular kind of guy who goes to a bar at five or six in the afternoon," she explained eagerly. "He's either commuting or traveling, or he has something to do in town later that night, and he's feeling a little lonely. Easy prey! The only thing you have to figure out is how to make them feel like they aren't getting a hooker, just a nice girl who 'needs a little help,' quote unquote. So having another pretty girl with you makes it seem less trashy."

Gradually, she became the den mother. When someone was in trouble, she would get the call. Like Manjun and Angela, she had gathered the invisible threads of a community around her. But she veered wildly. She would brood, drink, take anti-anxiety meds, then vow to change her life and go straight. Once she even landed a job as a human resources manager in a large accounting firm. Now everything looked different. The long hours, the office politics, the aggressive men who wanted to impress everyone with what go-getters they were. How gross it all was. And she *still* had to turn the occasional trick to make ends meet.

The last straw? A supervisor who offered her a raise in exchange for sex, a smug and grubby powermonger who assumed the worst about her. But if she had offered sex in exchange for a raise, she'd have been labeled a whore. She'd probably have been fired. What a bunch of hypocrites!

Instead, Margot drove up to Maine and took long walks in the woods. "I guess I owned up to who I was," she told me. "I knew I didn't want to work in an office. I knew I had a skill that men would pay a lot for. So the question was, could I do it in an intelligent way, without hurting myself, and maybe even save a little money?" Then she drove back to New York and returned to sex work with her eyes open. No booze, no meds. She started exercising, bought a computer and some financial planning software. She made sixty-five thousand dollars her first year. In time, she went from den mother to setting up dates and charging commissions. Business was booming. Madam Margot was born.

Margot's work as a sex broker was opening up a whole new upscale world to me. I was seeing things I had never seen before. She was so strong, so confident. Unlike Angela, who also had these qualities, Margot had no need to sell sex herself. She could make money and earn a measure of social power just helping other women do so. She wasn't abused or supporting a drug habit; she didn't have the social or legal obstacles that kept Manjun and his friends trapped in the underground. She had a line of credit and some investments. In the eyes of outsiders, she was just another middle-class woman living the good life in New York City.

Some people might ask, she said, Why suffer the risks and stigma of selling sex if you have other options? The way she looked at it, selling sex *was* her other option. "New York gave me a second chance. A lot of other places, I would have married again, had kids, been miserable. But here, I can reinvent myself. And you can judge me, you can put me down and call me names or whatever, but you can't take away the fact that I am *succeeding*."

As an immigrant, I recognized her defiant ambition in my bones—it was the ringing sound of the American dream. Is that possible? I wondered. Can sex work become a theater of aspiration like any other job? Can a prostitute even *have* an American dream?

Shine was taking me deeper into his world too. After church services one Sunday, he invited me to his family's place. They had the bay window apartment of a brownstone on a tree-lined street, a lovely location. Inside, I felt as if I was back in Chicago. Plastic covered the lone couch. A thick, dark blue shag carpet lay on all the floors. Religious pictures and symbols hung on all the walls; a few African prints and masks sat on side tables. Black-and-white family photos showed stern, hardened African-American faces in the middle of farmland. Everything seemed tied to the past.

Shine seemed amused at my interest in the pictures. "Just a bunch of country folk, ain't we?"

A giant black man, built like a tractor and at least six foot five, appeared behind us. Shine grabbed him in an affectionate bear hug. This was Shine's brother Michael, a former college basketball star turned real estate agent. The first time I met him, he put me through a hazing process that ranged from "Who do you know in Chicago?" to "How much do you know about black culture?" I still wasn't sure whether I had passed, because he generally gave me a wide berth.

"I'm going to get a plate of food," Shine said. "Sudhir, want something?"

"Coming," I said, turning back to the photographs for a last look. One was particularly haunting: a large print of a tall black man with a brown suit and a smart beige hat, black briefcase in hand, New York City in the background. He stood on a sidewalk with brownstones on either side of him. A child was walking past him. A green bicycle lay on the sidewalk, forgotten.

Michael was watching me. "Shine ever tell you about our father?"

"No," I said.

"Came on a ship right before the war. Got drafted. Sixteen children—that we know about!"

He laughed and continued speaking in an odd staccato style. "I'm the second youngest. Shine's the youngest. Three in jail. Me and Shine never been. Poppa lost his mind after 1990. When he lost his job. Depressed, couldn't get out of it. Drinking like you ain't never seen. Killed himself one day. Just shot himself in the head. In the basement. Shine and I were upstairs. He started shaking, I'll never forget it. We both knew what had happened. I got my blanket and wrapped my dad up. The bloodstain is still on the floor. Momma still ain't been down there. Shine won't go down. Ten years, and they still won't go down there."

Michael paused. He wiped his upper lip, which had a few beads of perspiration. "After that, ain't nothing been the same. Ain't starving or nothing, doing fine as far as that goes. But something is gone that ain't ever gonna come back."

I had met Shine's mother a few times, but she said very little except to welcome me and then walk to her bedroom.

"We moved Momma into a new house," Michael continued. "We fixed it up, bought the upstairs for my auntie. But she wanted to come back here. And the top floor, that's where my other brother stay."

"Shine never talks about it," I said.

"And he never will," Michael said.

It all made so much sense. Like his father, Shine was withdrawn and focused on an inner goal. Like his mother, he was a bit of a ghost in the world. This is what I was thinking when he called from the kitchen. "Sudhir, get your ass in here and try this mac 'n' cheese."

Country food. Feeling moved by Michael's story and the comforting family atmosphere, I walked into the kitchen to take a plate of gooey orange happiness from Shine's hand—a hand that was swollen and cut, yellow-black bruises flaring from a couple of red gashes. I couldn't help staring at it.

"This fucking kid Juan," Shine said, spitting out the name. "He's selling *downtown.* Can you believe that? I fire him because *I'm* selling downtown, so he decides to take me on. He found out which clubs and bars I work and now he's in there trying to sell his own shit!"

I knew Juan. He was barely nineteen. I didn't think he could get *into* bars and clubs, much less take on a well-connected gangster like Shine. Nor did I know he was a well-connected thug himself. What muscle did he have to ensure that he could withstand Shine's retaliation—which was assuredly coming?

It had started innocently enough, Shine explained. Juan wanted to be more than a runner and started recruiting a few customers, always giving Shine his cut. I remembered hearing Shine express some concern about this a few months earlier, only because he didn't think Juan had good people skills, but he shrugged it off because he had so much else on his mind. Then, apparently, Juan started making friends with some downtown bartenders. He told

Shine he was just being a friendly guy. But Shine suspected he was slipping them money to compete with Evalina, and that's when the confrontation began. Now he couldn't even get the punk to meet with him.

Retaliation had to come quickly and decisively or else Juan would detect weakness in Shine. But Shine and I both knew that this was no longer a ghetto dispute. A downtown bar was involved, which meant white people were involved, so the old rules didn't apply. Now Shine had to figure out how to deal with a dispute in the new world he was trying to conquer. Characteristically, he said he would be patient. Taking a deep breath as if trying to gather that patience on the spot, he said he would catch up with Juan at church.

"But his parents will be there," I said, shocked that he would transgress boundaries in this almost sacrilegious way. Even for drug dealers, churches were off-limits.

"That's exactly why I'm doing it there," Shine says. "If he runs, everyone will think he's guilty."

Pieces were starting to fall into place. The story about punishing Juan gave me an important glimpse of the perils of Shine's downtown experiment. At the same time, Margot was bringing me into her world, and soon I would be interviewing more of the elite white sex workers in her network. And even if Angela's efforts at marketing innovation and product development had failed, they'd brought me out of the ghetto and across many boundaries.

Then there was Analise, the ultimate insider. Around the time Shine gave Juan his beatdown, she started calling me and asking if I wanted to catch up. Of course, the answer was yes. I genuinely liked her as a person, but I was downright fascinated by everything she represented—beautiful and young and rich, she and her careless young friends were the end of all the striving, the focal point that organized the world. If you had told me at the time that Analise was secretly running an elite escort service, I would have laughed in your face. But that was the period when she was just getting started in the business, which might have been one of the reasons she reached out to me.

Our schedules clashed until one day she called and invited me to join her gang for a screening of her boyfriend's first movie, an NYU student film he had financed with about three hundred thousand dollars that he'd raised from family and friends. She had contributed a hefty sum herself, so she was listed as a producer. They held the event at her aunt's luxurious apartment on East Eighty-fourth, a Xanadu of mahogany and marble. Due to a last-minute crisis, I arrived very late. The doorman called, then hung up the phone and told me the party would be coming down.

A few minutes later, ten people tumbled through the front door, first men bearing bottles of champagne and then women in their slinky dresses and heels. Analise was crying and two women were comforting her. "Just ignore that asshole," said one. "You don't de-serve that shit."

That was my first glimpse of Brittany, who looked as beautiful and dangerous as a Greek goddess. Analise reached her hand out to me and whispered, "Sorry. Just come along. I'll explain later."

Then J.B. came out. He was hunched into a dark plaid coat and looked like he shouldn't be leaving his bed, much less the building. He pointed at us. "You fucking bitch! All of you fucking bitches! You have no fucking idea what I fucking do!"

J.B. wiped his mouth and staggered out underneath the green awning that extended over the sidewalk. He grabbed my shoulder and held on for balance, glaring at Analise. "You want the money? Is that what you want?"

Brittany stepped forward. "Why don't you just shut up?"

"It's none of your damn business," J.B. sneered.

"Yes it is, asshole. You're not getting into this car."

"Fuck that shit. I'm walking."

At this point, J.B. steered me toward Fifth Avenue. His friends followed.

"J.B.—get back here!" Analise yelled. "You're being ridiculous. We're all sorry. Let's just move on."

"Fuck you!" J.B. yelled back.

J.B. led us down Fifth Avenue, alongside Central Park. A guy named Michael came up to walk with us. "Don't worry about her," he said.

"It's her money."

"You can raise money, man. It's all about the material."

"See, she doesn't even get that. She's so fucking out of touch. I've got the *material*, man."

J.B. stopped at a bench, looking across Fifth Avenue to some millionaire's apartment building. One of his friends popped open a champagne bottle and handed it to J.B.

I took the moment to whisper to one of the guys. "What happened?"

"Sundance rejected his movie."

Meanwhile, J.B. was chugging. Then he burped and put his head in his hands. "All of you can fuck off and die for all I care," he said.

Then he stood up and swept his arm forward like a Shakespearean actor, gave a slight bow—and retched. It came out like a tube of chicken broth, one long projectile that nearly reached the street.

Michael just kept smoking and talking and so did the others, completely ignoring this bizarre outburst. "You should go out to LA," one said. "This is the wrong town for what you're doing."

"It was my first film," J.B. said. "First film. Does anyone get that? You know what my uncle Frank said? 'Better get a job, kid. Go work for your dad.' Fucking lowlife who steals from his own company."

Again, J.B. opened his mouth and let loose a stream of vomit.

This time it was less perfectly columnar and some sprinkles hit his shoes.

"My fucking brain is going to explode," J.B. said, dropping his head back into his hands.

Some of the other guys began to drift away, heading back toward the limo. They didn't seem disgusted, just bored. I was the opposite, rooted to the spot, completely mesmerized by this strangely nonchalant behavior. I'd seen friends vomit, but they usually moaned and groaned and promised not to do it again. I'd seen fraternity brothers vomit, but that was usually in the context of a wild bacchanal. I'd seen heroin addicts vomit, but that was like a medical event. I'd seen nothing like this matter-of-fact display anywhere else.

A few weeks later, I saw it again. This time it was Brittany. We were just outside the Plaza Hotel, walking north. She took two steps into the park, threw up in the bushes right next to the gate, and came back to finish her sentence. "She should go out there and try to find a place, and see how crazy it is!" We walked along fairly steadily with only a little weaving, listening to Brittany denounce her mother for the horribly unmaternal act of kicking Brittany out of the family's penthouse apartment. Then she darted into the bushes and threw up again.

Another time, outside a Chelsea art gallery, I saw one of the rich kids vomit into a trash can and turn to welcome friends while wiping his mouth. Then there was another J.B. episode. It began to seem as though every evening would end with some preppie youth stopping the cab or limo and taking a few minutes to launch the half-processed remains of the evening's booze and food onto the side of the street. They did it theatrically, turning the sidewalk into a stage, transforming themselves into the aggrieved and tragic protagonists of some great imaginary drama. I was aware of the risks of sociological voyeurism and the impulse to treat them like animals in a zoo, but I still couldn't help wondering: Was a certain style of drunkenness an aspect of class distinction? Was this some kind of socioeconomic marker, perhaps even a form of personal expression? Were they throwing up all the expectations they'd been forced to swallow?

One thing was clear: like Shine and Angela and Carla, these rich kids sure believed in the possibility of renewal. But theirs followed an existential purging so violent it seemed like a bid for redemption. Then they would pop another champagne cork and swallow some more renewal in a bottle. And the price of the bottle seemed to matter, as if it elevated their behavior above mere squalor. I wasn't sure whether to be disgusted or impressed. Was this the dark secret at the heart of the American dream? A Roman level of thirst and self-loathing? My colleagues in the history and literature departments talked breezily about the end of the American empire—I felt I now had some data points for their argument.

As I watched this play unfold I couldn't help but wonder about Carla's and Shine's respective strivings. If they were going to navigate these worlds, I hoped they wouldn't be required to show their excellence at purging. I started to have my doubts that they could survive it. I was invisible, but they, as blacks and Latinos, would inspire animus. Maybe Carla was right: animus was just the other side of sexual desire. Maybe Shine was right: you could simultaneously look down at blacks while wanting to party with them. But the people who seemed even less fit for life in this ruthless version of America—Angela and Vonnie and Manjun and Joshi and all the others—how long could they last?

How long could *I* last?

A few weeks after Angela and Vonnie moved out of their Brooklyn apartment, a spring thunderstorm hit New York. With the rain falling in great drifting sheets, Carla and I could barely see the sidewalk in front of us. We dashed from one awning to another. Fortunately, it was a quiet Sunday morning and we had the sidewalk to ourselves.

I hadn't expected Carla to be moving so quickly, but she was determined not to waste time. Maybe it was the specter of Angela and the fear of suddenly turning from the hot young thing into the cleaning lady. As we approached our destination, she stopped and looked straight into my eyes. "Can you tell I'm high?" she demanded. "The truth. Can you tell?"

Her last client liked to give "skiing lessons," and Carla was nothing if not a willing student. But the shadow of a store awning obscured her face. "I think you're okay," I said, trying to sound encouraging. In fact, though, the cocaine hangover was making her look shaky.

"That shit was really speedy," she said. "I hope I can do this."

"Just focus. And remember, you have something *she* wants."

Carla nodded and took a deep breath, trying her best to relax.

A police officer named Terry Wallace told Carla she should get off the streets and go to work for Margot Kerry. I had nothing to do with it. But as soon as I heard Wallace's idea, I thought it was brilliant. Since her beating, Carla had lost her swagger. Angela and Vonnie had replaced her. She was on antidepressants. Everything seemed bleak to her. She was so nervous, she asked if I would go along for comfort.

"My last job interview," she said in a doom-ridden voice, "a lousy cashier gig at a Target out on Long Island. I fucked the guy and *still* didn't get the job."

I saw Margot in the restaurant window and she waved. As I opened the door for Carla, I heard her take a few deep breaths and calm herself before crossing to shake Margot's hand.

Margot was now my perfect source. Slowly, as we got to know each other better and trust developed, she grew interested in my research questions and even offered to set up my next study, an in-depth look into the lives of elite women who had come to New

York to work in the upper reaches of the sex trade. I was already dreaming about the publications our alliance could generate. No one had managed to gather systematic, scientific information on this segment of the underground before.

I left them alone to talk, telling them I wanted to get some air. Next door, there was a magazine store. I browsed and mused about what I had just seen, a white woman and a Hispanic woman meeting for a drink. There should have been nothing remarkable about that, and certainly there were white women and Hispanic women who formed friendships in the ordinary world. But in the world of sex work, the meeting between Margot and Carla was almost inconceivable. Rich white men have always transgressed social barriers by having sex with poor dark-skinned women. Now these two were trying to buck history and economics to come together, a tiny revolution of the human spirit. I hadn't seen this in all my years of watching Chicago's sex work. Such were the opportunities that New York seemed to offer. Again, there were no guarantees and it isn't scientific to fixate on outcomes, but the boundary crossing not only brought distant people together, it gave them a chance to make a new social unit that defied categories and norms. In the next few years, however, I would interview dozens of madams and high-end sex workers and still be able to count on one hand this kind of socioeconomic and ethnic mixing. Lots of madams dreamed of creating ethnic "stables" to cater more effectively to the interests of rich white men; much fewer were interested in truly blurring the lines. In retrospect, this makes Margot and Carla's effort even more touching than it was at the time.

When I went back to the restaurant, I saw Margot squeezing Carla's shoulder while Carla wiped tears from her eyes.

"We were just saying how much we had in common even though our lives have been so different," Margot said.

Carla wiped away another tear. "Thank you for understanding, Ms. Kerry."

"I can't get her to call me Margot."

Taking my arrival as her cue, Carla said good-bye, hugging Margot. She thanked her again, then tottered out of the restaurant on her spike heels. Margot sat back down and let out a huge sigh. "These women are going to be the death of me," she said.

"Who, Carla?"

"Probably. She'll disappoint me just like the rest. They drink a lot, they're always on coke, they don't show up. Like this girl Louise—a huge, huge earner, used to be an accountant with Microsoft, but, man, is she living the life she never had in college."

Soon Louise would flame out, Margot said; then there would be a recovery period and possibly a return to work. Carla would probably go through the same spiral. The spirited ones always had big weaknesses. But Carla had ambition and she was pretty, Margot continued. Even if she didn't have much culture—or the right kind of culture—they could work on that.

This took me back to Angela and Vonnie's apartment, listening to their embarrassment about being "too Latina" to succeed in white New York, and to Shine's need to deal with Juan. Sociologists often have furious academic debates about the qualities people need to move across social classes. Is it hard skills like reading ability or computer literacy? Or do the "soft assets," like your accent or knowledge of the indie film scene, help you land the job? Margot's need to reeducate Carla was another cultural battle that was also an economic battle. Without knowing it, Margot was lining up with French sociologist Pierre Bourdieu, who called these soft assets "cultural capital." To really make the big bucks, Carla would have to learn to appreciate good food, to discuss politics and the opera—just as I had learned, with Analise's help, to negotiate the eating clubs at Harvard. More and more, the ability to cross boundaries with some cultural competence was starting to look like a *requirement* for success. Carla would need to learn to deal with wealthy white johns, to talk white and act white and perhaps even have sex in a more "white" style. In her own way, Margot was also crossing boundaries by building this bridge between the two worlds. The economic need to stretch made them stronger.

The problem is that this attitude can easily slip into racism. To Margot, difference was also an economic asset. "I'm sure she dresses like a little Puerto Rican slut, so I'll have to invest a few thousand in clothes," she told me. "But I do need a hot young ethnic girl."

She let the thought trail away and fixed her examining gaze on me. "But how are *you* doing?" she asked.

This was typical. Since that first meeting in the dark little Soho bar where I got dizzy, Margot and I had spent hours and hours in the corners and private rooms of many bars, and she seemed to move almost instinctively into a therapeutic mode—much as, I imagine, she did with the troubled young women who worked for her. It felt weird being in the same position as them, but Margot had a way of listening with such complete acceptance. I was hooked.

"Watch the drinking," she said. "Just slow down. What's the rush?"

Work wasn't going well. The documentary I had been making about the last days of a Chicago public housing project was an exciting new adventure for me, but I was nervous about the reception from my colleagues at Columbia and the wider academic world. Not only were documentaries a marginal activity for serious sociologists, they were easily cast aside as "journalistic." Elite universities were pressuring faculty to leave once they'd started to veer toward work that appealed to the general public.

Most of my fears would prove unfounded. As I showed some of the other professors the video, I got a surprisingly warm reception in some ways. Many told me of their own dabbling in photography, music, or art, which led to enthusiastic discussions about how to enliven sociology. But they also looked at me as if I'd just shown them a sweater I'd knitted, not a new professional venture. Film-making was a hobby. My takeaway was that it wasn't a great idea to become known as unconventional—a few of my colleagues even warned me that the same people who were "curious" today would come after me with fangs tomorrow.

A few months earlier, in fact, the chair of the sociology depart-ment had requested a private preview. The bad news was that the chair was Peter Bearman, the academic formalist who disdained the narrative school of engaged sociology. Though Bearman had been a strong supporter of my work so far, he could easily turn against me. We watched a DVD of the documentary in his apart-ment, just me and Bearman and his wife. When the movie ended, he applauded—and spent the next forty-five minutes detailing all of its terrible flaws. "Now you can get back to doing real sociol-ogy," he concluded.

"But I want to reach a bigger audience," I said. "I want to reach people who would never crack a sociology book. How is that a bad thing?"

He shook his head, a dismissive expression on his face. "It will never take the place of real, deep sociology," he responded. "Just don't be confused about that."

To be fair, his specific criticisms were actually very smart and helpful. But he had put his finger on my greatest fear. At a time when my marriage was falling apart and everything in my life seemed particularly unsettled and provisional, I was trying to cre-ate myself as something new, a filmmaker and public advocate who could step out of the trenches of dry statistics into a policy role. I wanted to cross the boundaries like the great sociologists before me, bold scholars like Herb Gans, C. Wright Mills, and Robert Merton. Maybe Bearman was doing me a favor. He was telling me that I couldn't pull this off, that *I* didn't have enough cultural capital.

I must have slumped in my chair. His wife jumped to my defense once again. "Peter, maybe you should try being his colleague instead of his father."

When I got to this part of the story, Margot smiled. "Women always want to take care of you, Sudhir. Be grateful for that. You love your work. Just try to get yourself back into it and focus on that."

She was right. What I really needed was a new project that I could dive into, a new world of data that no one else could access. *That* would cheer me up. Maybe it was finally time for her to help me get started with my study of high-end sex workers? We'd been talking about it for months. I could really use it now.

Margot frowned. She reached across the table, covering my hand with her own. "Can I tell you something honestly? You're not ready."

I took offense. I had been interviewing prostitutes and drug dealers since I was a grad student living on peanut butter and day-old bread. What could she possibly mean?

"Well, you seem, um, not totally together."

Margot's words hit me hard and sharp. As much as I tried to repress the happenings in my personal life, my troubles kept seeping out and affecting me in unanticipated moments. My mind shot back to my insanely quiet apartment, the one place where I didn't want to go. My wife and I were now living apart. We both knew that divorce was a fait accompli, but we were both stalling because it was a painful path that neither of us really wanted to pursue. We were trying to help each other move on and find a better life, which made everything so much worse. After one of our well-meaning talks about our "changing priorities," even a sappy TV commercial could bring me to the verge of tears.

Where once the inability to face my marital troubles produced panic attacks, now I was in full denial mode. I tried to make myself busy so I wouldn't have to deal with my personal strife. Taking on a few dozen interviews would be a great way to pass the time. Throw in a few strip clubs, hotels, and bars where I could hang out and observe the sex economy, and there would be only a few hours of the day left for ruminating on my failure as a husband. Thank God for fieldwork!

Margot clearly saw my desperation oozing out. She made soothing sounds, stroking my hand. "Listen, Sudhir. I could get you fifty women tomorrow."

"It's just conversation," I said. "I just want to talk. That's all. I mean, I really need a new project. I think it would be good for me to dive into something."

"You really believe that?"

What I believed was that she was getting way too psychological.

"You know who you are going to meet, right? Twenty-five-year-old girls who are beautiful and in pain. You're a sucker for that kind of woman, Sudhir. And they'll have stories, and you'll get wrapped up in the drama, and you'll want to save them and it'll be a big disaster."

"Margot, I have *never* slept with a prostitute."

She laughed. Then her expression turned serious. "Why don't you start with people who do what I do?"

I wasn't sure what she meant.

"*Managers,*" she answered. "You could learn a lot."

Until that moment, I'm ashamed to say, the idea had never occurred to me. I had seen the escort agency staff as people who were keeping me from talking to sex workers. "What would I study?" I asked.

Margot threw up her hands. "Are you kidding me? We make this whole thing run! We set up the dates, we lend them money, we find them drugs, we get their kids day care, we buy them clothes, we talk to their boyfriends who suspect what's going on. The other day, I negotiated a cash payment with a landlord under the table. Want me to keep going? I mean, the women just show up and open their legs. People like me do the real work."

Somehow, Margot's way of taking charge relaxed my fierce hold on the world. Why not let myself be guided by the generosity and insights of someone else, even if she happened to be a former Catholic schoolgirl from New Jersey who had become a Manhattan sex broker?

Margot's phone rang. "Sweetie, relax. Sweetheart—relax and tell me what happened . . ."

Margot covered the phone and turned toward me. "Sorry—two girls went to meet the same client." She thought for a second and added, "You should listen to this. These are two girls who keep calling me for help. They work for an agency downtown."

She looked around and saw that nobody was nearby, so she put her phone on the table and put it on speaker. "Are you both there?"

Two small distant voices in the phone said yes.

"Who had the guy first?"

"I did," one of the voices said.

"For how long?"

"I think six months now."

"Kelly, how about you?"

"He's been calling me. Maybe this is the fourth time."

"Okay, Kelly, you've had him a lot less. Did he mention Liz to you?"

"Um, yes, I suppose," Kelly replied. She seemed confused. "What does that have to do with anything?"

"Did he propose a three-way?"

"He made some jokes."

"Jesus, Kelly." Margot shook her head. "Never talk about three-ways. Did he ask you for a freebie too?"

"Yeah."

"He's playing you. Trying to push down your price. If you were working for me, I'd tell you both to dump him. It's not worth it. It's too crazy out there, and you need to help each other."

"Okay, Margot," Kelly said meekly.

Margot hung up the phone without saying anything more. She looked at me. "See what I mean?"

I kicked myself for not following this trail earlier. I knew that the lack of a friendly legal system encourages people on the fringes of society to find their own systems of organization. I had studied clergy members who intervene between warring gangs. I had seen block club leaders settle gang conflict on the street. Even in New York, all of this was playing out in front of my eyes. How many times had I seen the bartender in Mortimer's pub address a minor gambling dispute or a fight between a sex worker and her client? In Manjun's neighborhood, the cops probably could have made a separate side business just helping various underground merchants and their customers negotiate among themselves. Now, watching Margot, I finally realized that she also regulated her little slice of the underground economy through the constant phone consultations I had viewed until this moment as little more than annoying interruptions.

Now that I was finally paying attention, Margot filled me in on the backstory. She'd still been in her den mother phase when a girl named Karina called her out of the blue. She told Margot she had been walking out of a strip club in Union Square when a security guard beat her up and took her date's wallet, so they were holed up in a hotel and the man, a corporate lawyer, was freaking out because it was way past time to go home to his wife and children and he didn't have any cash or credit cards. So Margot grabbed some cash and rushed to the hotel, where she concocted an alibi and called a limo driver to take the lawyer home. Then she went to the club and negotiated a peace with the club manager.

Three days later, the corporate lawyer gave Margot two thousand dollars for her services, the club manager gave her one thousand dollars, and even Karina forked over a few hundred. "It was that night, I suppose, when I realized that I had a skill," Margot told me.

I thought of Shine. He always had a story about some conflict he had to resolve, warring gang members or some disgruntled local loan shark. At times, the issue concerned his operation, but often he was a third-party mediator for other aggrieved parties. Angela was the same. I'd always thought these were just positive stories that made them feel good to tell, or boasts after a few glasses of wine, not something central to their lives. But Margot had just told me it was all about making connections. That's why she called her agency Manhattan Nights, because she connected people for sexy nights and jumped into action if the night turned ugly. Glorious or dangerous, there was never a middle ground. It was a business but also a worldview, she said.

I felt a tingle going up my back. *Connections.*

Some of my original questions started to flood back. The global city was new for sociologists because people transcended borders and boundaries in novel ways. New Yorkers had side lives in Los Angeles and London, Londoners had business and personal affairs in Paris, Parisians owned real estate in Manhattan. Everyone assumed this pancultural connectivity was exclusively the domain of the rich, who could afford air travel and second homes, but all that I had seen pointed to another layer of connectivity: one among the laboring classes that was hidden from casual view, partly because of its relation to illegal and illicit realms. For the underbelly world, making connections also meant learning to communicate across unfamiliar landscapes. It required rapid acquisition of social capital. That was the way to prosper in new worlds where people's expectations and norms could differ. And since unfamiliarity always produces the possibility of conflict, these "language skills" could mean the difference between survival and defeat. Manjun, for example, had failed through shyness or fear or sheer time pressure to establish diplomatic relations with people outside his immediate social sphere. So when he became involved with local thugs, he couldn't access the right assistance. Angela failed in Brooklyn because her ties to the locals were too thin. Aside from Carla, she had no one to help her make the connections she needed. And Karina, as Margot told the story, was so thinly connected she had to turn to a stranger when she got in a jam. In each of these cases, a wider range of cross-border connections was the key element.

The pattern reminded me of international law. As any law school professor could tell you, people who make transactions across government boundaries (smugglers, for example) face constant trouble because the nature of their business precludes them from calling upon national authorities in times of conflict. So they have to provide their own security. More important, they have to reach across the real borders to create an alternate set of rules and norms. But because these rules are not written down or formalized through courts, they involve layers of ambiguity that create constant conflicts. The pressures and temptations associated with large sums of cash, sex, and drugs explain much of the rest of their trouble. In all these circumstances, informal ambassadors like Shine or Margot become valuable advisers. They have the ability to talk in both directions of the class divide and aren't intimidated by differences in race or culture. They have an ability to think on their feet, to adapt to the moment and the circumstance. In some ways it might be a matter of simple curiosity. They aren't fixed in place the way other people are, don't take comfort and identity from their surroundings in the same way. They are always looking over the fence to see what's coming next, always hunting out the next juicy bargain or sweet deal.

In sociological terms, these people are *brokers*. Usually this refers to local actors with social capital rooted in their familiarity of other locals—in a bar, a neighborhood, a housing project. New York was showing me a new side of this concept. Analise couldn't do background checks of the women who performed for her wealthy clientele, so she relied on cultural checks. As uncomfortable as Shine felt with his white clients, their mutual needs conspired to create a new Shine who could operate between the two worlds. Army brats and Foreign Service kids who spend years living in foreign countries often develop what they call a "third culture," a mixture of two worlds that isn't one or the other but something new. Perhaps I was seeing the Third Shine and the Third Margot. This was cultural capital of a particular kind, and my instinct and personal experience told me that the world would need more and more of it as time went on.

In the underbelly of New York, then, the future was being born. Or so it seemed to me in that moment of excitement.

CHAPTER 6

ADVENTURES IN ROLE PLAYING

In my office, I remembered the advice of my very first sociology teacher, Aaron Cicourel: "Stop every few months, and go over your data. This will help identify what you know and, more important, what you *don't* know."

I took out a pen and paper and began to make a list.

For the Urban Justice Center, I had conducted more than a hundred interviews with streetwalkers—good, solid work. I had some rich if idiosyncratic adventures with Shine in Harlem, a lot more of the same with Manjun and Angela and Margot, plus a lot of dry wells and a ton of doors slammed in my face. But I had learned something from every encounter and the evidence was starting to accumulate. My feel for New York was slowly starting to approach my understanding of Chicago. But I still feared I had small *n*'s and that size would matter.

Maybe the list would help. On the left side, I put a header:

LOW INCOME

I knew about the history of underground activity in Harlem. Shine and his neighborhood had given me deep lessons in how all of this had come to be, including the roots of modern-day black markets in central Harlem. That part looked sound. I also had solid contact information for immigrant sex workers, day laborers, gypsy cab drivers, nannies, cooks, and dishwashers. When the time was right, I could easily turn this access into a sociological study on their earnings, lives, and family struggles.

On the right side of the page, I put another header:

MIDDLE & UPPER CLASS

This category included Margot and Analise, money launderers, strip club owners, the doctors and lawyers who serve them. But I hadn't really conducted systematic interviews. Even though I had years of exploration under my belt, everything still felt impression-istic, especially compared to the more scientific approach of my colleagues.

From this list, as almost always happens, a question jumped out at me. Maybe this clunky scheme of low, middle, and upper class was itself a by-product of that old way of thinking about cities as bounded ecologies, neighborhoods separate in form and function with distinct groups living in each one. The sociologist Manuel Cas-tells calls New York and other global centers like London and Paris "informational cities" in order to highlight the move away from tra-ditional ways of carving up urban spaces. In informational cities, location still matters but the real currency is now mobile assets like information or connections. A new sociology of boundary crossers would have to study the role that networks—however fleeting they may be—play in refashioning this mobile world. But you couldn't look only at finance, real estate, and corporate capital. According to some economists, the underground economy likely represents some-where between 20 and 40 percent of an urban economy. This was too large to ignore. If my hunch about New York's black market economy was right—if the underground was organizing people in new ways that shrugged off constraints of the past, sending people across borders with a new mix of soft and hard skills—then it could very well be redefining the underlying organization of the city as a whole. Sociology couldn't neatly put Shine in his drug dealer box and Margot in her madam box and Analise in her Tiffany box and hope even to make sense of it all, much less grasp its potential scope.

Yes, this was the most meaningful question. Economists might try to pin down the individual ingredients people needed to jump up a class—education, experience, know-how, etc.—or they might focus on how big each class was and what percentage of income they made legally and illegally or how much the government lost in failing to tax black markets. But a sociologist could ask whether *new* classes were forming, new cultures and new ways of living that had the potential to make over the global city. *That* was the worthy goal, the paradigm shift that could effect meaningful change. Imagine a future Giuliani who saw the underground as vital to the city, a vibrant place that welcomed immigrants and provided a wide range of skills and services. He might then stop enacting what the urbanist Neil Smith calls "revanchist" policies, in which the modus operandi is to kick out the disenfranchised standing in the way of gentrification. He might even look at the informal and sometimes illegal adventurers of the underground as important new voices in the great urban chorus.

Actually, this was already happening in the developing world. Many governments had realized they couldn't stop people from bartering, devising off-the-books credit schemes, or failing to report their income, so they just accepted it and tried to make sure it didn't harm either individuals or society at large. For example, in the BRIC nations—Brazil, Russia, India, China—governments have put large sums of money behind programs that merge existing informal moneymaking schemes with modern enhancements like microlending and skills training. The point isn't to legalize prostitution or build a better drug trade, but to direct the resources of human will and aspiration in a more productive direction. Couldn't a New York mayor recognize these underground traders, brokers, and ne'er-do-wells in the same way?

With my pen in hand, I mulled over what I had learned from Margot, Carla, Analise, and Shine. They differed in many ways but all seemed to have one thing in common: the refusal to let race or sex or even wealth keep them in their designated social slots.

Once again, I wondered if they could be said to make up a distinct social class of their own, a kind of third class suspended between the two worlds they inhabited. Maybe that was too highfalutin' a question. But "criminal" was such an imperfect word to describe them, considered in the fullness of their actions. These people were seekers. As much as the peppiest young entrepreneur in any Silicon Valley garage, they dreamed of changing their worlds. And in their daily lives as ordinary citizens and consumers, their illegitimate earnings helped many legitimate businesses stay afloat. In that sense, they were pillars of the community.

Again, my instinct told me that the answer lay in connecting the underworld to the overworld. But here I was still facing the old problem of tracing those connections. Since the higher classes don't seem to give social scientists the same respect and deference as the poor—Margot seemed to take downright pleasure in treating me like a clueless child—I had to find another way to gain a more profound level of trust. Again I heard the voice of Professor Cicourel. "You're never neutral when you go out there," he told my very first class on fieldwork. "Understanding what *you* mean in *their* world is your greatest advantage."

What he meant was, you are never a "scientist" to people in the field, because they just translate your reality into their terms. So my role in the ghettos of Chicago became "poor graduate student." This isn't a question of concealment so much as the opposite, revealing what you want and who you really are. I just let people know the questions I cared about and the problems I wanted to solve so they could come up with their own ideas about how to participate. Instead of seeing my work as *extractive*—me sucking information out of them—I learned to think of it as *collaborative*: us working on joint problems together. Fortunately, it turns out most people like helping graduate students.

Now I had to find fresh ways to collaborate, a fresh role to inhabit. I didn't want to be a tourist, but I couldn't pass for a real insider either. I certainly wasn't a pimp or coke dealer or strip club investor. My real interest was basically unchanged from the grad student days: just to document their lives as accurately as possible. So if I was going to reveal what I really wanted and who I really was in terms that would translate effectively, maybe I should be . . .

A documentary filmmaker! It helped that I actually *was* a documentary filmmaker. I had learned that while the wider public often didn't see what academic knowledge would do for them, they seemed to find the idea of collaborating on a film more attractive. The academic articles could come later, when trust was built and I had a better sense of what research I might undertake. And maybe there would be actual documentaries; some of the stories had a lot of promise.

Of course, I ran the risk of annoying the stuffier solons of the academy. For them you wear either the scholar hat or the filmmaker hat, and the idea of any blurring in status is horrifying. But I thought the precise medium for storytelling was irrelevant and the important thing was to meet the audience where the audience gathered—not to be "correct" in some dusty library. Wearing the filmmaker hat would mean working in a different way with people like Margot: as collaborators instead of scientist and subject. And as soon as that idea entered my mind, I could see how she would welcome the change. It might finally erase the distinctions that were keeping us apart.

I would have to be careful. In the wake of infamous research studies like the Tuskegee trials, in which scientists let syphilis go untreated in order to study it, universities set up systems to verify the use of ethical methods. At Columbia, there were several boards that vetted research. I had always followed their rules closely, using false names and fake addresses so that no one could trace my notes back to individuals, and it had approved my formal study on sex workers. I also contacted these boards when I first started to hang

out with Shine, but when I explained I had no research questions and wasn't gathering data, just trying to meet people who
might help me reach such goals at some point in the future, it
stamped my activity "journalism" and left me to find my own way.
Still, I wanted to know whether there were any special rules for
filmmaking.

I asked for a meeting, which took place in a quiet conference
room, the footfalls of students echoing in the hall outside. "How
do I apply for approval if I'm about to interview women for a
film—not for scientific research?" I asked.

"Why are you making films?" a board member asked.

"Am I not allowed to make films?"

"You're a scientist. They usually don't make films."

"But I do."

I told them about my documentary on Chicago housing projects, which was soon to air on PBS.

One board member sighed. "Well, that kind of creativity makes
our lives difficult."

"Films are journalism," another board member said. "We don't
monitor journalism."

"So if it's journalism, I don't need to fill out any paperwork?"

"No."

They dismissed me with a request that I bring no more peti-
tions concerning journalism or filmmaking.

My instinct proved solid. Once I started talking about the possibility of filming a testament to her unique world, Margot
became much more interested in helping me. She said the hardest
places to access would be strip clubs, so she accompanied me to
several around the city and introduced me to the managers. Even
after the first hour in their presence, with Margot in the room, I
got a fresh picture of their jobs as a mixture of salespeople, security

directors, and personnel directors. They talked about the diversity of dancers they needed to keep on staff to cater to the wide variety of tastes men had, which increasingly included an indeterminate mixture of blacks, Asians, and Latinas they referred to using the blanket term "ethnics." From the drift of the conversation, it became clear they were hoping Margot would become their conduit to these populations, which gave me a new sense of the scale of her operation.

All of the managers said that, in a perfect world, they'd keep the sex work off premises. "Look, I know it has to happen," one said, "because men want it. But I can't stand the hookers that come in. Better they go to the hotels in the Bronx, where nobody gives a damn."

The newcomers were the worst, another said. "They think the clubs are going to be the safest place—off the streets, with security all around. Maybe they pick up a guy and go to a hotel, or screw them in the back. But these amateurs—that's what they really are—they're usually the first to get hurt because they don't know what's going on. Either their dates beat them up or my guys do."

The police officers I knew said much the same. They'd also seen a remarkable increase in the number of "amateurs," often women who began as dancers or actors and decided to sell sexual services on the side. The cops were also struck by the increasingly wide range of backgrounds of the sex workers they were arresting, who came from every country in Eastern Europe and Central America, plus Asia and Africa too. They rattled off strings of place names as if they were trying to win a prize for naming all the countries on the globe.

After the strip club introductions, Margot set up three calls with managers of escort agencies. The idea was the same: she would be on the line to back me up and intervene should I say anything amiss; I would talk generally about my research interests and see if I could establish a level of trust.

I wasn't quite sure how to prepare. The standard first step in sociology is a review of the existing literature, but there was no existing scientific literature on madams and pimps. The standard first step for documentarians is similar: have other films been made on this topic? The pickings were slim. I decided to treat these interviews essentially as prep work, asking the women to help me understand exactly how to approach their colleagues so as to ensure participation.

In this way, I was able to gather a surprising amount of information. All three of Margot's contacts were women in their thirties. Two were divorced, one engaged. Two had college degrees. One had a background in corporate human resources and the other two had held various administrative and sales positions. Working three or four nights a month, they made between eighty thousand and a hundred thousand dollars a year. Two rented, the third owned a condo in Brooklyn. Each employed five or six women and numerous irregulars who floated between sex trade and straight work. But these facts were less interesting than the way the managers answered the questions, using their education and savvy to calculate their responses on the fly. That was the main reason there was so little research on the role of the underground economy in the lives of the middle class and the wealthy, I realized. They were too smart for us. They could see us coming. And while participating in the cause of "scholarship" may have seemed a distant, abstract, or worthless pursuit to them, they all loved the idea of the documentary. Although I didn't know it at the time, I was standing at the dawn of the reality TV age, when the trade-off between shame and fame had begun to disappear. But instead of looking down on this as mere hunger for celebrity, I began to see it in the opposite way: as a beautiful desire to translate their experiences to the wider world in the most popular medium of the era.

So when all the boxes were filled, I couldn't stop thinking about

Angela and all the other low-income women who had revealed so much of themselves, exposing their most painful and intimate secrets to me with such heartbreaking generosity. All that data would grow deeper from a solid basis of comparison. I owed it to them to keep pushing. For that matter, I owed it to them to broadcast their story in the most effective medium I could. So I risked annoying Margot by asking each of the three brokers if I could talk to any of their employees directly.

Two refused outright. "I don't mind telling you about me, but I need to protect these women," one said.

The third was a manager named Darlene. Margot was called away just before we finished that call, so I took that moment to pop my question.

"I could probably introduce you to a couple of people," Darlene said.

That night, she gave my phone number to two of her employees.

The next day, both women called. I started with my usual "looking for advice" approach, asking them for the best strategies to win over the trust of their peers. Before long I had learned they were both white and twenty-five, earned about fifty thousand dollars a year working just two or three days per week, had high school degrees, and had come from the South to New York to be actresses. Both had been beaten up by a client at least once. Both had been forced to perform sexual acts against their will.

The first one stopped there. But the one who called herself Cathy told me she had plenty of time and was happy to answer any question I could throw at her. Thrilled, I asked her to name the hotels and bars she worked. She got out her date book and reeled off her last month of appointments with an efficiency that would have impressed Bill Gates. I asked about conflicts she had experienced, the biggest challenges she faced, the most annoying details—just throwing out whatever topic came to my mind—and she kept tossing back answers as if we were playing some fun information game. I wrote down the details as fast as I could, then ventured the uncomfortable question of what acts she performed and what she charged for them.

Cathy told me everything, adding amusing details wherever she could. "That guy, he actually was working for a publishing company," she said at one point. "I told him I kept a journal and he said he would really like to help me get it published—as long as I didn't put his name in it!"

Cathy told me about gypsy cab drivers who found her dates, probably some of Manjun's friends from Hell's Kitchen. She mentioned doctors who gave discount medical care or drugs. She talked about the emotional impact too. Even accounting for bravado, it was striking how differently she and the Angelas of the world viewed their lives. Instead of shame and fatalism, there was a note of defiance.

When she finally had to go, Cathy offered to hook me up with her friends too. She seemed to understand my n problem instinctively, actually volunteering concern that she would be able to get me a wide enough sample to represent the full range of upper-end sex workers operating in the city. "The industry is changing so quickly," she said. "You have to talk to as many people as possible. Some of us like hotels, some are online only. There's a wide variety."

Within a week, I had talked with fourteen high-end sex workers, all white, all from middle-class backgrounds, 80 percent from outside New York. They broke down into two basic groups. First, the aspiring artist type, who came to the city to act, model, or dance. They worked as massage therapists or physical trainers and supplemented their incomes through sex work once every few weeks, earning between thirty thousand and sixty thousand dollars a year. Sex work helped keep their American dream alive.

The second group came from the lower rungs of the business

world, mostly saleswomen, paralegals, administrative assistants, or human resource associates. They were a few years older than the aspiring artists; like Margot, many had turned to sex work after divorce or professional frustration. For them, hooking was just a way to get by and maybe even settle the score a little—to make men pay for their sins.

For all of these women, sex had become a general currency. In exchange for referrals, they slept with bellhops, hotel clerks, strip club employees, and gypsy cab drivers. For medical care, they slept with doctors and dentists. When money was tight, they borrowed from strip club managers, bartenders, and clients, and sex often became their means of repayment. Strip club managers were particularly notorious for using debt to force women to sleep with patrons and friends.

The material seemed so rich. Soon after, I got permission from Columbia to start a long-term research study and quickly landed a major research grant. I began to hire assistants. Separately, with my own funds, I also hired a videographer, filmed a dozen of the interviews, and began trying to raise money to make the documentary. Finally, all my efforts seemed to be gaining momentum.

Cathy called me again a month later. She was no longer working for Darlene. "I work for Tori now," she gushed. "I couldn't believe it when she said she was about to see you!"

At that moment, I was just heading out of my apartment for my first interview with Tori, an Ivy League graduate who managed a very exclusive agency on the Upper East Side and also invested in several strip clubs in New York and Florida. Her clients were such prominent people, she had been very reluctant to grant the interview, so I was surprised she had blabbed about it to Cathy. "Tori told you I was going to speak with her?" I asked.

"I'm the reason you're talking to her!" Cathy said. "Tori and I go way back. We took dance together for years. She wasn't going to call you, but I told her you were a nice person."

"I don't know what to say," I said.

"You don't have to say *anything*," she cried in her excitable way. "And I have something else that you are definitely going to like—one of my *clients* wants to talk to you!"

"A john?"

"Martin. He's a really nice guy."

This surprised me. Except for my inspiring experience with Mortimer, johns were the one part of the sex work equation I had barely explored. There was already plenty to do with the drug dealers and sex workers and I probably assumed that most men wouldn't want to talk about paying for sex. But Cathy said she'd been telling Martin about how open I was and that I never made her feel like a criminal. "I think he just wants to talk with someone," she said. "He hasn't been feeling so hot lately."

I didn't see myself in the role of analyst for frustrated men, I said.

Cathy became indignant. "You said you wanted to learn all about this world, didn't you? Well, he's part of this world. It wouldn't even *exist* without him."

A few days later, I found myself sitting across from Martin in yet another hotel bar. He was a tall, lanky man wearing a tailored tweed suit with a blue pocket square, his straight blond hair falling over his eyes as he spoke. He kept pushing it back as if each strand had been assigned a particular place on his head. "I guess it started about three years ago," he began, "when things started to fall apart."

I hadn't even asked a question! We were barely past hello. Slow down, I told him, and began taking him through my standard disclosure conversation: that I work for Columbia, that I wasn't actually studying johns in a formal way at that time, that I wouldn't use his real name, that I—

"I'm not worried," Martin cut in. "I trust Cathy completely."

"Martin, I'm *obligated* to make sure you under—"

"Did I tell you about how many guys I know are in the same situation?" he continued. "At least twenty! It's like the dirty little company secret. But we're not deadbeats, okay? I want you to know that. We are responsible people who are unhappy with our wives for one reason or another, you know, and we all have our personal flaws and compulsions. But we don't want to break up our families." He repeated his key line. "We are *responsible people.*"

But didn't compulsive and secretive behavior suggest something more serious? Wasn't sex addiction a possibility?

An expression of scorn crossed his face. "I read that stuff in the media. It makes no sense to me. Bottom line, my wife doesn't *listen* to me. Cathy listens."

Either he anticipated skepticism or my face revealed it, because he launched into a protest before I could even get out a response. "Most of the time, I don't even have sex with Cathy! I can count if you want—Cathy said you liked numbers. Last week, I met her twice—no sex. The week before, we were intimate once and not the other time. Before that, it was June and we had . . ." He thought for a moment. "Six meetings, I believe, and sex three times. So we're averaging 50 percent sex."

But if the emotional exchange was half the point, I asked, wouldn't it make more sense to have a real affair? Then at least you'd know your paramour wasn't being nice just for the money.

I still didn't get it, Martin said. Affairs were too risky, too irresponsible. The exchange of money *protected* him. "See, it's not like an affair, because I'm not interested in Cathy for anything long term. Cathy is good for me because she knows that I am married and I'm not going to leave my wife. She's there to take the pressure off. Hell, if my wife knew as much about me as Cathy does, she'd be sending her thank-you cards!"

"So seeing prostitutes is good for your marriage," I said, the sarcasm naked in my voice.

"Of course," Martin said. He seemed exasperated for a moment, then he asked me quietly, "Haven't you ever had marriage troubles?"

"Yes, as a matter of fact."

"Then you understand."

If he meant the hunger to be with a friendly young woman who did not think you were a bad and repulsive person, I certainly did. But it offended me to be drawn into his world in this way. I wasn't here to talk about me. I was the scientist, not the subject. (I realize now how defensive this sounds, but I was raw enough from my personal troubles, and the act of observation seems to require a certain protective distance.)

"It sounds like what you really need is a marriage counselor," I said. "Or a psychologist."

Martin shook his head. "I'm not into the therapy thing. This feels better. Talking to Cathy, that feels *a lot* better."

With that, he began to unspool the message he'd come to deliver, an odd mixture of apology and boasting. "The thing you have to understand is, guys like me, we're big earners. High achievers. We were jocks in school, we're rising stars at investment banks and law firms, and we aren't going to a goddamn therapist to sit there and whine about how Mommy didn't love us. That guy is a loser. But a guy who spends a thousand dollars to command the attention of a beautiful young girl, especially if he doesn't even fuck her, that guy is a player. And when that guy goes home, he's going to be less stressed out and angry. He's *going to be a better husband.*"

As Martin continued, he chose his words carefully, loading them with just the right amount of emphasis, putting on a performance that was supposed to impress me with its brilliant, blinding honesty. "You're a good listener," he said when he was finished.

With a bit of embarrassment, I realized that I was filling the role Cathy usually played for him. At the same time, I was starting

to fantasize about yet another documentary, about the complicated lives and complex motives of the high-end john.

"I think a bunch of my friends are itching to talk to you about this," Martin said. "Do you mind if they call you?"

"I—I—I don't know what to say," I stammered.

But Martin's phone was vibrating on the table. "Sorry, that's my office. Gotta go."

He rushed out, leaving me sitting at the table.

When I got home that night, my empty apartment greeted me like a tomb. I hated coming home. All the things my wife had left behind reminded me that I had failed. The coffee table mocked me. The lamps rebuked me. I wanted to burn them all. On one visit to my parents' house I was so upset, I threw away nearly every trophy, picture, and memento I had saved from my childhood, as if those years were somehow responsible for how badly things had gone wrong. All this made me more eager to plunge into a new round of interviews.

But sometimes even that backfired. One spring night, I came home and saw I had a voice mail message. I felt that little burst of hope. Maybe it would be something good!

Instead, it was Margot with shocking news. "Carla just robbed a client," she said.

What!? I couldn't believe it. Little frightened Carla, so recently the victim of an assault? Who had been so excited to work for Margot? Who had been so determined to break out of her cultural trap and achieve something? It seemed impossible. Just a few nights earlier, Margot was telling me that she'd sent Carla out on three dates so far and all the clients had given very positive feedback. She finally had that fiery young ethnic girl. She was thanking me. What could possibly have gone wrong?

The voice mail continued with more detail: Carla had gone to an expensive hotel with a businessman, attacked him, stolen five thousand dollars, and fled. Now he was threatening to call the police unless he got his money back.

That was all she knew. Carla wouldn't return her calls. "You're part of this," Margot said. "You have to help me find her."

This was now officially one of my worst nightmares. I was a researcher, a disinterested academic. I couldn't get involved in sorting out assaults and robberies. But I felt I owed Margot. And Carla was in trouble. I had to think of her too.

Do the right thing, I told myself. Picking up the phone, I punched the numbers for Margot's office. I was prepared to tell her that I would go to Carla's apartment immediately and do whatever I could to sort this out.

Instead, Margot started yelling at me. "I can't believe you spoke to Darlene's girls! Why would you do that without talking to me? Didn't I *tell* you I didn't think it was a good idea? And then you go and do it *behind my back*?"

Taken completely by surprise, I felt my voice get shaky. "I—I'm sorry. I thought Darlene was going to tell you."

How could this have happened between her message and my call? It couldn't have been twenty minutes.

"She did tell me! She told me *she's really pissed* because that girl Cathy told you all this shit she shouldn't have told you!"

I wheedled and pleaded, insisting Cathy hadn't told me anything confidential or damaging. But Margot wouldn't yield. She'd trusted me and I took advantage of her and now this little twit Cathy was telling all her friends that I was going to help them organize for better pay and better working conditions and maybe even make them famous with my documentary.

"*What?*" I said.

"Yeah, you're like Cesar Chavez for these women. Darlene thinks you're trying to poach her girls."

"Poach her girls? That's absolutely insane."

"That's what I was trying to tell you, genius. When these psychotic ladies find someone who listens to their sob stories, they think he's Prince Charming. And suddenly it's Professor Venkatesh this and Sudhir that and I have Darlene screaming in my ear."

She went on for some time, telling me I should have listened to her and my judgment was suspect and thanks but no thanks for the offer of help with Carla but there was real life involved here, it wasn't some kind of *research project . . .*

When she hung up, I felt horrible. I had made my fair share of fumbles in my work, but this was on another level. I knew that doors opened only a few times before they closed forever. I had finally gained enough access to carry out a study of sex across the entire region if I wanted—I was ready to make appointments with strip club managers, hotel clerks, bartenders—and I had blown it all by becoming too eager. My dreams of success were falling like a mist.

The worst part was, Margot was right. I should have anticipated this kind of problem. In nearly every study I'd done of illegal worlds, I had experienced the shocking speed of rumor. That's why I was usually so patient, waiting months to ensure that people knew exactly what my intentions and research questions were. This was all because of the divorce, because of my impatience and my hunger. I should have gone more slowly. I got greedy. And I really should have kept Margot in the loop. She was the one who was speaking up for me, opening doors for me. What would I do now? Was there any way to win back her trust? Or was it hopeless and broken like every other goddamn thing in my miserable life?

The answering machine taketh away, but the answering machine giveth also. After Margot's message there was a second one, from Martin. With great excitement in his voice, he said he wanted me to meet him for a drink. He named a private club on Forty-fourth Street.

I said I'd come right down.

On the way, I thought about telling Martin what had just happened with Margot. If anyone knew how difficult "easy women" could be, he would be the guy. And we'd bond and I'd get the access I needed and write the study and make the documentary and all would be glorious again. But as I got closer to the club, walking past the elegant hotels of Midtown, the idea began to disturb instead of comfort me. This was the portal to the high-end sex trade. The doormen I passed were actually middlemen. The valet could put you in a cab to a brothel. Looking through Martin's eyes, I saw a glutton's feast. But when I looked through my own eyes, even though I was after information instead of sex, I also saw a glutton's feast—and *I didn't want to have anything in common with Martin.*

Inside the bar, Martin was sitting with two other well-dressed businessmen. They were loud and happy, well into their first drink at just past three in the afternoon. They greeted me as if they'd known me for a lifetime. "Sit, sit," one of the men said, pushing a chair into a more welcoming angle.

Martin was grinning. "I told you there'd be interest in this," he said.

The men shot out their hands. "I'm Jonathan," one said. "This is Nate."

I ordered a drink as Jonathan continued with the story he was telling, something about a fight at the office. When my drink came, Nate cut him off. "Enough about the office. Let's talk about sex."

They all looked at me. I looked back at them. Nobody wanted to start.

Finally, Nate laughed. "Let's start with this—what do you think about us?"

I didn't know what to say. First I had to get to know them, I said.

"It's not a crime," Nate said. "What we're doing is not a crime."

"Actually, paying for sex is a crime," I said. It felt cleaner that way. But oddly, that seemed to spark them.

"Paying for a good time is not a crime," Nate said.

"You're writing a book?" Jonathan asked.

"Not sure. I've been moving to documentaries lately."

Jonathan studied me for a moment. "No faces, right?"

"Yeah," Nate said. "You gotta put us behind a screen and disguise us with those Darth Vader voices."

The last thing I wanted to do was expose them as individuals, I explained. I was going to add that using false names to protect privacy was actually part of the university rules, but that just reminded me that I had no interest in studying them. I started to get anxious. I wanted to get out of the world of johns.

But Jonathan took a breath and made up his mind. "Ask me anything. I have no shame."

Again, I wasn't sure what to ask. Jonathan helped me. "You're looking for the Big Reason. The Big Why. Why do we do it? Why put our marriages at risk? Why risk the scandal? But it's really not that complicated."

Nate shook his head in violent disagreement. "It *is* complicated. I mean, it sure can *get* complicated. That's why you have to keep seeing different women. Don't get attached."

"And what if they get attached to you?"

Nate looked glum. Clearly, attachment was a big issue that I'd never considered.

Jonathan leaned closer and confided, "Nate just went through this. What was her name? The one who rented an apartment on your block because she thought you loved her!"

Nate put his head in his hands, theatrically ashamed. "I should never have taken her to the fucking Caribbean."

"One ride in first class and she's yours forever," Jonathan said with an evil laugh.

Nate began telling the story, his voice ranging between comedy act and confession. Then Jonathan jumped in with a story of his own, the prison of his marriage to a woman he married too young.

Eventually, Martin stepped in. "Sudhir, the thing all men ask themselves"—he always used my name before he said what was really on his mind, I noticed—"is a very simple question. Do you want to do it again? Knowing what you know, risking what you risk, do you still want to meet the next lithe young woman in the next expensive hotel?"

Jonathan rubbed his hand over his jaw. "I have to get out of my fucking marriage."

Nate asked if I was married. I nodded.

"So you know what it's like."

I nodded again, not sure how far I wanted to go with this.

"You just stop listening to each other," Nate continued.

"You stop doing a lot of things," Martin said.

"I know," I said. "I'm separated."

As if I had said the secret password, the three men exchanged glances that turned into smiles. "I knew it," Nate said. "I knew there was a reason you were so interested!"

I glared at Martin. He knew damn well he'd all but forced me into this meeting. What had he been telling them?

"What's it like to be separated?" Jonathan asked.

"Separation is *hard*," Nate said.

This led to a discussion of comfort, which they viewed in a surprisingly straightforward way. Because women had wounded us, each in our own way, all men need comfort. And because women had wounded us, each in our own way, there was only one way to heal that wound. And only when the wound healed a little could we go back to our normal lives and our normal wives.

By the end of 2004, after nearly fifteen years of research, I could count on two hands the number of conversations I had had with johns. But every single conversation had one feature in common:

they all wanted to confess, to be heard, to create *community* around their desire. None of them wanted to believe they were doing anything harmful. They all wanted a way out of the isolation of their secrecy. In fact, while my mind wandered, Nate began arguing that the need for comfort somehow made prostitution legal—or, at least, "not a real crime."

All the men grinned. In fact, there was a big poker game coming up at the end of the week, right here at the club. *You should come! It would be great!* "Just come and meet everyone. You'll learn everything you want. They're great guys."

"Let me think about it," I said, mumbling something about objectivity and detachment. But after we'd said good-bye and I began walking back to the subway, I asked myself what I was doing with these men. I felt bad because it was so obvious they wanted to talk, to share, to escape their isolation. But in sociology there's a rule of thumb: just because something is interesting, that doesn't make it relevant. I was studying the experiences of sex workers at the higher end of the income scale. Did I really need the views of johns?

I walked on past the fancy hotels, past the doormen and valets and clerks who all played a role in this vast interconnected web of sexual commerce. Musing about a documentary was one thing, I told myself, and the idea that I might break ground on a hidden world excited my ego. But on a scientific level, I had to stay more focused.

Or was I just afraid?

The truth was, these men were *exactly* the kind of thing I was looking for, another connection between high and low. But they were also a mirror. Their loneliness was my loneliness, their need for comfort identical to my own. And looking in that mirror was not something I wanted to do.

As I walked past another hotel, under an old-fashioned gold marquee, the doorman gave me a welcoming nod. I ducked my head and hurried for the subway.

. . .

Once again, the phone broke the gloom inside my apartment. Margot was calling again, this time from somewhere on the street. The lively sounds of cars and construction came forward whenever her voice stopped. "You gotta come help me, Sudhir. I need to find Carla right away. Things are messed up, I don't know what's going on, and I can't find her."

Margot sounded confused. This was not like her.

"I'm on my way—but what happened?"

"*Carla* got beat. I had it backwards. I just found out. I feel like a real asshole, Sudhir. That guy was talking at me and I don't know Carla all that well and I just—I fucked up. I should have trusted her."

The new story was that the client had a penchant for a type of sexual role play that involved physical abuse—actual slapping and hitting. When Carla refused to continue without a lot more money and the eager client went to get some, she called a friend for help.

I could picture the scene. Carla wouldn't want to fail. She probably thought, *Just stay put and solve the problem or else Margot will fire me.*

But Margot thought it was her fault. She felt terrible about it. "I've seen this happen before," she said. "These young women, they get beat, they go through a bad stretch, they don't trust anyone. I should have worked with her more. She just seemed so strong. And then this guy beats her too."

Now Margot was worried that Carla would give up and go running back to the projects—where, ironically, she probably faced a much greater likelihood of violence.

This was definitely a possibility. I thought of Shine. In his world, violence was routine, practically a requirement. Years of bitter experience had taught them there was no other way to enforce their unwritten laws. But for people like Carla and especially Margot, violence was still shocking. In a way, on a professional level, this actually *helped* Margot by giving her a market for her conflict resolution services. But it also meant that she needed to prove and re-prove the utility of her soft approach. Taking on the Carlas of the world made it difficult since they were likely to ratchet things up by taking disputes and inflaming them. And looking at it from Carla's point of view, that was another reason moving up was so scary. When you exist between worlds, the rules are in flux and you don't know how to handle things. Soft or hard? The old way or the new way? Which do you choose when your life might depend on it?

There was yet another ugly complication. The john had hired a private detective to find Carla. This was surprising because he was a prominent lawyer from Washington D.C., and usually people like that fade into the woodwork when things get dicey. But he was so furious at being "cheated" he actually seemed willing to risk his reputation, or perhaps he felt this was a necessary preemptive strike to save his reputation. So despite her distress over Carla's pain and suffering, Margot really needed to find her and talk her into giving back the money. It wasn't fair, it wasn't right, but it would really be better for all of them.

This was way out of my pay grade. "Maybe we should talk to a friendly police officer," I suggested.

"I told Michael already. There's nothing he can do."

"Margot, just to be clear, I cannot be involved in anything criminal," I said. I enunciated each word.

Then I said to hell with it and went out looking for Carla. The Lower East Side was her home neighborhood, so I headed there. It didn't take long to find out that she'd been living with a friend and working out of a local bar. And in that bar I found her. "Margot's looking for you," I said. "She knows that bastard beat you up and she's sorry."

Carla broke into tears. She'd been so miserable, she said. She didn't want to disappoint Margot, didn't want her to know things had gone so wrong. She would have taken the beating for five thousand dollars. She was planning to! She *never* should have called her ex-boyfriend. "This is my ticket," she kept saying. "I have to get out of here. Look at this place. I need to do something different with my life."

I told her about the private detective. Then I told her Margot wanted the money back.

Carla wailed. "I don't know how to get the money back!"

The guy who had it was Ricky, the ex-boyfriend. Ricky was really mad about what had happened to her. He wanted to go after the john and demand more money and possibly even beat him some more. If she asked him for the money to give *back*, he'd probably beat her up himself.

"Maybe I could just work it off?" she asked me, her expression a mixture of fear and hope.

That was not a message I wanted to carry. I didn't even want to think about it. I just told Margot how to get ahold of Carla, and a few days later she called to say she had defused the crisis by paying Carla's debt out of her own pocket. Carla did not need to know that Margot had first gotten the figure reduced to a grand.

"Carla needs to get back out there," Margot told me, "or she'll feel like it was her fault. You don't want to go through life feeling like a victim."

Margot always seemed to work her magic in the direction of more sex work, I thought. Funny how that worked out. But maybe it wasn't as calculating as it seemed—maybe she understood these women and their struggles because she was tuned to their unhappiness. That would explain why Carla's setback bothered her so much. She was really a big-hearted person who identified with her employees.

Then she'd gone and ruined it. "I need to find some pretty young brown girls," she said. "Black girls too. The next big sex trend is going to be all about jungle fever. Trust me."

. . .

Two months later, Margot called and said she had some news for me. She was creating a finishing school for hot young black and brown women. "None of them trusts each other, none of them likes each other, they can't cooperate like normal people. So they're fighting and doing stupid things and making bad decisions."

Like in a sex-work *Stand and Deliver*, she was going to help turn them around. Classes began the following week. Maybe I'd like to come.

A week later, Margot's apartment looked like a makeshift classroom. Five attractive young Latinas sat on couches and chairs while Margot paced in front of them. "What's the first thing you do in the hotel?" she asked them.

"Tell the bartender what room you're going to," said Carla, like a proud student.

"Right," said Margot. "You can't always call me because your phone may not work, or you may lose it. So you have to tell the guy at the bar."

Another one said she didn't trust the bartenders. They would look at her funny when she talked, and sometimes they kicked her out.

"You *have* to trust them, okay?" Margot said. "They work with me."

Margot explained how to open up a bank account to keep the cash away from their family. She told them not to wear dark makeup around white men, to lighten their hair if they could do it without looking trashy. She told them not to say too much and to keep their smiles coy. She talked to them about buying fewer things of higher quality, thus saving money while advancing their cultural capital.

"What's the first thing you do after you get your guy naked?" she asked.

"You take *your* clothes off—duh," one answered.

"Wrong."

Other answers came. "Get the money." "Jump on the bed." "Slide to your knees." Margot shook her head each time.

Finally she said, "You tell him how big his dick is."

Carla snorted. "So we lie to him?"

Margot nodded. "If he's fat, you tell him you love a big guy. If he's skinny, tell him you love his six-pack. And you *always* tell him that nobody ever made you feel like this before."

The women were skeptical. Sex work in the projects was much more cut-and-dried. If they laid it on too thick, they said, the johns might get pissed and hit them.

But Margot knew her clientele. Over the next six months, Carla and her friends doubled their income. A $75 session became $150, and sometimes tourists mistook them for equals and paid as much as $250. A few even did well enough to leave the projects, especially after Margot helped them find apartments where they could sleep with the landlord in exchange for rent. Which is why I was so surprised the day Margot, after chirping along about how much progress they were making, suddenly broke into tears.

"What's the matter?" I said.

"Watching them make one stupid mistake after another. It's making me crazy."

But she didn't have to do it, I helpfully pointed out. I had been thinking for a while now that the jungle fever market was a risky experiment for her. The profit was in the upscale market—that's where everyone wanted to be—so why would she want to move in the other direction? Especially since she had begun talking about her long-term goal of moving out west and starting a beauty salon or other small-business venture. Why saddle herself with so many temperamental, troubled women?

"It's what I do," she said in a voice of gloom. "It's the same thing

I do with *you*. I manage them, I manage you. I'm responsible for everyone."

"You're not responsible for me," I said.

She exploded with a scornful laugh. "If it wasn't for me, none of these girls would be talking to you."

She was upset, but there was no reason to talk to me that way. "If it wasn't for you," I said, "I'd have found somebody else."

"Please, Sudhir. I'm tired. I don't have the energy to deal with your ego right now."

Awkwardly, I made some forced polite excuse and left. Out on the sidewalk, the sunlight was too bright and I had a dislocated feeling. The good-bye had been too abrupt. I shouldn't have reacted so emotionally. Maybe I had gotten too close to Margot.

I looked up and down the street, not sure what to do with myself. It was still early and I didn't want to go back home.

As 2005 rolled around, I started to think about what I'd learned. It was time to go back to the office and make another list: "Things I Learned About Life in the Global City by Looking Underground."

a) Definitely, New York is not Chicago. Say good-bye to the old-sociology idea of life revolving around tight-knit neighborhoods.

b) In the new world, culture rules. How you act, how you dress, and how you think are part of your tool kit for success. (It's a dangerous thought because it could easily lead to blaming the poor, but it's been increasingly accepted by other sociologists.)

c) The ability to cross boundaries is vital. New York forces multiple social worlds upon you whether you like it or not, and even porn clerks and drug dealers need to learn to cross social lines smoothly.

d) The poor are just like you and me . . . except when they're not.

e) _____

As I reached that last one, I realized again that I'd better focus my research or else I would keep drifting. I had to ask myself why I kept reaching this impasse. As much as I wanted to reach the upper reaches of New York, only a few avenues seemed to be feasible. In fact, only one: *sex.*

Maybe the world was trying to tell me something. Maybe sex was the ideal means of crossing the boundaries that defined and connected New York City. This most intimate of behaviors, which all humans are trained from birth to consider private and individual, might be the secret thread drawing New Yorkers from all walks of life together. I considered the facts as I understood them so far. As the sex economy changed with the times, every social worker, escort manager, cop, and porn store owner had his or her own theories and reasons to explain the changes, but all their stories had two common features: the new conditions and the great sums of cash floating around. The escort managers talked about the large numbers of women from middle-income backgrounds who were arriving in New York with a surprising new openness to the idea of using sex work to supplement poorly paying straight jobs. The social workers and strip club managers talked about the struggles among different ethnic groups who were all competing for their piece of the Big Apple pie. The cops talked about the turn from the drug cultures of the past to the incredible sums of money that "classier" sex workers were able to earn—some were pulling down a hundred thousand dollars per year or more, raising the ambitions of ordinary streetwalkers and sending them, like Angela, into new neighborhoods and more ambitious pursuits. Finally, the city was experiencing a wave of ethnic mixing and permeable class barriers unseen since the glorious turmoil of the late nineteenth century, when the first large waves of European immigrants gave birth to the ideal of America as a vast melting pot.

Were these theories accurate? Did they hold true for the city as a whole or were they merely small phenomena among a few special classes? As soon as I completed my latest series of interviews, I would have a broader range of hard data. But everyone I met seemed to be telling the same story.

Which brought me to the problem of Martin. Sociology insists on moving from the specific to the general, and I believe in sociology. I remembered some advice Herb Gans gave me when I arrived at Columbia: if my story could be written by a journalist for the *New York Times*, then there may not be a reason for me to write it. He was trying to tell me that things that were interesting weren't necessarily useful. And the fact was, I had no real sociological question to ask about Martin—just a vague interest that might someday turn into one—and it was frankly hard to picture the foundation or branch of government that would finance a study of high-end johns who work on Wall Street. It was time to get more rigorous. I would tell him that I could talk to him now and again as a friend, but nothing more.

The next time we met, I arrived at the hotel first and ordered a drink. Looking around the bar, I saw a pair of attractive young women sitting together nearby. Were they colleagues having a drink after work? Or sex workers pairing up for plausible denial? Either way, the sight of them steeled my resolve. No more hanging out for the sake of hanging out. I had plenty of work to do on the sex workers themselves, an actual suffering population. Martin was history.

I looked up to see him standing in front of me. "I'm taking your advice," he said.

"What advice is that?"

"I'm going to tell my wife. It's the right thing to do. *You* taught me that."

Sitting down, he pursed his lips and made a *pop* sound, a definitive smack to demonstrate the intensity of his determination.

Several other patrons at the bar turned to look and he did it again. *Pop, pop.*

"Martin," I said, speaking with the special emphasis you'd use with someone who might be in a coma. *"I—never—said—any—thing—about—telling—your—wife."*

Martin smiled radiantly. "You helped me see things clearly," he said, removing his wire-rimmed glasses and cleaning them with his crisp white handkerchief. This was one of his trademark behaviors, along with cleaning his glass rim, tapping the table, making thumbs-up signs, and now this new smacking sound with his mouth. He seemed to manifest himself in weird physical gestures.

"Martin, we've had this conversation before. What you do with your life is really not—*really* not—my business. Maybe you should speak with someone?"

He shook his head in a definite way. He had made up his mind. "It's time I moved on," he said. "You helped me understand that. You listened to me. You didn't make me feel stupid or strange or abnormal. That's why I want you here when Marjorie comes. You should be here for the end of the story."

"Marjorie is coming here?" I said, my voice incredulous.

"She should be here in five minutes."

"Jesus, Martin. Your *wife* is coming here? Does she know what you have planned? What are you going to say exactly?"

Martin laughed at my anxiety. "Look, I'm going to tell her about Cathy and me, about our relationship. Lord, I feel liberated."

Somehow, I knew I would end up the bad guy in this. His wife would turn against me in shock or embarrassment just because I was there at such a bizarre moment.

"There's going to be all sorts of surprises." Martin chortled, and a chill came over me. I reached out and took hold of his forearm, noticing the soft silk of his jacket. Even *I* didn't want this level of access into the personal lives of others.

Martin took out a white manila folder. His face beamed with

the beatific expression of a penitent returned from confession, an expression I had seen before after particularly far-reaching interviews. "I gathered some notes for you. I thought I owed you something. Take it as a sign of gratitude. Some of my friends, the ones you met—we all thought it was something great you were doing. A lot of them felt the same as me. It's just not something so easy to talk about."

"Martin, please. I think we should slow down."

But Martin kept talking, so pumped up he barely heard me.

"You should have this. I think this information will help you."

Martin pushed the folder in front of me. I stared at it, wondering what he meant by "information." Martin practiced law, but he was also an accountant. We had talked in detail about the financial structure of the upper-end sex industry. I sensed that the papers had some hard data on his personal expenditures, and perhaps that of his friends. Despite my resolution, this was tempting.

"I interviewed them. My friends," Martin said, proud as a student submitting his senior thesis. "Well, sort of. I mean, I did my best. I don't know if it's perfect—you know, from a *bookkeeping* perspective."

Martin rubbed his hands together—another new gesture.

"Martin, you're a lunatic. I can't take this."

"No, no, no. You deserve it . . ." he said.

His voice trailed off. I looked around the bar. As dinnertime approached, the room was filling up with well-dressed middle-aged women in elegant dresses, their sparkling jewels echoing the dripping chandeliers above. Some were busy with their phones. Was one of them Martin's wife? When Martin started his confession, she would look over at me and know that I already knew the whole story, that I was there to witness her reaction, and she'd be completely justified in hating me. With each woman who passed, I felt a growing sense of doom.

When I turned back to Martin, he was saying how much pain I was in. Not him, me.

In fact, all the guys felt bad for me.

That was it, the proverbial final straw. Sociology has to stop somewhere and what better place than this—the definitive example of too close for comfort, and *way* too close for objective science. I muttered some words of apology under my breath and bolted out of the restaurant, leaving Martin to meet his wife alone.

But on this dash past the glamorous hotel marquees to the safety of the subway that would take me home, new questions nagged at me: In a world of shifting borders and permeable barriers, was my anxiety a symptom or a clue? What did too close for comfort *mean*?

I was about to find out.

CHAPTER 7

BOUNDARY ISSUES

S hine said he had some news for me, so we met at a bar near my
office. He told me the church confrontation didn't work. Juan
just denied selling coke right there in front of everybody. Now
Shine was moving to plan B.

Before he could say any more, we were interrupted by a very
upset young black woman. "They asked me to leave!" she cried.

Shine put down his soda, turned, and looked her up and down.
Her wide eyes made it clear she'd been doing coke, and her hands
were shaking, so it seemed she was probably coming down off an
elephant-strength buzz. She even had the little bluish black blotches
hard-drug addicts get on their faces. "Who? Where?" Shine asked.

"The dude at that bar downtown. Said I shouldn't come in
anymore."

"What did he say *exactly*?"

"Said, 'You got to get out of here.' But this dude was in the
bathroom and he was about to come back, so I said I had a friend
who was still in the bathroom. And he said, 'I don't care. You gotta
leave.'"

"Did you get to everyone?" Shine asked.

"I *couldn't*. He told me to leave!"

"Next time, wait outside. Don't leave people hanging like that if
they're waiting for shit. They get nervous, shit happens. I got to tell
you everything?"

I was surprised Shine was using someone so strung out as a runner. The transition from the street crew really wasn't going well,

apparently. He seemed disgusted. "Wait over there," he told the woman, pointing to a seat in the corner. "We got to talk when I'm through with the professor." She started to obey, but he stopped her with a question. "Did you see any East Side niggers there?"

"I don't know . . . It was a pretty big place."

"Was everyone white?"

"Yeah, I guess. I mean, there were some talking Spanish, Do-minicans or something."

"How many of them?"

"Like two or three?"

Shine looked like steam was going to come out of his ears. *"Was it two or was it three?"* he said.

People looked over. This wasn't normal for him. Something was wrong.

"Three. Just a bunch of young dudes having a beer."

"I don't think so," said Shine. He took out his phone from his coat pocket and walked outside to make a call. The girl went off to her appointed space. I sipped my beer.

A few minutes later, Shine walked back in and sat down. He didn't say anything and I could tell he wanted some time to cool off, so I put a few dollars on the table and said good-bye.

Later that evening, he called to explain. Shine's access to the bars depended on the bartenders who received a fee for allowing his runners to come and go. As he suspected, Juan had paid one of them off. This meant that Shine's drug runners would no longer be allowed to come inside—tall black women in Wall Street bars stood out, so it was easy for the bartenders to tell who was a run-ner. That son of a bitch Juan was taking over his sales spots, Shine said. Which was bad enough on its own, but it was also dangerous, since Shine and his runners were now walking into potential law enforcement traps—what if the bartender called the police the mo-ment one of Shine's employees walked in? Without an agreement, there was nothing to stop them from dropping the dime. The cops

the only thing I could think was, How could law-abiding, God-fearing parents stand to watch that? How could they bear it, knowing they couldn't call the police because that would only make things worse? What kind of society had we created?

I guess Shine could see the distress on my face. "I'll tell you about it later," he said. We sat at the table without saying much, eating his mother's comfort food. I felt very melancholy. This was not a side of him I ever wanted to see.

When we were finished, we went for a walk down the sidewalks of Harlem and Shine told me the story. For five hundred dollars, he'd hired an older man named Tito to help him track Juan's whereabouts. Tito lived in the neighborhood and could move around without being detected. He had spent over a decade in jail for drug trafficking and nobody would pay him a living salary after he got out, so he served as a hired gun for underground traders. He'd do anything from party security to beating up deadbeats to shaking down local business owners.

Tito's report was thorough. Juan had four young women, girls really, who lived with their mothers in Harlem and worked in stores or offices downtown. They found customers and Juan came down to meet them. Tito also learned that Juan was looking for a basement apartment in the Bronx, which was significant because basements were popular places to store drugs and weapons. Juan was even starting to interview young guys to run for him. And though he didn't have security guards, he usually traveled in a group that was bound to be armed.

Tito suggested that Shine grab Juan as the young man was leaving a building on 134th Street, where one of the girlfriends lived. A small alleyway that separated two brownstones would make a splendid spot for a beating.

In the meantime, Shine did make a few more stabs at settling the dispute. He got a female to carry a message. Juan ignored it. Then he approached him on the street. Just find your own bars,

Shine said. Take Brooklyn and give me Soho. But Juan had an attitude. He said he'd developed clients and bartenders and turned them over and now *he* should get a cut. "You owe *me* money. I want my money." The claim itself was innovative, a revolution against the established pecking order, and the thing that angered Shine even more than a goddamn nineteen-year-old runner asking for an equity stake in his business was the idea that he'd *told* the kid he didn't want him cultivating customers in the first place. Now the little bastard wanted a reward for ambition Shine never wanted him to have. Offer shares to a crewmember? The idea was outrageous. The whole system would *collapse*. He could always find another person willing to accept a day's pay for a day's work.

Under different circumstances, I might have laughed—Shine sounded so much like an archconservative denouncing unions and the minimum wage. But in this world, the loss of market share led to consequences that were immediate, personal, and painful.

Juan was much smaller than Shine, but Tito helped hold him down while Shine applied his form of human resources counseling. He focused on Juan's face, making sure to open some good cuts that would leave a lasting impression on the young man. A "bunch of good shots to the mouth" drove the message home.

Shine shook his wounded hand and smiled. The thing was, right up until the last punch, Juan was muttering about the money he was owed. Shine had left the kid lying on the ground in a pool of his own blood and he still wouldn't give up. He'd be back.

"What if he brings his cousins with him?" I asked.

Shine just sighed and stared ahead. We walked a few blocks in silence. Then he sighed and cursed Juan's name a few times before saying he would probably have to go into business with the little bastard.

"Are you kidding? After what you just did to him?"

"Had to do that, man."

I didn't know what to say. It was so unemotional, so

Machiavellian—so *professional*. There was something simultaneously frightening and attractive about Shine's ability to dispense
force in this dispassionate way, as if he had given a mild rebuke to
a subordinate—nothing personal, just business.

The immediate concern was more basic: Shine couldn't just ignore the bar downtown. It would look like he was showing weakness and that would tell Juan and his cousins to move back in,
which would open the gates to all kinds of trouble. This wasn't like
the regular business world. Burger King could shut down a fran-
chise without worrying about Mickey D coming to whack him.
But if Shine fought for the territory the way he would up in Harlem, it would freak out the white boys and the cops who protected
them. He was back at the practical problem of crossing this particular border. He still didn't know how to handle the white bartender or the upper-end clients. He couldn't bring Tito to each bar
Juan's crew had taken over. What he needed now was the ability to
surf through an unsettled period when the context was changing
from what had come before—the quality sociologist Ann Swidler
has called possessing the right "cultural repertoire." In a period
of flux, when the old way of behaving is not working, a broad set of
experiences and references seems to give a person the ability to find
new rituals and mechanisms of success. Failing that, the only solution is to find a broker, or "rabbi," who could support him.

The A train rumbled under our feet and Shine turned to look at
me. He held my eyes and smiled with an odd, amused expression,
resigned and a bit puzzled.

"I'll give him the bars. I mean, he'll have to pay my cut—I
won't just *give* them to him. But I want out of those goddamn bars
anyway. That's the kind of thing that gets cops all excited. They
don't give a fuck about some street corner in Harlem with grannies
and schoolkids walking by, but a bar full of white boys getting
shitfaced must be protected at all costs."

I understood his point. If he stayed in Harlem and sold to the locals and the few middle-class white tourists, he was considered a nuisance but not a threat. But what would that leave him? I wondered. If he gave up the streets *and* the bars, what was left?

He read my mind. As we paused at the curb, respecting the red light only as long as it took to check the traffic—the code of the New York pedestrian—he smiled and slapped me on the shoulder. "Art," he said.

"Art?"

"Galleries. Openings. Those people got tons of money, and they like to party. And it's a scene where you can be . . . colorful."

He grinned.

It sounded like a good plan, I said, but it also sounded like an even harder nut to crack than the bars in Soho. How was a guy like him going to find his way into a world like that?

Shine seemed amused. He knew I'd been hanging out in artsy circles since beginning the documentary work, so maybe he thought I was being proprietary. "You think I never heard of Jackson Pollock? I've been to the goddamn Metropolitan. I went there on *school* trips."

I said nothing.

"Anyway," he said, "my cousin's an artist. Evalina—you know her. She's *in* a show that's opening on Saturday down in Soho. No shit, artsy types just like yourself have welcomed her just like she was one of them."

I sensed a dig there, a hint of competitiveness. Was he saying I didn't welcome him as an equal? Could he really be nervous about status after telling me he'd just beat a man and left him in a pool of blood?

"Why don't you come?" he said, grinning now. "That should be fun for you—you can see me work *your* crowd. Might even be some friends of yours there."

I said yes, of course.

. . .

This brings us back to where the story began, to the gallery opening when Shine and Analise first met and the shocking scene—shocking to me, at least—when Analise came to my house and told me she was in the same business as Margot. Of all the connections between high and low I could have imagined or desired, this was the least possible crossing of the last possible boundary.

By that point, so much had already happened. In Hell's Kitchen, I had learned the secrets of one New York neighborhood's underground economy. I had seen people and places changed by the rapid globalization of New York. I'd determined that the sex trade would be a fitting way to write about the boundary crossings that defined contemporary New York and followed the natural connections that had led me out of the ghetto. Margot and Darlene and their friends were giving me a new perspective on the underground economy throughout the city. But Analise was about to remind me how little I knew.

We didn't see each other for a few weeks after her confession. Then she called with an unusual request. In all our time together, we'd rarely met outside of public places. This time, she wanted me to come directly to her place, a ground-floor two-bedroom just off Gramercy Park.

When I got there, the decoration process was still under way. Framed prints and lithographs leaned against the wall, a paint can sat on spread newspaper, furniture had been shoved against walls waiting for placement. She immediately brought up J.B. He had left for Los Angeles to develop some new film projects. Her money had been "wasted on a movie that's never going to get into Sundance." Her face was drawn.

Now she was trying to make a break. This apartment was part

of it. She had asked her mother for a raise on her allowance and rented this place, a new place for a new life. "Look!" she said. "It even has a garden." Ever hopeful—that was the Analise I'd known before. I grew hopeful too. She was going to dump the idiot boyfriend and abandon her life of crime.

She made tea and took me out to the backyard.

"Check this out," she said, opening up a laptop on a small round cocktail table. On a second table pushed next to it sat a portable file box with about two dozen manila folders marked with different-colored tabs. Each sheet had a weekly revenue and a monthly "intake to date" sum scribbled, and scratched out and updated. That way, Analise didn't have to flip through the pages inside the folder, which also provided data on historical revenue, biographical information, hotel rates, and services performed.

These were the records for her escort service. "So you're not going to quit," I said.

"I'm going to do it *better*," she answered. "I have to winnow this down," she said. "I've got about five or six reliables, I figure, and ten I don't know if I can trust."

She started describing the challenges. These were privileged, willful young women long on looks and short on business sense. They were giving away "freebies" to potential clients, getting drunk, forgetting to cultivate relationships. It was ridiculous. She even tried sitting them down for some basic instructions on how to handle difficult situations, but they were too busy texting or dreaming about a trip to St. Barts to pay her any mind. So they kept making the same mistakes, kept losing money, and kept putting themselves through unnecessary dangers.

"I really can't help you," I said. "I mean, I'm not sure exactly what it is you want me to do—or say."

"I just wanted you to see how I'm dealing with things," she said. "I mean, I'm trying not to be stupid. I don't want to do this forever, but . . ."

She stopped, then narrowed her eyes as if she was looking at the truth behind the truth. "All I know is, the more money I make, the more confident I feel. Like, if I have *money*, I can finally talk back to my parents."

We laughed—who doesn't know what that feels like? My story wasn't so different. I was obsessed with data instead of money, but we both had chosen to focus our efforts on worlds far more hard-edged than those we were born into. The more I could penetrate the underground, the better I felt about myself. If it was marginal, criminal, or tinged with outsider status, count me in. The seedier, the better. My recent divorce had multiplied the impulse, pushing me to the margins among the outcast and the criminal. At times I told myself I was following in the footsteps of Robert Merton, examining the links between the deviant and the mainstream. But why so many risk takers, why so many criminals and class traitors? Since the day I walked into the Chicago projects, I'd felt more comfortable with those the rest of society had written off as expendable.

I sat down and examined her color-coded file system. "I can't believe how organized you are," I said.

She brought out a long, eleven-by-fourteen piece of paper marked up like a time line. On the top, in pencil, there were years that delineated columns: 2008, 2009, 2010, and so on. All the future dates were listed neatly, each a half inch apart, as if time moved in linear beats. There looked to be various milestones and markers of achievement, some indecipherable. On the sides, she had scribbled various notes, indicating rows: "Kate," "India," "Paris," "Hamptons real estate," "Cash," "Trust."

"This is your future?"

"I told you, I'm doing this for a year or so, and then I'm gone."

There was a blank space under "Cash."

My mind started racing. This was a golden opportunity, the leap into the upper classes I had dreamed of making, and it was coming through sex. It was too good to be true. At the same time, I felt terrible about it.

"What's the ideal number?" I asked. "For you to quit, I mean."

I was looking for an out, probably. Or at least a termination date.

"Not sure," she responded.

Analise grabbed the client folders and started making piles. These eight were good. Clare, too temperamental, no dates this month. Jo Jo, always busy. Twice a week, trip to Miami.

"Let's call Amy. I'll put her on speaker."

"Who's Amy?" I asked.

Amy was a possible new girl. She'd just come down from Connecticut College, a little young but she said she'd dated a bit already to get through school.

The phone stopped ringing and a voice said hello.

"Amy, how are you?" Analise shouted. She turned on the speaker and laid the phone on the table. "Listen, I'm putting you on speaker and my friend Sudhir is here, helping me figure stuff out. I want to talk to you about some things."

No problem, said Amy, but she had to take a minute to walk outside and find a private spot. Analise and I waited.

"Hey! I'm back. Sorry, I'm at a press event for BMW."

"Oh, you're still doing PR?"

"Yeah, it's my dad's friend's company. But they're only hiring part-time right now."

"Well, so that's what I wanted to talk with you about," Analise said. "I'm a little worried you sounded unsure. You said you dated in Rhode Island?"

"Yes, I did date in college a few times—"

"But you realize it's going to be different here," Analise interrupted. "This is New York."

"Well, a lot of the men were from Boston," Amy said.

Analise snorted.

"I think I'm ready," Amy pleaded. "I know you probably need a firm commitment, but I want to do this and Kimberly said you were a great person to work for. I think I could really be good for you."

Analise came back with a tone of cold precision. "What I need to know is, how many days can I count on you?"

"At least two," Amy said. "Maybe three, I don't know. And what I meant was, the men I dated, they weren't off the street or anything. They took me to plays, to these amazing dinners. One took me to Maine for the weekend. They were serious men."

"So you can travel?"

"Yes," Amy replied quickly. "I can do that. I don't have anything that I need to stay here for."

"Do you have a pet?"

"Yes, a small cat."

"But you're cool leaving it?"

"Oh, yes—I just did. Went to St. Barts. I have a friend who cat-sits."

"What about friends? How are you going to deal with your friends?"

"They know I date. My girlfriends, I mean. Some of them do it too, so it's not a big deal. I don't know. I guess I could do whatever you needed. I don't have to tell them."

"Well, that worries me, to be honest. It's never a good idea to talk about your business. Or my business."

"I would never do that," Amy said. "But my girlfriends, they got me into it. But they weren't very good at it. I was the best one."

"Why?" Analise asked.

"Well, I really like to listen and have a good time. Guys at college are just so boring and these guys were taking me to all these amazing places."

Analise rolled her eyes. Infatuation with rich men bored her. "How much do you need to make?"

"I live in Chelsea. My parents own the condo, so that's all good. I get five grand from them for other stuff."

"That's not enough for a girl in the city!"

"Tell me about it!" Amy said.

"Long term?"

"Well, I guess I want to be an agent. My aunts, they're both agents. One does actors. I think I could really be good at that."

"I would need you to make me the priority," Analise said. "At least for six months. I mean, I can't have you not show up for shit. I won't take that, okay?"

"Of course."

With that, Analise signed off. To me, it seemed that Amy was perfect and Analise was on the verge of hiring her.

Instead, her expression turned to scorn. "Really, does she *really* think I'm going to give her a shot?"

Amy seemed smart, devoted, able to put off peer pressure. What more did Analise want?

"I don't hire whores," Analise said.

Sometimes Analise and her friends used the phrase "in the middle" for women who liked to hang out with elites but who were not elite themselves. It was considered the height of gaucherie. Analise walked toward the kitchen and opened up a cabinet in search of vodka. "I can't do anything with that. Except worry. I'd rather have a bunch of Brittanys than that boring girl."

The problem with Brittany, she continued, was that she was wild and willful and despised the men she dated.

"That can't be good for business," I said.

"Are you kidding? It drives them wild. They can't wait to get her naked and put her in her place."

But Brittany was starting to act increasingly unstable—throwing up, passing out, fighting with clients and bartenders and cab drivers and even police officers. Analise was going to have to do something about it. And even with that, she was still worth a

know that I have certain professional obligations regarding confidentiality and—"

Analise launched into a fairly precise version of my standard predisclaimer disclaimer: "Although Sudhir is not currently engaged in a formal study, he is a university researcher," etc. It was impressive. She even parodied my formal diction. And of course, neither of the two women blinked a false eyelash. She was their boss. What did she expect them to say?

Letting out a sigh, I reached into Analise's cigarette box myself. If you can't beat 'em . . .

Jo Jo winked at me. "Long day?" she said. I shrugged a little, acknowledging that it had been, and Jo Jo scooted her chair over closer to me. "Analise told me what you do—gangs, drugs, women of the night. You must have an exciting life."

At this point, she actually batted her eyes. She wasn't trying to be subtle.

"I'm in bed by nine," I said.

"Why are we *so* interesting to you? It's just sex. Sex and money—oldest things in the world."

"Yeah, except it's a *lot* of money. And you're already rich. You're white, you take vacations around the world. I bet you have maids."

"Of course," Jo Jo said.

"That doesn't mean anything," Kimberly said. "Everybody has a cleaning lady. Even my cleaning lady has a cleaning lady."

"Still, you have so many other options."

Kimberly took over. "You seem pretty judgmental for a sociologist. I'm not sure why anyone talks to you when you say shit like that."

Fascinating, I thought. On the lower economic rungs, the reaction to direct questions like mine is much more humble. But Manjun didn't have a cleaning lady. Angela didn't have a cleaning lady. "Objectively, you *have* other options," I said. "Most of the women I study don't."

"Whatever," Kimberly said.

Jo Jo said things were complicated, launching into a meandering history of her family that went back to the American Revolution. "I went to Yale," she said. "Got my degree, came to New York, tried the nine-to-five thing. No, thank you. Jesus, that was a living hell. So my dad cut me off. He says it's good for my character."

She cackled.

With Analise, she was making ten thousand dollars a month.

"Are we fucked up? Probably. I take Vicodin, snort coke, get drunk off my ass. But who doesn't? I don't see a lot of psychological masterpieces out in the straight world."

Listening to them made me think about Angela and the problem of the "soft" assets she didn't seem to possess. Relative wealth and the accompanying sense of privilege gave these women something cultural that was important for succeeding in this world—simple nonchalance, a sense of entitlement that nothing could threaten. The critical difference was that it came so naturally, while Angela and Carla and even Margot had to make an effort. I could relate. Just as I had learned about wine and opera to look like less of a fool in Harvard's eating clubs, those women had to study the ways of the rich men they wanted to attract. But Kimberly and Jo Jo were like creatures from another planet, exuding a sense of privilege so serene it seemed to justify itself. My first thought was that money could never buy this, but then I realized that *only* money could buy it. My Columbia colleague Shamus Khan captured its essence in a study of the boarding school elite: *ease and privilege*.

But that was my take. What did Jo Jo and Kimberly think separated them from other women? I wondered. If another woman wanted to work for Analise, what qualities would she need?

Jo Jo began with confidence. "Basically, she can't be . . ."

She stopped, struggling to find the right words.

"Jo Jo doesn't want to be insulting," Kimberly said.

Jo Jo sat forward. "Here's what I mean," she said. "I was at Zanies the other night. The club was kind of empty. I was waiting for my date—he got caught in traffic. I saw this girl get dumped by this guy. Really weird. He just threw down the money and left. I knew what was going on. She was from an escort service. I could tell. So I went up to her and tried to calm her down. Said I knew what that feels like. After about an hour she says she wants to leave her agency and asked if I can help. You know what? Not a chance. Why? She was, like, this working-class girl. Fucking Julia Roberts. What the hell does she know about the ballet or fine art? I mean, you are *never* just sucking someone's dick. Sometimes you don't even do that. They have to feel comfortable with you in public."

"And you have to know when to shut your mouth too," Kimberly added. "Those girls, the Puerto Ricans and white trash, they sleep on fucking bunk beds. Our guys aren't going to trust their reputations to some chick who hangs around the hotel looking for business."

Jo Jo seemed a bit disappointed in me. "So that's it? That's what you do for a living? Spend all your time talking with girls like us?"

"I don't meet a lot of people like you," I said. "Usually just Puerto Ricans or white trash."

"Funny," she said.

I didn't reply.

"Anyway, it's not that fucking complicated. We like money, and this is a fast way to get it. What's the big deal?"

I thought of Manjun, and how eagerly he tried to show me the divine in his degraded neighborhood. The poor I'd studied always seemed to need to rationalize their behavior, even if it was to make *Scarface*-style boasts about how little they cared about social norms. They had to make peace with their god somehow. Here it was the opposite. Not only did Analise and Kimberly and Jo Jo never feel pressed to justify their actions, they seemed to feel that victory was found in *refusing* to justify them.

Another mystery to explore.

. . .

The next time my phone rang, it was a friend telling me that Analise was in the hospital. I made some calls and finally reached J.B., who was still in California trying to become the next Harvey Weinstein. Some old guy got drunk and started beating on Brittany, who locked herself in the bathroom and called Analise for help. Analise tried to help and the client turned on her, giving her the beating he'd wanted to give Brittany. "Fucking Brittany," J.B. said.

"Analise should have called the cops," I pointed out.

"Yeah, right."

J.B. didn't get back for two days, but maybe business really did keep him, because he looked very upset when he finally got to the hospital. Usually he acted like a weary tour guide waiting for the last group to take their pictures of a monument; now he looked stunned by the sight of the monument burning down. "I couldn't have done anything," he said. "There was no way I could stop it."

He said it as though he'd already said it to himself a thousand times.

We were standing outside the hospital, waiting for visiting hours. He lit a cigarette as I shivered, my hands shoved deep in my pockets. It was late March, when a blast of cold seems so unkind in the face of the coming spring, and all I had was my professorial corduroy jacket. My sympathy was stifled by the knowledge of what he'd really been doing out in LA. While taking a break from failing at making feature-length indie movies, he was putting his cash into porn films and partying late into the night with his new porn friends. I knew Analise wanted him to quit going out to LA, where he only seemed to lose their money. To which he would respond: "Look what *you* do! What right do you have to judge *me*?"

"She could at least appreciate how hard I work," he said.

I mumbled something.

"The real problem is my family. I mean, she's in the hospital. That could get the wrong kind of attention."

That sounded like a canned phrase, perhaps one he had heard in his childhood: *That could bring the wrong kind of attention, son.* From previous conversations, I knew that what he meant was attention from the media, which would inevitably get to the one person in the world he most feared.

"So what happens if your old man finds out?" I asked.

"Um, I'd have to dump her. No question."

I was flabbergasted. "You're kidding me," I said.

"Do you know who my father is? I used to spend summers working on the docks up and down the East Coast. Dad had invested a lot of money—importing, shipping, trading, all that stuff. When people got upset, you know, when things were getting a little bothersome, do you know what Dad did? Brought down some Hells Angels to beat the shit out of the strikers. Dad's *insane.* He'd probably go after Analise's whole fucking family."

Now I was worried. "Could he really find out?" I asked.

"When you're doing international work, you need deep contacts in the law because half the shit that goes on your ship is never declared. You can't break the law on that scale without help. Somebody probably already called Dad. Man, it's going to suck when I see him. It's just going to suck."

J.B. reached into his pocket for the last cigarette, crumpled up the pack, and threw it on the ground. He was wearing a dress shirt with thin pink stripes and a sweater thrown over his shoulders. He looked like JFK on a boat, steadying himself for the next wave.

"Wish my sister was here—she always knows how to handle things. But she lives in London with a fucking Paki who owns hotels."

He noticed my existence and said, "Oh, sorry—I don't mean you." I was supposed to understand that he meant *Paki* Pakis, not an assimilated person like myself who understood important cultural intricacies like the Hustle and "Keep on Truckin'."

"Kathryn knows how to take Dad on—because of the marriage she had to deal with a bunch of shit from everyone and now no one talks to her, so she doesn't give a fuck. She never backs down. And her kids, man, they *hate* the old man. And he hates them back, which is hilarious. You should see him fighting with these little five-year-olds like they were real people, getting drunk and calling them all sorts of nasty names. And they just stand there and laugh at him."

Already, I was imagining a study on intermarriage among the wealthy. Did intimate contact with another race stiffen all their spines in this way? Genuinely curious, I asked J.B. how she would handle the situation.

He let out a big sigh, I'm not sure why—either from longing or disappointment in his own ability to cope with his father. He glanced up toward Analise's hospital room. "She'd be up there instead of down here smoking a cigarette," he began. "And she'd be working the phones like a madwoman—she'd get my brother to fly out here, and he'd make my dad come too, and then when everyone was gathered she'd just come out and say it. 'Analise has been doing blah blah, making money blah blah.' And you know what? We'd all probably end up being fucking *proud* of Analise!"

Did his brother know? I asked

J.B. nodded. "I told him."

So why not call him? If he could work magic on the old man, why not ask for some help?

He looked ashamed. "He's in Tokyo. I don't want to bug him." But his voice was wistful, as if he really wanted his brother's help. I didn't know much about his brother, but I knew he was older and successful in his own right. I imagined J.B. had asked him for help many times in the past. Too many times.

He looked at his watch. "I better get back up there," he said.

Thrusting his hands deep into his pockets, he headed down the sidewalk toward the hospital doors.

I didn't see Analise the rest of that month. She'd gone to the Hamptons to convalesce; I was busy finishing up a semester of teaching. She finally returned to New York in May 2005, which I remember because school was almost out. When I went to visit her at her apartment, she opened the door with her bag already slung over her shoulder. "Want to help me run an errand?" she asked. We headed right out again.

She still looked slightly shaken. She had lost some weight too. We started walking west toward Chelsea and she fell into a desultory account of the days just past. The beach house was the perfect place to gather her thoughts, the sand got into everything, she told J.B. she didn't want to see him for a while, the social scene was crazy but she avoided that.

"How's he taking it?" I asked, steering her back.

"Junebug? He's pissed. Says it's all my fault—I should quit the business before something worse happens."

"And what do you say?"

She cackled, giving me a glimpse of a more cynical Analise. "If I quit, where are you going to steal the money to launch your cinema empire?"

Was this how these events were going to affect her? I wondered. I pictured a pilgrim's progress from innocence to experience that left her with the same Machiavellian approach to life she despised in her own parents. The psychology of entitlement *required* a victory. Was that the difference between her and the girls who didn't "get" it?

Maybe she felt guilty, because she softened her tone. "You should check in with J.B. sometime. He likes you. And you're both making movies now—maybe you can do some business."

"I don't exactly make his kind of movie," I said.

"I realize that. But all that porn stuff is a side thing. He's going legit, or at least he will be. I think he's making some kind of urban-thriller-lower-depths thing. You can talk about aspect ratios or whatever."

She stopped at a plain red metal door in a brick wall, putting her hand on the knob and grinning at me. "And you always wanted to hang around rich people—excuse me, investigate their secret codes."

With that, she pulled open the door and led me into the building, which turned out to be an art gallery under construction. A pair of workers were running wires and putting up wallboard.

"This is what kept me going," Analise said. "I kept thinking about this place."

"Is this yours?" I asked, surprised.

"Yes! I mean, not yet, but soon, I hope. Kate owns it now."

She'd been talking about doing something in the art world for years, but it was only when the money started pouring in—a few weeks before J.B. started stealing it, in fact—that she realized the time had come. Her friend Kate happened to be looking for investors, so it all came together quickly. She even managed to convince her mother to chip in a few dollars. With time and more money, she hoped to invest enough to become a partner. Impressed, I realized she was playing the game on a level almost inconceivable to Angela or even Margot: not to make the rent or lay up a nest egg, but to build wealth. They were selling piecework; she was creating leverage. Her sense of entitlement unleashed her ambition.

She led me to the back, where an older woman was issuing instructions to someone over the phone. "If they want us to host, it will have to be after December. Tell her we're getting full, so she better act fast."

She looked up at us and spread five fingers, the universal hand signal for *Give me five minutes*. Analise led me into another small room, where the walls were raw and the desk was a door on saw-horses.

"My office," she said.

My heart leapt. "Your *office?*"

For the first time that day, Analise gave me a big smile. "Boy, do we have a lot to talk about."

Again, I thought of Angela. Her Brooklyn apartment had been the first step toward some kind of financial stability, a small-business dream to clean ill-gotten gains, sign up for a credit card, and someday maybe even move back to the Dominican Republic with a little retirement savings. I'd lost count of the number of times she'd dreamily narrated this story, as though she was the lonely office worker staring at a postcard of Tahiti in her cubicle in mid-January. Manjun and Santosh and so many others did the same shuffle between illegitimate and legitimate economies, flout-ing the law when they needed to but always hoping for the day when they would be freed up from sex work altogether. For Analise and her crew, the jump between legal and illegal was more like a game, and losing didn't mean death or prison; it just meant "Go back to Start. Do not pass Go." To Analise, the chance to invest in Kate's gallery was just a chance to advance to the next round and talk about herself with a new clarity and purpose. She wasn't slum-ming; she was an *entrepreneur.*

Just at that moment, the other woman called her name and we went back to the main room. This was Kate. She seemed to know all about me. Carrying a pack of cigarettes and a cup of coffee, she led us out to a small backyard and the requisite smokers' table and began to explain the situation as if I had come for that exact pur-pose. Which I suppose I had, without knowing it.

"Analise is going into the art business. It will take a year or two, but not much more than that."

I looked at Analise. She took a deep breath and presented her case as if I were a jury—just as when Shine tried to convince me he had philanthropic intentions when he beat the crap out of the young black men who worked for him. "I decided I'm going to be really good at this, and I don't care about the consequences."

Was she serious? Was this some kind of psychological mechanism to allow her to keep moving forward?

"I was foolish—I admit that. I put myself in a vulnerable position. Because I was doing things halfway, playing at it like a little rich girl. So I have to decide, am I going to let some drunk asshole run my life? Some guy who beats up women? That's who gets to make my decision? Or should I find a way to *deal* with it?"

At this point, Analise's speech became halting. She still hadn't figured out all the details, but the intention was clear. She was going to escalate her work as a madam. For the foreseeable future, which she expected to be of short duration, she would throw everything she had into the trade. Earn enough revenue, launder it through Kate's gallery, where she would slowly build up an equity stake, then get out of the game. The key was to dive in deeper and focus her energies on running a productive business. She vowed not to get beat up in hotel rooms anymore, as if that was something she could completely control. She began talking about the ways she would be helping the Jo Jos and Kimberlys of the world, though she didn't push it very far, because even she knew that charity didn't suit her. But she was clear on the main point: no more lollygagging; time to get serious and make a real go of it. In the great American tradition, she was determined to offer the best possible service for a good price.

Female empowerment seemed like an odd issue to bring into this decision, but it wasn't the first time I'd heard prostitution put in those terms. Streetwalkers and high-end escorts alike talked about the autonomy and feelings of self-efficacy they earned from the skillful sale of their bodies. And they were always talking about their savvy exit strategies. Managers like Margot and

Analise were especially prone to this. In fact, nearly every escort service manager, madam, and pimp I'd ever met loved to talk about the day they would quit. Very few really enjoyed directing other women to sell their bodies, and the ones who did often turned to drugs to numb their pain and guilt. Some of this was endemic to the life of any hustler, however. I had heard Santosh and Shine speak of similar dreams. This seemed to be a natural product of the strange relationship to the future people have when they start experiencing success in the black market. They realize that the only real future is with the thieves that come after their money and the police who come after their freedom. So they pretend the future is bright.

Shakespeare said it best: if you have no virtue, assume one. But watching Analise put on her new disguise as full-time-madam-for-a-while brought the illusion and the danger home to me. I could see how it helped her push ahead through her fear, but if she actually started believing in her fictions, where would she stop? What dangers would she overlook?

I also had an intuition that the relationship with Kate was not going to work out. It was just a feeling, but the thing about laundering money seemed like a bad sign. Analise was taking on too many risks. She was wealthy and she didn't need to worry about hiding and laundering her cash. That was the kind of thing Shine and other ghetto entrepreneurs had to worry about. So why go into business with Kate? What did Kate give her that she felt she was lacking? Something didn't feel right.

Maybe Kate sensed my skepticism. She tapped her cigarette against the edge of the metal table as a reflective expression came over her face. "I've known Analise since she was a baby," she said. "Our families spend summers together."

The phone rang and she said she'd be back in a minute, crushing her cigarette under the toe of her stiletto. Analise began filling in the rest. A musician, Kate quit school to travel and her father cut her off. Her mother still sent her money through their lawyers, but she didn't touch it, said she'd give it to her kids when the time came.

"Why an art gallery?" I asked.

"A lot of men come here," Analise said. "She gets to know them real well."

I sighed.

At least she'd finally decided to let go of Brittany, she said. "She's acting totally crazy. She's calling up people at their offices and setting up dates herself."

Point by point, she filled me in on the rest of her business plan. There were planned investments in new artists, especially beautiful young females who would attract wealthy men to the gallery, exhibitions and liaisons with galleries in Paris, Rome, Mumbai. I couldn't tell whether the illicit activity would be going global as well, but this was still the upper-class version of Shine I'd been searching for. Analise was also moving "downtown," and using new connections to create new moneymaking schemes and capitalize on the worlds she could bring together. "Reach out and touch someone" was being given an uglier meaning. I did my best not to be judgmental, but I felt I was seeing a life unravel in front of me, with little of the empathy I felt when watching Carla or Angela succumb to similar pressures and desires. I realized then that the distancing effect of being a professional observer actually allows you to feel things you can't feel as easily with your own friends. You expect more from people closer to you. You allow yourself to get angry with them. Maybe this was another reason I tended to study the poor. Maybe I really did find safety in their difference, even though I kept telling the world that treating them differently was patronizing. It was something to think about later, when things were more calm.

unwinding one business, developing another, learning a complex new culture, and avoiding the cops. No wonder he looked so harried.

But no matter how sordid the world, there was something heroic in that dogged expression of Shine's. He wasn't going to give up. He was going to take on his sea of troubles or die trying. Drug dealer and thug he may have been, but sometimes it was hard not to admire him.

To the police or the city government, Shine's attempt to fire young men and hire new staff might look like empty scenes from a TV crime show—a little tension, a whiff of danger, nothing more. In fact, Shine was deftly managing one of the most significant transformations in the inner-city labor market to occur in decades: the decline of the vibrant crack economy that had given thousands of part-time jobs to the disadvantaged. Refusing to fade away like so many of his peers, he approached the problem in a way that was methodical, precise, and keenly self-aware—just the attributes the manager of a complex business would need.

Adaptations like this are another thing too many sociologists ignore. They tend to see people living in the margins of society as people stuck in some kind of rut. Successful people are proactive, they're seekers and strivers adjusting and readjusting to the world around them, the thinking goes, so the poor must have lost their drive somehow, or never had any. Or in another variation on the theme, the poor live in neighborhoods that rarely change, that remain economically and racially segregated, while the world around them is eating Asian fusion and watching British actors play American cops on TV. It's the old myth of the "undeserving poor," always a justification for cutting back on social programs. But Shine and Angela and Carla and Manjun were just as hardworking and conscientious and proactive as anyone in the middle or upper classes. Just like big-time capitalists, they took huge risks and struggled to keep up with New York's fast pace and endless competition. Though their personal income levels and the socioeconomic status of their neighborhoods might not be shifting greatly, they were not the passive subjects so many sociologists used to fuel their paternalistic claim as all-knowing fathers for societal orphans. In fact, they were quite dynamic in both thought and action, and they also scrambled to keep up with a world that was transforming blindingly fast, even if the benefits of all that creative destruction did not accrue to them quite as rapidly as to wealthier strivers.

As my tone may hint, this is a pet peeve. For the last decade, I've been fighting the stereotypes of the poor that began to pervade American society after the publication of the infamous Moynihan Report in 1965, which argued that the history of slavery and generations of single-parent matriarchal families had created a "tangle of pathology" that made it difficult for many inner-city blacks to enter the social mainstream. The truth in this analysis took a backseat to the blaming, it seemed to me. White families had high divorce and addiction rates too, but their entry into the job market wasn't blocked by patronizing assumptions about their tangle of pathology. Suburbs also bred family dysfunction, not to mention some of the highest rates of alcohol and drug addiction, domestic abuse, and other forms of delinquency, but you didn't hear people talk about the tangle of suburban pathology. Poverty has been growing faster in the suburbs than in the inner city since 2000, but a dozen years later the cliché of the urban poor remains intact. My argument, based on the experience of my years in the Chicago ghetto, is that the poor are actually *more* resilient and economically creative because they have much bigger obstacles to overcome— just as a small house built by hand can be much more impressive than a mansion built by experts.

I was sentimental to focus so much on positive outcomes, I

knew. As any sociologist worth her degree can show you, American society is built in such a way that social class divisions are reinforced every day, not overturned. We tend to end up in social and economic positions much like preceding generations of our families. That's partly why social scientists can predict where one will end up by capturing only a few personal attributes, like race, education, parents' income, and so on. In the last twenty years, in fact, American class divisions have grown so durable that social mobility has all but frozen. Still we worship at the altar of meritocratic advancement, telling ourselves that success is just one lucky strike away.

How the sameness of class gets reproduced is not always easy to see. I've always preferred the sociologist Elliot Liebow's description, written nearly a half century ago as he observed "streetcorner men" in our nation's capital: "Many similarities between the lower-class Negro father and son . . . [result] from the fact that the son goes out and independently experiences the same failures, in the same areas . . . What appears as a dynamic, self-sustaining cultural process is, in part at least, a relatively simple piece of social machinery which turns out, in rather mechanical fashion, independently produced look-alikes." Exposure to the same circumstances is not going to yield highly novel outcomes for most of the poor. Expecting advances for the masses when the conditions don't change is folly.

Nevertheless, another rule in sociology says, *Don't let aggregate data explain individual behavior.* This is called the "ecological fallacy." Though Shine and Angela *could* end up looking a lot like their parents, trolling the ghetto and eking out a living, this was not necessarily a guaranteed outcome. And that's why outcomes are themselves deceptive. They tell you little about the aspirations that drive people to rise above their circumstances. Not only Shine and Angela but Carla, Manjun, Vonnie, Santosh, and dozens of others at the bottom of the income spectrum militantly refused to accept their predicted fate. They wanted something more, and were clearly willing to take great risks along the way. And the ingredients in the recipe seemed increasingly to include the ability to work across the city, not just in familiar neighborhoods where friend and foe knew one another intimately, but in parts of the city where the rules and norms were completely unknown and often upsetting.

Was that the magic ingredient? If so, what were its secrets? I wasn't certain, but clearly some of my subjects had more of this skill than others. As I kept discovering, mixing with strangers in unfamiliar worlds is no simple task. Santosh alone seemed to be succeeding on both sides of the spectrum, working smoothly with the undocumented but just as smoothly with the mainstream world. Manjun was out of the race. Angela was on the bench for a while, again. Carla and Shine were still in the running. Even if I never left the low-income world, I would feel I was seeing an amazing event, a veritable pageant of the human spirit. Despite the harshest of climates, they were so resilient and ever seeking.

But as a sociologist, I reminded myself again, I wasn't there to showcase survival. That wasn't what the people themselves were after. They never thought of themselves as victims seeking to overcome great odds for a few bread crumbs. In their eyes, they were pursuing an American dream in the Big Apple just like anybody else. It would be insufferably patronizing for me to talk about them as survivors. A question more true to their dreams would be: what traits helped people win and how did they acquire them?

To answer that question, I still had to get myself out of the ghetto and into the winner's circle. This was still proving to be surprisingly difficult—until the day I reached into a notebook and took out a small piece of paper that my friend on the police force had given me back when Manjun disappeared. At the time I'd been fixated on contacting Manjun and took it as Officer Michael's way of distracting me. Then the saga of Angela and Carla took over my life. But now I remembered talking to the officer about my dreams made their bust, Juan walked in, and everyone was happy—except Shine.

This fight with Juan was costing him. How much worse would it get? And how could he raise the heat without scaring the white customers and killing the whole business?

"All it takes is for one of those dudes to let the police know where I'm hanging out," Shine said. "I'm out there with no protection."

What it added up to was, Juan could use his relationship with these white customers to hurt the guy who'd given him the idea of forming relationships with white customers in the first place—a bitter twist indeed. And Juan's cousins were high-ranking gang members themselves, which meant that Shine had to work within a very narrow framework of acceptable street justice or risk violent retaliation. "That boy could fuck me over pretty quick," Shine muttered.

That was another surprise. Street-savvy entrepreneurs like Shine never admit vulnerability. They can't risk a chink in the armor. He knew he could trust me, but still—dealing in bars outside Harlem had clearly put him outside his comfort zone. A small shift in the cocaine market and all that was solid in Shine's life was melting into air. Marx would have been fascinated, Milton Friedman amused. The creative destruction of capitalism—*change or die*—was sending this resourceful and determined man into bars where he didn't know the manager, to hotels filled with security he'd never met, to white customers he didn't trust. And "die" wasn't a metaphor.

The frustration I'd seen on his face at the bar that day spoke volumes. In sociological terms, Shine was coming to the painful realization that he was missing some aspect of cultural capital, that he wasn't quite in line with the tribal codes of this new world. He could pull off the small talk—half the battle and no small accomplishment—but the rules of conflict still eluded him. And conflict was a sine qua non of life underground. People in Harlem's black market understood physical force. He could threaten a person or even their family members and everybody knew the limits. Nobody would dream of going to the cops, so you solved problems on your own, but self-reliance also increased the likelihood that force would be used. In sociological terms, physical confrontation was a social norm that had to be dealt with off the books.

But the white bartender? Who knew how someone like that would react? Shine kept muttering about the right ways to settle conflicts in the "white world." If you couldn't beat someone up, he wondered, what worked? Persuasion? Rational informed discussion? The whole thing was giving him a headache. He had tens of thousands in the game, he said, and he'd better figure things out before he lost the money and his reputation along with it. The only thing he knew for sure was that whatever he decided to do, he'd have to do it fast. "I might not be around for a few days," he said.

I didn't ask what he was planning. For my own safety, it was better not to know.

It took a while to find the right time," Shine said. His voice was very quiet.

We were alone in the kitchen of his mother's house. This was the first time I'd seen him since the day the tall black woman had come into the bar all coked out a few months earlier.

"Juan?" I asked.

He nodded.

My stomach lurched. His original plan, I remembered, had been to face him down at church. I pictured that skinny kid, imagined his dignified working-class parents standing at the church door talking to the priest. I saw them look down at the sidewalk and the expressions of horror and shame as they saw Shine confront their son. In a research study I would have filed this under "informal regulation mechanisms of the underground economy." Now dozen Amys. "I don't want to hear a girl say she dates 'serious' men from Boston," she said in a withering voice.

This disappointed me. Analise had been so welcoming, so open. She was the one rich girl I knew who was—speaking of class traitors—always ready to open her arms to outsiders. Now she was policing the very boundaries that kept women like Carla and Angela on the bottom.

Under the loose pages before us, Analise's brand-new cell phone began to vibrate toward the edge of the table like some kind of burrowing animal trying to escape.

As Analise reached for her phone, two women came through the patio door. I wasn't sure if they had just arrived or if they'd been in the apartment all along.

"It's freezing out there!" one of them shouted.

Analise didn't look up. "Yes, that's right. I'll need a large—no, a large. Yes, I know, but last time you gave me the smallest room in the hotel. A *large*. Okay, how many times do I have to say this? Do you speak English?"

The rest of us laughed. Analise could be so unforgiving.

"I want the room on the sixth floor, 623. Okay? And if you don't give it to me, then the three nights I book each week will go down to zero."

Analise looked up at us, rubbing her hands through her hair. "I give these idiots five thousand dollars a month. No appreciation." Then she made a quick introduction. "Kimberly, Jo Jo, Sudhir."

Both women had blond hair with dark roots; both were dressed casually in sweats and tights and leggings as if they'd just come from the gym or a revival of *Flashdance*. Jo Jo was smoking one of those long Nat Sherman cigarettes. We shook hands and exchanged rote smiles.

"I worked three nights this week," Jo Jo said. "I need a break. I'm going to Aruba."

"Too bad. Mr. X wants you Friday," Analise said.

Jo Jo pouted unconvincingly—apparently Mr. X was a valued customer.

"And me?" Kimberly said.

"I'm on the phone," Analise answered, waving Kimberly away.

"This bitch gets a full week, and you can't get me anything?"

Interrupted once again, Analise widened her eyes and cupped the phone. "Those are all *return* visits," she said, her voice cutting.

Kimberly glared at Jo Jo, who laughed and preened a little. "What can I say? They like my style."

"Fuck you," Kimberly said, taking a cigarette from the brown box on the table without asking.

There was a moment of silence; then Analise started talking on the phone again. "Hello? Yes, hi! Yes, it's me—you recognized my voice? Oh, Lord, that's so lovely in this day and age. Thank you. I'd like two tickets, but they have to be in the box—my client can't see very well and his hearing is not so great. Of course, five hundred sounds reasonable. Just hold them at the box office and I'll have a car come by in an hour to pick them up."

When Analise hung up, Kimberly asked in a sullen voice who was getting to go to a Broadway show.

Mercilessly, Analise shook her head. "The tickets are for Brittany, and not for Broadway—the Met."

Kimberly looked puzzled. "They're going to a museum?"

"To the *opera*," Analise said.

Her cutting tone made me fear for Kimberly's future as an escort, which snapped me awake. All of this was so sudden and novel, such a peculiar and fascinating new revelation about this remarkable person I thought I knew. This wasn't some happy little clubhouse for rich kids.

"I think maybe I should take off," I said. "You guys are—"

Analise frowned. "Oh, don't worry so much. No secrets here."

No secrets? It was *all* secrets. "I can't just sit here unless they

Vonnie returned after ten minutes. Carla would be okay, she said. She'd lost some blood and needed some stitches. Father Madrigal was inside. He wanted us to return to their apartment. The police were coming and it wouldn't be good for them to be here.

"I'm not going to leave," Angela said, stubborn in her loyalty to Carla. Vonnie tried to convince her the cops would be attracted to "three hookers" standing outside the hospital, but she wouldn't budge.

Finally, they agreed to go for a walk. They spent the next hour strolling through the neighborhood around the hospital and debating their options.

"I sometimes wonder what it would take for me to kill a man," Angela muttered.

The question hung in the blustery air. Her friends looked at each other, and then over at me.

"*Dios, Dios . . .*" Angela's voice trailed off. She rubbed her eyes and leaned on a rusted steel post, blowing into her cupped hands to stay warm. She shifted her weight back and forth, breathing heavily. An old pain in her right leg made standing in one position uncomfortable. She burrowed inside her pocketbook and pulled out three ibuprofen tablets, swallowing them quickly without water.

An ambulance passed by and turned toward the emergency room. The four of us looked up simultaneously. A group of twenty-something hipsters passed by us in a hurry, blowing smoke from their cigarettes.

"I mean, they just make you so angry. They get you real close to wanting to do it," Angela continued. Her voice grew shaky.

Vonnie reached over and pulled Angela into her chest. Angela started to cry again, the third time in ten minutes.

"You cannot protect people, you understand," Vonnie said. "God protects—not you, sweetie." The neon sign of the corner bodega flickered above.

Finally Vonnie's phone rang. It was Father Madrigal. The police would want to talk to each of them the next day. "Please, go back to the apartment," he said.

Reluctantly, the three women agreed. I rode back with them and got them settled in with some hard-earned vodka-and-Cokes. Out on the street again, drained and hammer-eyed, I went looking for a cab.

T he hospital discharged Carla two days later and she returned to her parents' house. When the other three women and I dropped by that afternoon to see how she was doing, the cuts on her face were still stitched and covered with bandages and the bruises on her arms had ripened to an eggplant purple. "I used that knife just like y'all told me," she said. "Cut him *real* good."

But her bravado had a brittle quality. We could tell she was still scared. Anxiety and fatigue covered her like an invisible film.

At the hospital, she said, she'd told the nurses she'd been beat up by her boyfriend and begged them not to call the police. But they did. If it hadn't been for Father Madrigal, the cops would have spread the story all over the neighborhood. At least he convinced them to be discreet.

Not that it would do any good. "He's going to come after me," she said.

No, he won't, we all assured her. The police would catch him first.

"I've been getting calls . . ." Carla said, trailing off. When the women dug it out of her, it turned out she had given the guy her number. He was calling and hanging up. It had to be him. And he knew about the apartment too. The one thing Vonnie had feared had now come true.

"You told him?!"

"Not exactly."

dangled off his wrist—not exactly corporate, but not quite "street" either.

"You win the bet?" the barman asked, cleaning a few glasses.

"Knicks lost," Shine said. "Again."

"Man, you don't learn, do you?"

There was a pause and then the barman said quietly, "I'll be on a break in about twenty if you want to grab a smoke."

Shine nodded. Although he showed no expression, just the usual somber ghetto warrior face, I knew he was growing a little depressed about his inability to find customers. He knew he had to be patient, but the days without revenue were starting to pile up. So far the staff of this bar had been perfectly happy to "grab a smoke," but hadn't introduced him to any potential customers. He knew he had to take the time to build relationships, but how much time?

"Hey, man. You're back," a voice said. A young man with shiny black hair combed tightly back over his head (with a liberal dose of gel) came over and patted Shine on the back. "Michael. Remember me?"

The young man made a motion to the bartender for another round and gave Shine another pat. "Come over—join us. I'm getting killed in this game. You should take over."

We looked over at a group of young white men and women, all standing with beers or pool cues in their hands, all fresh and new to the city, their youth contrasting with the stained wood and stained-glass lamps.

Shine hesitated and for once I could see through his armor. He was nervous. *Welcome to the club*, I thought.

"Yo, Chris! You want to play?"

Shine looked blank for a moment, then snapped alert. "Shit, that's me."

I'd wondered what name Shine was using in his life outside the ghetto. Now I knew. "Laugh at their jokes, Chris," I suggested. "White people like that."

"Fuck you," he said, punching me on the arm and stepping past me toward the pool table. I swiveled my seat to watch him. He towered over the others around him, not just because he was taller. His presence simply took up more space. He was silent, they were chatty. He was still, they were jumpy. His black skin shone.

A young woman approached the group, clearly interested in talking to Shine. But he ignored her. She smiled, but he kept his movements small, as if he was wrapped in plastic, probably because he believed that too much expressiveness "makes white people feel threatened," as he put it once.

The woman started talking to him, asking questions and not letting monosyllabic answers discourage her. I decided to weave my way over and listen in. When I got close enough, she was talking about the thrill of Manhattan.

"I want to do something special," she said. "*That's* why I moved here. Isn't that what New York is all about? I mean, you live here. You *know* this."

"Right, right," Shine was muttering.

"I mean, I'm not going to be working in this shitty office job for long. I'm going to have this really cool fashion line, for everyone. Like this! See this dress—do you think people in New York would like it?"

"Sure," Shine said.

"Hey, Abbie! You have to meet Chris—he knows everything about New York. Abbie's going to be an agent. She's got this amazing job. She gets to go hear music all night."

"Right," Shine said.

Finally, the barman came over and asked Shine if he wanted to step outside for a smoke. Michael said he would join them.

When they returned, Shine said it was time to go. He didn't

. . .

Toward the end of that summer, I decided to take Analise's advice and check in on Junebug—in my mind, that's what I still called him. I had seen him a few times since the night at the hospital, once at a screening and once in his production offices, when he was a completely different person—much more at ease and in control. He even got me to suggest some "urban" story lines for his next movie. Now that he was in production on a legitimate film, I was curious to see how he was managing the transition.

I dropped by his new office a few days later. The scale of his operation surprised me. At least ten production people were drinking coffee amid legal pads and laptops, a pair of whiteboards were covered with scheduling details, props and costumes awaited final touches. "Sorry, Sudhir," he said. "We're running a little late." Then he turned to his crew, all business. "The new pages won't be here until Monday, but everything is the same in terms of the schedule. So let's try to get the casting done—which means you, Jimmy. Try to focus on the job instead of chatting up the hotties."

When they were finished, J.B. asked me to step outside on the roof to smoke a cigarette. "Never go into business with friends. My dad keeps telling me that."

"Those guys are your friends?"

"I went to boarding school with them."

"Lost any yet?" I joked.

J.B. smirked. "I'm not sure I ever had any to lose."

They were all part of an investors circle, he explained. They had money but no experience, and they all wanted to get into movies, so they'd each put up a half million bucks for a shot at the glory of cinema. "Which means that everybody gets to give their input," he said with another cynical laugh.

They had been doing this for a few films now, starting with

student films and then porn and now this. I asked how much money they'd spent so far.

"A lot."

"Lost much?"

J.B. laughed. "I put fifteen grand into dot-com stocks just before the crash of 2000. I'm never playing the market again."

I understood the lure of films, I said. You could reach such a wide audience. But I couldn't conceive of gambling away thousands of dollars.

"That's the difference between you and us," he said, shaking his head as if in pity. "We know you have to get in the game and stay in the game. Because once you're in the game, you're *in the game*."

Back inside, I handed J.B. an outline I had written for him—Carla's story, basically, starting with the beating and then her push into the escort business. I expected him to put it aside and read it later, or not read it at all. Instead he asked me to sit down and leaned back in his desk chair like a mogul, holding the pages in front of his face. A few minutes later he tilted forward and slapped the pages on his desk. "These are *great*," he said. "Let me pay you for this."

"I'd rather get to know your rich investor friends," I said.

He laughed. "Never going to happen."

"I don't want to *poach* them."

He knew what I was after. He cocked his head and gave me an appraising look. "What do you make of this tribe, Mr. Anthropologist? Figured it out yet?"

With that, I knew I could eventually get him to cooperate. Despite his cloak of cynicism and the standoffishness that seemed to be part of having money, he was as susceptible as most of us are to Carl Jung's great maxim: *The desire to reveal is greater than the desire to conceal.*

"I have a few theories," I said.

One theory, in fact, was that my initial assumption about the

remoteness of the rich was wrong. I had a hunch that Analise's newfound commitment to life as a madam and J.B.'s playful resistance to my interest both shared the same eager motive. Analise wanted to prove that her skills and savvy outweighed her wealth, and J.B. wanted me to see him as something more than a category (preferably, as the next Samuel Goldwyn). Both wanted me to see them as making it on their own. They wanted me to recognize them as authentic themselves rather than mere products of their gilded environment—which struck me as bitterly ironic, since poor people, authentic almost by definition, rarely seemed to give a damn about whether they made it by pulling up their own bootstraps. Those who had so little were only too happy to take help from anyone willing to give it.

But J.B. just laughed and slapped his hand down on my pages again. "Don't waste your time, Sudhir. This is the real stuff—real poignant human shit. We could make money with this!"

The next time I heard from Analise, she was calling to ask for advice. Her frustrations with Brittany had put her on a roller coaster. One day she loved her, the next day she wished they had never gone into business together. Today she was ready to get rid of Brittany forever but wasn't sure how to do it. The parallels to Shine and Juan struck me again. Brittany was feeling the same kind of cocksure rebellion as Juan: *Look how great I'm doing! I can make it on my own! Why do I need to carry this guy?*

Having Tito arrange a beatdown didn't seem appropriate, so I had to tell Analise that I had no great ideas to offer. But, of course, I'd be thrilled for an opportunity to observe as she fired her.

"We're going to meet at the gallery space on Thursday," Analise told me. "Bring your brass knuckles."

When I arrived, Kate and her staff were in the front of the gallery preparing a photographic exhibit on street life in New York

City. Pictures of crowds crossing Times Square were interspersed with shots of small family businesses in Canarsie, East New York, Astoria, and other communities in the city's outer boroughs. The pictures were simple and beautiful. Most were taken by European photographers because a prominent European car company had underwritten the exhibition.

I went straight to Analise's office. She looked good, elegant as always and perfect for a gallery. The first words out of her mouth were: "To be honest, I'm not sure I ever imagined doing this without her. That's my fear. Not that I couldn't do it, but we're kind of joined at the hip."

I pictured Juan's face, that stubborn refusal to accept how things had changed. "I thought your mind was all made up," I said.

Analise hesitated, biting her lip, and I could see how deep the problem went. Underneath all the confidence she was trying to exude, she was deeply anxious about the unknowns ahead. Brittany and J.B. weren't just employees or business partners. They were a part of her foundational network, and I was beginning to understand that the business of border crossing was more complicated than just mustering the courage to explore new worlds. It also meant leaving old worlds, or negotiating a new relationship to the old worlds. The poor ghetto entrepreneurs who feared leaving their own little fishbowls weren't just afraid they'd be eaten by bigger fish; they were also afraid of being greeted as outsiders when they tried to return home. Even Analise, with all her entitled individualism, still needed the comfort of a network. Crossing boundaries didn't mean leaving your friends, family, and former business partners in the dust; it meant trying to keep the old while finding the new—not so much developing new networks as *extending* the networks you already had. Margot was the exception—her friends and family had shunned her. But for Analise, Brittany wasn't just a friend and contractor but also a reminder of who she was and where she belonged. Shine could have just moved to another bar and left

Juan behind, but that would have left him a little more alone. The underlying challenge was existential: if in a world so big Juan was just a loose end, wasn't Shine kind of a loose end too?

"Yeah, but anyone can *say* those things!" Analise laughed. "You have to *do* it." Then she sighed and shrugged and let out a small laugh. "I guess the problem is, the men she brings in are the most steady—it's never just a date here and there. It's the guy who wants to come back. And that's all Brittany. She gets them to return, like, several times a month! No one else is that good."

Brittany arrived at the gallery an hour early. We were both surprised. She walked into the back room, where we were sitting, and immediately lit a cigarette.

Smoking wasn't allowed in the gallery. Analise was about to tell her to put out the cigarette, but Brittany read her mind. "I don't care! This is not my greatest day, Analise. But you wanted to talk so here I am."

Analise didn't seem to know how to start. I sat silently, trying to disappear.

"Well, are we going to talk or not?" Brittany said. She was obviously high, no doubt on cocaine.

Analise took a deep breath. "You're screwing up," she said. "*A lot.*"

"That's one way of looking at it."

"Oh, yeah? What's the other way of—?"

Analise stopped herself in midsentence. She tried to calm down.

"You don't do what I do," Brittany continued. "That's the fucking problem, Analise. So unless you know how to make it out there, I'd try to be less fucking bossy. You've been a real fucking pain in the ass lately and I'm tired of it."

That got Analise going again. "You're pissing people off," she said. "Showing up late, not showing up, showing up wasted out of your fucking mind. You can't piss everyone off, Brittany, and just think it's okay and nothing will happen."

Brittany just puffed on her cigarette, as if she was alone at a bus stop.

"The hotel, Brittany," Analise continued. "You really think it was okay to yell at the bartenders, to trash the room, and then just leave the guy sitting there like that? He has a wife, Brittany. You can't just . . . *expose* people like that."

"Fuck you, Analise. Really. I mean, I can't take it anymore."

Analise stared into her hands. She took out a cigarette and started walking toward the door.

"That's it?" Brittany yelled. "We're done?"

"I don't know anymore, Brittany. You're such a fucking pain to work with. You don't seem to want to work with me, and to tell you the truth, I'm finding it hard to work with you."

"You know what, Analise? I'll make it easier for you. *I'm* done. That's it. How about that? Does that solve your problems?"

"Yeah, it kind of does," Analise said, her lips pursed in anger.

Brittany got up and stormed out, which left Analise looking stunned. She walked slowly out of the office and toward the back of the gallery into the garden.

Analise had broken up with Brittany many times, but they always forgave and forgot, or almost did. This dated back to their school days, but it was actually not an unusual pattern in the escort world, where sex workers frequently quit on a manager or agency only to come crawling back a few months later. Economists call this "sunk costs." It was hard for Analise or Shine to get rid of people because they had already invested so much time and effort trying to make it work. Friends just call it loyalty.

But this time, it was different. After storming out of the gallery, Brittany started making moves on some of the other girls who were working with Analise. She was better at finding customers, she told them. They could make more money working for her. This betrayal Analise took hard. The next time I dropped by the gallery to find out how things were going, she excused herself for a quick trip to the bathroom that left her sniffing and starry-eyed. She fell back into her chair and let out a big sigh. "I have to do something, or else I'm finished."

"What do you mean, 'finished'?"

Brittany had poached five of her best clients, she said. "I can't risk having a catfight, you understand? I would rather just get out, just stop everything, than let the news get out that I'm fighting with her. Can you imagine what would happen? I mean, she's got such a big mouth."

"Well, maybe it's a sign," I said. "I mean, is this *really* what you want to be doing your whole life?"

Analise shook her head. She had a better idea, apparently. "Shine is going to help me."

So there it was, the arcs of my story connecting. I wasn't too surprised. After Shine and Analise met in the art gallery, I had a sense their lives would intertwine. Of course, I hated the idea. They would have met at the party anyway, but I couldn't shake the feeling that I was responsible. And I was jealous too, I have to admit. But the scientist in me—thank God for him!—was excited. The connection Analise and Shine had made was precisely the point I was trying to make with my work. The global city was bringing together people of varying classes, ethnicities, and backgrounds, and here was *une liaison dangereuse* as poignant and lucrative as any other. The novelty wasn't necessarily the upstairs-downstairs quality. That was as old as the city itself, or older—you could reach back to Mesopotamia to see slaves and nobles courting. But here was a business venture that blurred all the ready-made distinctions between legal and illegal commerce, that required the collaboration of two brokers to translate the languages and codes of two different worlds. Shine provided the coke, Analise provided the clients. Shine provided the muscle, Analise identified the parameters of the conflicts. As much as I didn't really want to see this play out, it made complete sense. The question was, how long would it last? Could they survive the inherent tensions that had sunk Angela?

The truth was, the change in Analise depressed me. When I was a kid in college, the idea of entropy struck me hard: all that is solid melts into air, creative destruction, and so on. A factory is always one innovation away from becoming obsolete. Everything is always in the process of falling apart. The bourgeois succeeded because they *didn't* cling to tradition. Instinctively, despite all their protestations to the contrary, they embraced entropy.

Entropy rang true to me because I was going through so many personal changes. It rang true in New York's underground too. Everyone was constantly on the precipice of change. You had to learn how to get out, change your focus, accept losses, fail quickly, and move on. Success required self-awareness.

This was the theory. But in practice, I hated to see Analise going through this particular episode of creative destruction. Shine too. They both were failing, but their ambition and nerve wouldn't let them quit. It was heartbreaking. Maybe their resilience would help them solve each other's problems, or maybe they'd drag each other down to destruction, exposure, and arrest. There were dangers I knew all too well, dangers that could sink them. One was obvious. The police are all about patrolling social boundaries, and many of them hate the sight of "salt and pepper" mixing in the same shaker. But police actually arrest few black marketers. There are simply too many of them, and an arrest could spark violence from newbies fighting for market share. The real hazards would be linked to the inner demons that fueled their ambitions—greed, jealousy, reckless behavior, an inflated sense of their capacities. Selling drugs or running an escort service isn't what usually lands you in jail, after all. It's the inability to approach your involvement in a moderate way. Too many people want to be a kingpin. The handful who grow slowly and never deal with strangers are rarely caught. That's why crossing boundaries screams *"Danger!"*

Examined with colder eyes, the adventures of Shine and Analise could be a fascinating experiment. Two very different people with very different cultural assets, both were struggling to thrive in the invisible economy. Which assets would be most useful? Which would be most destructive?

From what I'd seen so far, I would have to conclude that the low side of this particular high-and-low equation had more power. Shine understood the black market and didn't shy away from the messiness. He had a better sense of when to push forward and when to pull back. He was protected by his ghetto cool, his mask of indifference. Like other drug kingpins I'd seen, he knew that today's failure could be tomorrow's success, and slowing down or taking a loss could be the key to staying in the game for the long haul. But Analise didn't seem to have those instincts. Her ambition and elite recklessness clouded her judgment. She wanted to be in control of everything and also wanted to throw all caution away. Maybe this too was an aspect of her elite culture code, a privileged person's refusal to scale back to a more modest operation that would let her scrape by without the glamour of a big success. But there was danger in the way she kept talking about some happy place in the future when the dirt of her illegal enterprise would be magically washed away. She thought that people like her made the rules and could break them too. But dreamers don't thrive in the world of crime. The underground is perfectly suited for the self-aware business manager who knows her limits, and what the market (and the cops) will bear.

The whole thing was like watching a car crash in slow motion: you're helpless to stop the inevitable and wincing with every crunch of metal. But too close for comfort also meant that I couldn't turn away. For better or worse, I had to see what would happen next.

CHAPTER 8

EXIT STRATEGIES

Margot called, asking if I'd like to come watch some of her missionary work—lately, she had been helping her "contractors" organize their financial lives, teaching them basic investment principles, persuading landlords to give leases without background checks, even cosigning loans. She was becoming more and more obsessed with the idea of exit strategies. "We all exit," she told me more than once. "You can do it at thirty or fifty, but one day you're going to stop—and then what? These girls have got to learn to *think*."

Obviously, she was talking to herself.

This was a subject scholars of sex work rarely explored. Many of the women at Margot's level of the industry had high school diplomas and college degrees. They certainly had acquired experience as skilled hosts and conversationalists. They had learned to navigate complex social situations and negotiate with a wide variety of people. But they couldn't exactly put their skills on a résumé. How did they make the transition to a normal life?

Today, she had invited two prosperous escorts, Morgan and Fiona, to her apartment. They were both very attractive, very well-dressed women with Prada on their backs and Blahniks on their feet. I had previously interviewed Morgan extensively—I was up to 150 interviews now, a good, solid data set—so there was already a level of trust when we all sat down.

Margot poured tea from an English china pot. She offered milk and Splenda but no sugar or half-and-half. Then she dove in.

"Listen, I want to tell you something. Based on my experience, you're going to either die, get caught, get a disease, or lose all your money. I want to help you avoid that."

Morgan and Fiona looked at each other. "That's a bit of a surprise," Morgan said.

"Yeah, we thought you were going to ask us to go into business with you. I was thinking, where's the champagne?"

"How silly of me. You're the first hookers in history to put away a few grand. I should be asking *you* for advice."

"You called us, Margot."

"I did. 'Cause I want to help you. Sudhir's the researcher, so he can correct me if I'm wrong, but most of the women who get to the point you're at begin to fade away."

Margot looked over at me and I shot her a look that said, *Thanks for dragging me into this.* But I played along as best I could. "Most of the women I've met do start to run into trouble because they're not smart with their money," I said. "Planning for the future is not a strong suit among the people I've interviewed."

"We're not idiots," Morgan said. "We save a *lot.*"

"You have *cash,*" Margot countered. "And even then you had to fuck that apartment broker to get a lease. What if you can't fuck the next one?"

Actually, it had been more complicated than that. Morgan had persuaded the broker to waive his fee and sponsor her at the bank, which enabled her to pass a credit check. In exchange, she had been sleeping with him for approximately three months without collecting any money.

"Fiona, you're no different. You've fucked half the city because you can't get a credit card."

Fiona scowled and began fiddling with her cigarette pack.

"Look, you guys are smart," Margot continued. "A lot smarter than the other bozos I know, God bless them. At some point, you're going to want to do something different. So I have a proposal for you."

Morgan shrugged her shoulders, giving in. Fiona followed her lead.

"My estimate is that you each have about five thousand in the bank, maybe a little more but not much. You think you're going to build it up, but let's get real—on the cab ride over, you probably talked about going to St. Barts for a week or at least down to Miami Beach, right? You work so hard, you deserve it. And there's *guys* there! There goes the five grand. And you have to buy clothes, right? There goes another two grand. And I bet your credit cards are maxed out if you have credit cards, so you're blowing stupid money on bank fees."

Margot paused and watched the truth sink in.

"I'm not telling you to live in a cave, but you need to *change your relationship to money*. Here's my suggestion. Start lending out some of the cash you've saved. At a decent interest rate. Don't rip people off, but start turning your cash into *profit*. I've done this. I'm telling you, it changes your way of thinking. Instead of money for things, you think of money for *money*—for the future."

Morgan looked interested now. "How much could we make?"

"By the end of the year, your five grand could be seventy-five hundred. Without fucking anyone."

Seeing that she had them, at least for now, Margot continued in a rush. Find women and give them cash advances, get them to pay back a little each week, never let them skip, and keep *all* the money in the bank. She used a credit union on Long Island, where she opened an account for each woman and linked it to an account she controlled; each week the money just got subtracted from their accounts into hers. Then they had to start doing straight jobs, just a few hours a week but enough to get a legit paycheck. Waitress, hostess, whatever. They would have to cover the years without straight jobs when they went looking for a real one.

After thirty minutes, Morgan still seemed skeptical. "Maybe you're right," she said. "But still, lending money . . . what if they don't pay up?"

That was the beauty of small sums and weekly payments, Margot explained. "You never lose too much. And it doesn't happen as often as you'd think. Most hookers are basically honest, not that they get any credit for it."

Morgan still wasn't convinced, but by the time they left, Fiona said she wanted another meeting once she'd had a chance to think it over. Or maybe she was so grateful finally to be getting her nicotine fix, she just wanted to make nice. I closed the door on her and turned to Margot.

"No way this is going to work," I said.

Margot sniffed. "I'm not an idiot. If I can get one out of ten to see the light, that's fine. And you don't know everything."

We sat down again. She told me that she'd been telling some of her contractors—she always called them contractors now—that she was quitting the business soon. At first they all thought she was crazy. Lots of midlife crisis jokes. But soon they started to call her up—always secretly so that no one else would hear—to ask how she was going to do it.

I could see that Margot was in some kind of pain, probably feeling guilty for her role in their lives as sex workers, and guilty for abandoning them too. This was common, something I'd seen many times in all illegal work, whether it was street hustlers earning a few dollars a week or high-level drug traffickers pulling in hundreds of thousands a year. Some kind of guilt always ate at them. But most couldn't even dream of another life. That was what made Margot different. And part of this, I couldn't help feeling, was the inspiration of New York City itself. Margot knew she was a player in the big show. She wasn't just good; she was one of the best. That gave her a kind of social capital I hadn't considered until now, the confidence to make a change. And even while she was pining away for a quiet house in the Southwest, she still day-dreamed about the many businesses—dancing clubs, catering and entertainment businesses, cruise ship tours—she could start in New York. Each one fed the same underlying fantasy of helping other women to avoid subservient relationships to men.

I thought this over and shook my head. "Margot, you're going to miss all this."

She winked at me. "You are too."

I laughed. She was right.

"You love being out there at two a.m. in some shitty little club," she said.

"And you love running hot girls like Morgan," I said.

"Yeah, but *you* think you're different. You tell me how nuts the rich kids are, how amazing the poor people are, how much you feel for all the poor, suffering hookers. But we're *just like you*. That's what you can't admit."

She was right again. This time I didn't laugh. "I'm here because they don't have a voice, Margot."

She shook her head as if she was disgusted with me. "*They* have a voice, Sudhir. They talk all the fucking time. *You* don't have a voice is the problem. You feel like they could *give* you one. So you run to them—the feeble, the sick, the criminals, the crazies. Why do you always go to them? Think about it. Why do you always try to find in them *something about who you are*?"

Margot was onto something, I knew. I didn't like it, but she was right. I'd been doing this same kind of work for twenty years. Even though I was now aiming for the middle-class women and the rich, the motive wasn't much different from when I studied the Chicago projects. I wasn't exactly going for the wealthy lawyers or accountants. Even when a few called, like Martin, I ran away. I wanted the loners and the outcasts. I felt alone and different and sought out acceptance and wisdom from those who were equally stigmatized.

Thinking about it amplified my discomfort. I didn't want to study these worlds forever, I kept telling myself. But even as I spent my nights in the underworld of New York, I was also occasionally flying back to Chicago to follow the journey of the public housing families I'd studied over a decade ago as their homes were demolished and they found new places to live. More than 80 percent of them were ending up in neighborhoods just as poor and segregated and crime-ridden as the project towers they'd left. Dozens of tenants would call me just to talk about their inability to find a home, pay rent, or control their son or daughter in the unfamiliar new environment. Kids were dying; parents were going to jail. It was Groundhog Day, ghetto style. The definition of depressing.

With the wounds of my divorce still fresh, I also couldn't help resenting Margot a little bit. Her question turned me back inside. Was I studying the poor out of some prurient desire to feel better about myself? Many social scientists study inequality for their entire lives—I was hardly the only one—but there were probably fewer than a dozen who chose direct interpersonal contact over weeks and months and years. The surveys and phone interviews other researchers used helped them maintain a healthy emotional distance. I defended my need to see misery firsthand as a search for truth, but was truth an excuse for voyeurism under the cloak of science? Were my own prejudices and needs driving my search?

But what would I do if I didn't do this?

I left Margot and went straight to a strip club to do an interview—three interviews, actually.

My *n*'s were getting bigger all the time.

. . .

As 2005 was coming to an end, Angela called to say that she was leaving for the Dominican Republic. She was feeling depressed and wanted to be around family, she said. But she had a parting gift. She had found some Eastern European women and some Latinas who had managed to penetrate the upper reaches of the sex trade. They had all agreed to talk to me. If I came over to say good-bye, she would give me their phone numbers.

When I arrived at her apartment, she was making Sunday dinner. The smells reminded me of the old Brooklyn apartment, and I almost expected Vonnie and Father Madrigal to walk in the door.

Instead, Carla showed up. "Surprise!" she said.

They were friends again? How did it happen?

"Margot!" Carla said. "I learned a lot from her."

"Carla is like a queen bee around the bar," Angela said, so proud she might have been talking about her own daughter. "Helps everyone. I'm so proud of her."

I knew that Margot was having a positive effect on Carla, if you can call changing from streetwalker to escort a positive thing. She was proud that Carla had become a "great date" and was now booking about four high-paying clients each month. Taking Margot's advice, Carla had decided to stay in a subsidized apartment back in her old neighborhood and save her money to buy a condominium in the Bronx.

"I have a picture of the building hanging above my bed," Carla said.

I smiled, picturing Margot telling her to "visualize" her goal.

But Carla parted ways with Margot on one point. Margot thought Carla should limit her contact with friends and family in the projects. Get up and go to work and stay out of the drama, she'd said. *Your friends will drag you down much quicker than anything you might do.* Culturally and emotionally, Carla couldn't accept that. Leaving the fishbowl was not so easy.

I could see it from both sides. After all the drama surrounding the rich client who'd wanted to beat Carla up, when Margot finally started helping me again, I began beefing up my *n*'s with a much wider range of upper-end sex workers. I had spoken to women who worked in suburbs and in cities; some worked part-time, supplementing their regular jobs, while others saw sex as a full-time vocation. Some just danced at clubs—avoiding physical encounters—while others were phone sex operators. Soon I'd have enough to launch an expansive study of women who worked in three cities—Miami, New York, and Chicago. What particularly fascinated me was that their backgrounds were so different from either the streetwalkers I'd associated with Angela or the blue bloods in Analise's employ. The women Margot found all hailed from small towns in states like Arkansas, Kentucky, and Pennsylvania and worked as far away as Chicago, Los Angeles, Washington, D.C., and Miami—the global city as a network of cities. They approached their work in a much more businesslike frame of mind, changing their names and pooling expenses to buy condos and using a variety of Web-based platforms, from Facebook to Craigslist. One group had even formed an investment circle to take advantage of tips and advice from their rich clients.

Margot kept trying to impress these lessons on Carla. "They never look back and neither should you!" Margot liked to say.

But Carla would never leave her friends and family. She would probably never even leave the Lower East Side, despite that picture of the condo in the Bronx. In fact, she had already used some of her savings to give loans to a few friends who wanted to try what she was doing. They needed clothes, didn't they? She even had dreams of becoming the Margot of Avenue A and was already, for a small commission, helping some young streetwalkers with dates and advice. "Sudhir," she said, "these women *need* me."

The words were eerily familiar. Like Margot and Shine and Angela and Manjun and all the rest, success meant nothing to Carla unless it was reflected in the people she cared about. Her social capital was also her social cost. I couldn't shake the thought that philanthropists never won in the black market, or that Carla's charitable instincts were a reflection of her anxiety about her own future.

When she went off to make a phone call, I asked Angela what she thought about all this. Wasn't Carla risking her investment? Wasting time and energy she needed to create her new life?

Angela shook her head. "If Carla was meant to make it out there, *mi amor*, she would have done it by now. I'm just happy she's not on the pills."

"But I thought the whole point was to get out of here, get off the streets?"

"We're not like you, Sudhir. She's nobody without us. She couldn't put on her *panties* without us."

She laughed at that, then became serious. Margot wanted Carla to be white, she said. And that just wasn't going to happen.

I remembered the words of the contractor back in Chicago who'd told me he hated taking jobs in white neighborhoods. "The ghetto's like a fish tank," he said. "You struggle all the time trying to make enough to get out of the tank, but as soon as you get out there and feel the heat, you try to jump back in." This was more complicated than fear of a white planet. If you spend your life on the edge of a cliff, you know you need people to help you in times of trouble. Carla had had the experience of that rich white client who'd beat her and got his money back. She had no recourse, no established social system to support her. Why would she want to put herself through that? But in the ghetto, everyone knows everyone and everyone owes everyone and there's always someone who would do you a favor—who *has* to do you a favor.

This was the diametric opposite of Analise and J.B. and their dreams of heroic individual achievement, which explained a lot. There was no doubt where my sympathies lay. But the problem was, Carla's choice exposed her to new dangers. If she was trying to manage teenage streetwalkers, you didn't need a psychic to see another slow-motion car wreck coming her way.

A few months later, I found myself in another kind of fish tank. This one was an elegant Park Avenue apartment with a Lichtenstein print hanging on the wall and a small ivory Buddha sitting in a wall sconce lit by a small spotlight. Analise's friend's place. They were in Bermuda for the week.

I drifted into the kitchen, where Analise's guests looked like they were straight out of the J. Crew catalog—young men dressed in mock turtlenecks and blue blazers, a few skinny bored girlfriends. A full spread of sushi, caviar, champagne, and holiday cookies on the counter. Copper pans hung from a rack on the ceiling; a giant stove looked big enough to feed an army.

And the black marble countertop made a splendid surface to cut cocaine on, judging from the lines spread out in a boastful array.

And there was Brittany, swaying through the room in a gold Carolina Herrera dress with one naked shoulder. She had landed in trouble and come running back to Analise, of course, and she was worse than ever. She'd gossip about Analise's escort service to anyone who would listen, talk openly about trips to Paris with clients, brag about sleeping with UN diplomats because they "had immunity and so no one goes to jail!" Her sense of privilege seemed to undermine the modesty and self-awareness a person needed to think tactically, which made the threat of some kind of explosion constant.

As Brittany sloshed around the room, a single thin strap worked overtime to keep the dress on her shoulder. To me it seemed to evoke their whole hanging-from-a-thread operation. On her right ankle, she wore a sparkly diamond chain that added another touch of decadence to her black-heeled shoes. With one arm around an unsuspecting man, she put a hand gently on the small of his back and used the other to raise up her skirt just enough to show her panties. Then she laughed like it was all a big joke.

Shine stood idly at the living room window, an unlit Kool dangling from his hand. He looked sharp in a black beret, clutching a rocks glass filled with whiskey and Coke. His sleeveless shirt made a display of the tattoo on his biceps, a crucifix with a legend written in calligraphy beneath: *He Knows.*

J.B. was talking to him. "I'm probably going to the Rose Bowl," he said. "It's incredible, man. Maybe someday I'll take you with me."

Shine looked at him with thinly concealed disdain. "I guess I prefer the Sugar Bowl myself," he said.

J.B. said one of his films had run into "creative" problems, so he was back to making porn to raise some fresh capital. His grand plan was to use some of the girls who worked for Analise. He fiddled with a new pack of Dunhills and sighed. "Analise and I want to leave," he said.

"The party?"

"The city," he said. On a sailing ship, one of his father's smaller vessels. It would be a good break from all this, once the porn flick was finished.

Shine scowled, doubtless thinking the same thing I was—nice fantasy if you could get it, and J.B. probably could. But lesser mortals could not.

Shine smiled and gave me a curious look. "Well, you finally got out of my neighborhood." He turned away and looked out the window toward Harlem, as though he wanted to be saved from what New York had become.

A few minutes later, Analise started banging on a bathroom door. "Brittany! C'mon."

From inside the bathroom, Brittany groaned. "That fucker told me this shit was clean."

Analise shook her head in disgust. "I bet you don't even know the guy's name, do you?" She hit the bathroom door one more time and told Brittany to get her shit together, goddamn it. A moment later Brittany came out, looking dazed. "Did Michael go home? Where did that fucker go?"

"I gave him to Jo Jo," Analise said.

Brittany shot her a furious glare. "Fuck, Ana!"

"You're too wasted," Analise said, her voice icy.

"You're like my fucking mother sometimes," Brittany said.

During their breakup, Analise had told me that she and Brittany would always be in each other's lives. Now I saw what she meant. They were locked in the same battle forever, Brittany insisting she was indispensable and demanding constant emotional stroking, Analise forever trying to turn Brittany into a slightly less controlled version of herself. I wandered away in a state of melancholy tenderness and spent the rest of the evening standing in the kitchen talking to Evalina and one of J.B.'s depraved preppy filmmakers. At different times, I glanced across the room and saw Analise and Shine together, or J.B. and Analise together, or Analise and Brittany together. I had a feeling that they were all in a space capsule together, floating in a weightless world.

Finally Analise walked over to me and asked how I was doing.

"This is weird," I said.

She led me out onto the balcony so she could smoke a cigarette. Shine was already out there smoking.

"You okay?" Analise asked.

"I'm okay," I said.

"You don't look okay, my brother," Shine said.

I tried to laugh. "Truthfully? Don't you think it's strange that you two are working together? Don't you think it's strange that you and Brittany are back together? And what about J.B.?"

But Analise shook her head. "The problem isn't us," she said. "The problem is you."

Shine nodded. "She's got a point, Sudhir."

I was completely floored. My Harlem broker had met my Upper East Side broker and together they were running a citywide brothel, and *I* had the problem?

"I'm going to be honest with you," Shine said. "Since I've known you, you been meeting up with all these people—Manjun and Angela and Carla and Martin and Margot and all these people—and you don't *do* nothing with it."

Why were they attacking me? I was an academic trying to penetrate a variety of subcultures in hopes of writing that great book or documentary. I had done studies. I was gaining access, entrée, insights. This was Margot all over again.

Shine continued. "You think I'm uptown and she's downtown and how the fuck can we hang out? *Fuck* you, man. Why the fuck not? You doing the same thing. You teach them rich kids uptown, you make films downtown with downtown people. What makes you so different?"

A good question, I had to admit.

"I'm done with this shit in a year," Analise said. "Shine will move on to another level. None of us are fixed in place, Sudhir. But *you* are. You go from story to story and group to group but you're always in the same place, looking in from outside. And now you're freaked out because you don't know what's inside and outside anymore."

She was right. That was it exactly. How odd that the ultimate insider, America's daughter, understood me better than anyone. I was trying to make a box big enough to fit everyone into and she and Margot just climbed right out and pointed at the box *I* was in. They finally broke through my Chicago framework and put me in that New York state of mind I'd heard so much about. It was probably the same reason Martin freaked me out so much, because his world came too close at that vulnerable moment in my life. I couldn't maintain my borders.

"But that's what's so great about this city—everyone who *wants* to be different *gets* to be different. It *doesn't matter*."

With that, she threw her cigarette off the balcony and followed Shine back into the party.

Shine shot me a look as he walked away. He didn't need to say anything because his expression said it all. *You can't stand there watching or the wave will hit you. At some point, you gotta choose.*

A few months after that, Angela called. Carla had been beaten up once again. She had gone to a hotel room where one of her teenage protégées was working. The date was going bad, the woman called Carla from the bathroom, and Carla arrived to find the man tweaked out on coke and the girl locked in the bathroom. The man beat Carla so bad she couldn't answer questions in her hospital bed for three days. When she came out of her daze, she kept telling Angela how proud Margot would have been.

Angela wanted me to put her in touch with Margot. "Carla won't listen to me. Says, 'Only Margot understands what I'm trying to do.'"

Margot had been in the Southwest, looking for a new place to live. But I got in touch with her and we made plans for the three of us to visit Carla at her apartment.

When we got there, we found Carla propped up on some pillows that looked as if they'd been borrowed from a child's bedroom. She was all bandaged and bruised and crazed from painkillers and humiliation. She wanted revenge, she said. She was going to get Ricky to go kick that motherfucker's ass into the next world.

Margot took a small chair and pulled it next to the bed. She stared at Carla, ignoring her talk of revenge. Finally Carla pulled herself up on the pillows and spoke through clenched teeth. "Why is it that you can do this, but I can't? I'm no idiot. It's not fair."

"Stop feeling sorry for yourself," Margot said. "That's the worst thing you can do."

"It's not *fair*, Margot," Carla cried.

"Fair? No, it's not. But why am I here?"

Angela and I were standing at the back of the room, by the door. I saw Angela look at Margot curiously, wondering what kind of strategy she was using. I was wondering the same thing.

"Carla, why am I here?" Margot repeated.

"I don't know," Carla said meekly.

"Well, if you don't know, I don't know either." Margot looked around the room, taking me and Angela in too. "I'm done with this. I'm getting out. You want to whine and bitch, you do it to Sudhir—*he's* not going anywhere."

"I'm not whining," Carla said.

"Yes, you are! You're whining! I'm so sick of listening to whores whine about their pathetic fucking lives, Carla. If you want to play in this game, you have two choices: either you let the girls get beat up or *you* get beat up. Someone's going to get beat up. Which one do you want?"

Carla didn't know what to say. "I don't know. I—"

"Well?" said Margot. "Which is it? Them or *us*?"

"These are my friends," Carla said. "I'm not letting no asshole beat up my friends."

"See, that's your fucking problem, Carla," Margot said, standing up to leave. "Those hookers are *not* your friends. They *work* for you. They're the thing standing between you and a better life. Get your head together and stop being a whiny little bitch."

With that, Margot walked out of the room. Angela and I followed her through the dank hallway, into the dimly lit elevator, and outside the housing project building, a twenty-floor monument to government paternalism that seemed particularly futile on this sad night. In fact, I thought, Carla and the building had a lot in common. She wanted to be there for her friends and offer a helping hand as they tried to make it as prostitutes in a world that was the definition of nasty, brutish, and short. She wanted to be their Angela and make them feel good about themselves, she wanted to be their Margot and make them learn to better themselves, but all she had learned from her journeys across all those borders was how to get her ass kicked. Now Margot was telling her the same thing all the critics of government support said. Low-cost housing and welfare and health care and that sweet Angela love just made you weak. To win at this game, you had to be tough. You couldn't be their friend. You had to be like Shine. You had to know when to cut your losses and move on. It was, in the end, a business.

At some point, you gotta choose.

I'm sure Angela and I were thinking the same thing. Carla was running this race handicapped. She didn't understand what it really meant to manage people, how to motivate them to survive the nightly abuse and also motivate *yourself.* That was what Margot had lost, the reason she was quitting, the reason she was so bitter. She had begun to succeed as a manager, she had often told me, the day she accepted that *somebody* was going to get hurt. Being violated was part of the game. But at least she could choose not to be the victim.

It was all so sad. Angela was going to go back upstairs, at least. God bless her for that. She shrugged her shoulders and started to wipe her eyes.

"I'm sorry we had to meet like this," Margot said, and now the compassion was back in her voice.

"Yes," Angela said. Just that and nothing more, but it said everything. She squeezed my hand.

Six months later, Carla killed herself.

. . .

The calendar turned again. It was now 2007, a full decade since I first came to Columbia University and the city of New York. I was in a strip club in northern New Jersey looking for new venues for another study of the sex economy. I needed to find club managers and dancers who would talk about the journey so many of them took from dancing to full-time sex work. In this bustling industrial corridor just outside New York, the strip clubs were small neighborhood places where the TVs showed the game on mute while women danced to loud rock and roll. The owner of this one, a gruff but amiable fellow named Jimmy, had studied sociology at a community college and liked to talk with me about growing up in the working class. Twenty feet away, a young Latina woman was sitting on the lap of a burly white man wearing a green Caterpillar hat. She reminded me of Carla. With each beer, the burly man grew rowdier. Jimmy got up a few times and made a move in his direction, and each time the man waved him off with a promise he would calm down.

Suddenly, the burly man threw the young Latina down and put his foot on her throat. He poured his beer on her face and then dragged her out of the bar by her hair.

Jimmy went into the back of the bar and grabbed what looked to be a short baseball bat. I followed him outside, along with a dozen other customers. The burly man had pinned the young woman against the outside wall of the bar and he was smacking her in the face with his open palm.

Jimmy walked up to him as the burly man wound up for one more strike to her face. Just as he put his fist in the air, Jimmy clobbered him with the bat across the back of his neck. The man lost his grip and the girl fell and Jimmy swung the bat again. *Whack! Whack!* The man fell down next to the girl.

Then Jimmy pulled the girl up and told her, "That's it—you're done. I don't want to see you back here. I told you nicely that you weren't ready, and you didn't listen. So get the fuck out."

He turned to the small crowd and told them to go back inside. "People are trying to sleep. Let's be respectful."

I slid down against the wall. My knees were weak and I was about to throw up.

Jimmy came over and grabbed my arm with the same hard grip he'd used to drag up the Latina. "No," he said. "Don't do it."

All the faces of all the women I had seen in situations like this came swimming into my head. Carla. Angela. All the horrible stories I had heard.

"Don't go there," Jimmy said.

I tried to talk, but it just came out like this: "I can't . . . I can't . . . I can't . . ."

A week earlier, the night we had met, I had told Jimmy that I was nearing the end of my work. The nights were too long, I explained. I was getting worn out. "Bullshit," he'd said. "You're scared—I can see it. You want to save these women, and you don't know how, and it's eating you up." He felt the same way, he said. All these crazy women reminded him of his wife. Men were protectors, and it didn't matter whether she was your wife or some low-rent streetwalker. It hurts to see them like this. Especially when you can't do anything about it.

Now he said, "You *can*. Go home, but come back. Come back once. After that, you can stop. But you have to come back once."

He lit a cigarette and gave it to me, then lit another one for himself.

"You can sleep here if you want or you can go home, but it's important that you come back. Get back on the horse."

"I'm done, Jimmy," I said. I started to cry and I buried my hands in my face, embarrassed that he was seeing this. The study I wanted to complete, the book I wanted to write, the documentary film I hoped someday to complete—I was sick of everything and ready to throw it all away.

"Someone has to get beat," he said. "That's the game. Someone gets fucked up, gets a beating. You can't change it. Go home."

He walked back into the club as I sat and sobbed. *Someone has to get beat.* First Margot, now Jimmy. The image of Joshi came into my mind, arranging his toy soldiers on his knees. It was all just too hard to accept.

Finally, I pulled myself together and called a cab. On the long drive down those dark industrial streets toward the lights of Manhattan, a strange thought came into my head. In the ragged alleys of Newark, in the strip clubs of Manhattan, in the back of a porn shop in Hell's Kitchen, on the elegant sofa of an upscale madam, I had found a community. Like Mortimer, the dying man who depended on the kindness of prostitutes; like Martin, who found comfort among his fellow johns; like Angela, with her tolerant priest and the small army of sex workers who loved her, I also had people looking after me. And I had the advantage of growing success with the research that mattered so much to me, a morale booster if ever there was one.

With the help of Angela and Margot, I had gathered enough contacts in the upper-end of the sex trade to launch a study of several hundred women in several cities, and I finally managed to build a big enough sample of women to satisfy the scientists of mainstream sociology. But the truth was, all my scientific detachment about the "informants" and "research subjects" was a dodge, along with my glorious collection of n's. Margot was right about me. In a vast city where I felt alone, in a country where I had been struggling to find my own way, I had searched out a small army of weary soul mates who did their best to point me home. And this wasn't some character flaw or research failure but the business of life working itself out, especially life on any kind of margin. These improvised communities gave support and also resonance. Their lives rippled through me, my life rippled through theirs, we extended our support systems outward through one another and into the beyond that threatened and beckoned us. The only real difference was that I was also taking notes, quantifying and categorizing, applying the tools of science to the journey we were all taking together.

And Jimmy was right too. I had to come back. Even if it was just for one more night, I didn't want this to be my last memory of the underbelly world. I owed all of them that much. I owed them so much more.

I saw Margot one more time. She said she wanted to hear my proposal for the regionwide study of the sex economy in New York. But when I showed her my list of the issues I would be studying, she gave them a quick glance and went back to talking to me as if I was a client. "Make a list. You want interviews? Fine. You want to meet more people like me? Fine. Cops? Whatever you want, let me know. But do it quick because I don't know how long I can do this."

A few months later, she quit the business and moved to Arizona. I never saw her again.

Angela called me once from the Dominican Republic, but I didn't even get a chance to speak to her. She left a message on my answering machine saying she wanted to put the past behind her.

Shine I met a few more times. Once it was back in the old bar, having a drink at the end of the day. He had a bad cough and was as gloomy as an accountant at the height of tax season, loaded to breaking with everyone's miseries and lies. He asked what I was doing and I told him I was giving everything up for a while—no more sex workers, no more johns, no more rich kids. I was even taking a break from the documentaries. It was all too much for me. I couldn't figure out a way to hold it all together.

"It's probably a good time to take a break," he said.

I sensed the pity in his voice and rejected it. "It's not a break, Shine. I wanted to map all the patterns and figure out the code. I wanted to find a way to connect everything. I wanted to show that people like Angela and Carla and Manjun weren't so different from people like Analise and J.B. I wanted to show them a way out."

That was the truth. This wasn't about science. I wanted to show them a way out and I had failed. "I *failed*," I said.

With that, emotion welled up from so many places. Memories of the porn store, of the apartment in Brooklyn, of the time I accompanied Carla to that diner to meet with Margot. I even remembered the magazines I looked at in the newsstand when I left them alone to get to know each other. *Foreign Affairs*! I felt like crying and kept pouring the feelings into a soliloquy about New York and my fear that I would never really figure out this enormous protean city no matter how big a study I could build. "*I failed*," I said again.

Shine met my eyes. He took a deep breath and glanced up at the television and put an ice cube in his mouth, sucking on it pensively. When he looked back, I got the feeling he had returned from a distant place. "Did I ever tell you how my older brother died?"

I shook my head.

"Nigger came back from the Middle East, post-trauma or whatever they call it, all depressed and hopeless about everything. Violent sometimes, real jittery. He used the same word. *Failed*. 'I failed.' I told him, 'Don't ever use that word. Say *changed*, brother. Say, *I changed*.'"

Shine put his drink down. Our eyes met.

"And you?" I asked.

"When I was little, I used to go downtown. Did I ever tell you that? I used to go and look at all the art. Man, I loved it."

"Your brother told me," I said.

"So there I am, hanging with all these white boys. I'm thinking, man, if I could put that art up in *my* house . . ."

"You want to open up a gallery?" I said.

He nodded. "Maybe. Maybe I do. And white folk helped me figure it out—shit, I never thought I'd say that!"

At that moment, I realized that Shine was going to be fine. He might even turn into a big success. My hunch about his low power was right. He had a way of accepting his past and all the fumbles, mistakes, and missed opportunities, and he was perpetually *open* to new worlds and new opportunities. He had a way of forgiving himself. Maybe it was those childhood trips to the Metropolitan. Maybe it was New York. Failure would never define him. Longevity did. And in the underworld, that was half the battle. Learning to step back, reassess, reimagine.

As if he could read my mind, he turned the tables and asked me a startling question. "Can you still write a book?"

"What?" I said.

"Can you still write a book?"

He said it as if this was the obvious question only a simpleton would overlook. And the truth was, it was precisely the question that was secretly tormenting me. I owed it to Angela and Carla, to Manjun and Analise and even Shine himself to rescue from the stream of time all the moments and truths they had shared. Maybe their little piece of reality represented the whole or maybe just a part, but it was still human and true and added something to the sum of knowledge. And telling the story was another way to extend their explorations a little further out of the fishbowl.

But it all felt so far beyond me. I still had so many more questions than answers. Thrown, I made a tree-falls-in-the-forest joke. "If you write a book and no one reads it, did you really write a book?"

He laughed, and in that moment I saw that he wasn't worried about me either. He had a hunch about my powers too. The thought gave me strength.

. . .

My last serious conversation with Analise also took place in a bar, but it was much different from my conversation with Shine. While she nursed one vodka tonic after another, she talked about turning over her operation to Kate and either investing her free cash in the art gallery or pulling her money out. Or she would go to India and help expand her uncle's school. Then on to Paris, where there was an opportunity to open up a clothing boutique. Her world was a Romper Room of second chances, a tribute to the endless vistas of globalization as practiced by the rich.

"On August fifteenth," she said, "I'll be in India and it will be like this never happened."

The alternative was turning into a version of her mother, staying on the Upper East Side and living a comfortable life without meaning or challenge.

"Most of my people have no purpose," she said. "They have causes, but no purpose. The best I can do is to keep on going."

But I was still reacting to her weightless vision about the global Romper Room ahead. It didn't seem fair that she had so many options and others had so few.

"The problem with your people is that you all believe this is *your* world," I said. "You guys make the rules and you can change them whenever you need to. Dabble in prostitution or go off to India and teach the little brown children—and there are never any consequences."

"Let's be realistic. I'm done with New York. And isn't that what you wanted? For me to quit 'dabbling in prostitution'?"

All I could do was laugh. "I don't even know where to begin. Most people I see are so utterly aware of consequences. Squatters, drug dealers, gang members—they're all acutely aware of what the future might bring."

"But so are all my friends," she said. "It's a basic human trait to be curious about how you act and what will happen. That's why I'm going to India. I get to reinvent myself. My family is here, but I can leave them for a while. I can be someone else, which is what I always wanted."

I knew I wouldn't see her again. Even though I had never launched a formal study of Analise, I had been in this place before many times when previous studies neared completion. The exchange is never a simple one. As hard as it is to spend years observing someone in the criminal world without developing all kinds of complex feelings, good and bad, it is equally difficult to be the one who is observed. The time comes when the thing just naturally wants to end. So I decided I would treat her the way I treated any research subject when the study was over, just close the book and move on to the next tribe—which was, I suppose, exactly what she was doing too. It's natural to blink before you turn the page.

But before I got a chance to say good-bye, she asked about my plans.

As Shine suggested, I tried to begin my speech with "I changed." And as I spoke, I realized I actually liked her approach to reinvention. Like Shine, she had the gift of being open and it was her strength as it was his. India had been her Metropolitan Museum, perhaps, the thing that gave her a talent for detachment from her class. I wished I could have embraced the same detachment so quickly and decisively myself.

"I'm not sure what I'll do. Probably write a book on sex workers. But part of me really wants to make films."

She gave me the look of disbelief she always gave me when I talked about making documentaries, even though I had already made three of them by that time. Doubtless J.B.'s film career colored her opinion. But I also think she might have been telling me that she didn't think they were my real talent. And I knew she was

right too. What I was good at was listening to people for a long time, the way I had listened to her. *That* was what mattered.

But I wasn't as decisive as Analise. Maybe I didn't have that luxury. Instead, like Shine, I had to sit for a while and let it all sink in. I had to figure out a way to bring together all the worlds inside myself, the ethnographer and the scientist and the filmmaker and the guy who hung out with strangers until they became friends. I had seen something unique in New York, I was sure of that. Even my colleagues at Columbia had become supportive, encouraging me to keep taking the roads without street signs, the roads that led across borders most people didn't know existed. In a short while, those roads would take me into worlds I could never have imagined entering, from the Department of Justice to posh Madison Avenue advertising agencies, where listening to people's stories and uncovering sociological truths turned out to be just as rewarding as it could be in academia. After all my anxiety and growing pains, the university's long history of interdisciplinary exploration and emphasis on public involvement made it a perfect intellectual home.

I contemplated making another list: "What I Saw and Heard and Felt in the Underbelly of the Global City." Instead, I just started writing about the people I had met and the stories I had heard. For the first time, I wasn't judging New York based solely on what made it different from Chicago. It was possible for me to imagine my experience there on its own. I had come to New York as a sociologist trained to see the city of the twentieth century, with its fixed ways that spoke lovingly to the traditions and bonds that made America so inviting, the importance of neighborhoods and the power of community. At the same time, on a personal level, I arrived in this city famous for welcoming newcomers as a newcomer eager to take advantage of the city's willingness to permit reinvention and rebirth. I discovered that the new globalized open city suggested, in itself, a radical new approach that would echo the world it was absorbing.

But the global city didn't wipe out the older virtues. In this sense there were more similarities between New York and Chicago than I first realized. Place still mattered in New York, neighborhoods still had meaning in New Yorkers' lives, and the ordinary sense of home was still rooted in familiar neighborhood ecologies that lent comfort and security. But the global city also retrofitted and turbocharged these behaviors for a bigger stage. Because New York created connections at dizzying speed, but many of them didn't last—*the key to success was the talent to use and lose improvised social ties.* Exploit them when they could serve you and discard them without too much grief when they didn't, just as Santosh put away the memory of Manjun and moved on with his life, as Margot packed up and left the women she had tried so hard to save, as Shine and Analise shrugged off their old costumes and stepped into new roles. The recipe for success seemed to involve a particular form of self-awareness, a gift for detachment from the fixed comforts of neighborhood and class and identity even as one sought to leverage them: forgive your sins, let go your failures, create yourself afresh, and live for another day. After all, there are always new opportunities. The city constantly changes. So why not you?

Was this possible for everyone? Hardly. In fact, most of the people who tried to float ended up sinking, especially if the measure of success was class mobility or economic advancement. Most of the people whom I met when I arrived in the city were now either dead, isolated, stuck in some rut, or remaindered to daily survival with little but their regrets to sustain them. Nevertheless, the very same people exceeded my fondest sociological caricatures. Whatever box I used to define them proved limiting because they didn't define themselves by their outcomes.

There is a famous Chicago saying: "We don't want nobody nobody sent." Translated: go at it alone, dream of making it by yourself, and you'll end up alone and defeated. The protections of clannishness create their own limitations, many of which are clearly

mental. But in New York there is a greater sense that boundaries are rooted in perception alone. They are not permanent obstacles. Over and over, the experiences of everyone I met showed me that a strange encounter or changed circumstance was an opportunity to be seized. Manjun could have left the porn shop when he found out that it was linked to the sex trade, Margot could have walked away from her Wall Street suitors when they offered to pay for sex, and Shine could have remained content to roam about his back- yard rather than befriend Midtown bartenders. The connections that New York forged were not a fun form of tourism but opportu- nities for economic mobility and social advancement. Unlike Chi- cago, where relentless ambition was frowned upon as a sign of unneighborly behavior, New York gave you license and added fuel to the fire. It *encouraged you to question your station in life*. And, yes, some people failed. The old stories of race and class still had rele- vance, though they were less predictive. Margot and Analise walked away with more money and new opportunities, while Angela and Manjun and Carla found it harder to escape. But Shine and San- tosh learned from their ethnic and social limitations and continued to press forward.

The threads connecting the global city may be invisible, but they can be found *in stories*. Just as when a pioneering group of Chicago professors went out, a century ago, into a city reeling from the turbulence of immigration and massive economic changes and wandered the alleyways and skyscrapers gathering up stories with- out judgment or evaluation, giving birth to a pragmatic, boots-to- the-ground, uniquely American school of sociology, stories were once again the best and possibly the only way to make sense of a chaotic place like New York. Because each story *was* a thread, and only by weaving them all together could you make anything whole. The classic New York stories of aspiration and transgression are sociologically useful not just because they evoke the voice of the storyteller, putting flesh back on the *n*'s abstracted by science into data, but because they *reveal the structure of the city itself.* That first scene at the gallery when Shine and Analise crossed paths, for example. As a data point in a computer graph it is almost meaningless. But seen through the pattern laid down by our accumulation of stories it becomes yet another tale of improvisation in a world of shifting values and social roles. And if the upper-end madam and the ghetto thug were both improvising their supposedly fixed social roles, if their way of relating and even their styles were subject to such rapid revisions—as if they were merely a fiction agreed on between two people—then it was a short step to admitting that succeeding in a life of crime wasn't so different from making art. The global city, like the canvas, provided the structure, but the rest was in the individual's hands, making each Angela and Manjun a kind of artist whose art and job consisted in crafting the latest, most up-to-date version of themselves and offering it to the city for final judgment. Is this the "me" that will finally make it?

As I mentioned earlier, a diverse group of leaders, from government leaders to foundation presidents, has begun to make similar arguments. The skill, ingenuity, and resilience of those taking an "alternate economic path" in life cannot be boiled down to the laws they transgress, they say. From Accra to Chennai, Shanghai to São Paulo, global cities in their sheer enormity have taught us that the underground economy gives millions of people their only chance at survival. We ignore their needs (and potential contributions) at our own risk. If this book helps encourage that trend, no outcome could make me happier.

Some time after this, I did see Shine one more time. It was at a party somewhere on the East Side. We didn't really have that much to say because we'd said it all already, but I remember that we stood together and looked out the window on the glittering city below us. I thought of describing the films I had made, the studies completed and the tenure achieved, evidence that I had changed instead of failed, but I managed to suppress the urge. We stood side by side in comfortable silence. The city below us was as endless and baffling as it was when we'd met ten years before, and it would still be just as endless and baffling a hundred years from now, an infinite array of options and challenges and invisible threads waiting to gather us into its numinous weave. And maybe I still didn't see the pattern complete, maybe I would always have more questions than answers, but I had to keep extending my little community of words out into the world just as Shine had to keep selling drugs and dreaming about that art gallery. Because this was New York City, and those twinkling lights were a million different worlds beckoning us with their delicious possibilities of knowledge and commerce. We might not know all the answers, but at least we knew what we had to do.

We had to *float*.

ACKNOWLEDGMENTS

My colleagues in the Department of Sociology, the Committee on Global Thought, and the Institute for Research in African-American Studies provided vibrant intellectual spaces to grow and mature as a sociologist. Herbert Gans challenged me to write intelligibly so that I might contribute to a more enlivened public discourse. William Julius Wilson remains a caring and generous mentor. Saskia Sassen, Farah Griffin, Steven Gregory, David Stark, Shamus Khan, Alford Young, Alexandra Murphy, and Eva Rosen were wonderful interlocutors. Doug Guthrie saw me through this journey, patiently telling me to exercise patience. Katchen Locke was supportive and wise throughout.

Ann Godoff saw a book early on, where I saw only scribbles. I couldn't have taken a step without her leadership. Suzanne Gluck taught me how to find my voice; the authors in her orbit find themselves enriched beyond words. John H. Richardson held my hand—and sometimes my pen—and taught me how to tell a story. David Lobenstine read early drafts with the right mix of insight and prodding. I'm indebted to Andy Celli for his grace and counsel, and to Stephen Dubner for constant encouragement.

Jonathan Knee, a terrific writer and colleague, gave generously of his time, scanning each page with the eye of a master storyteller. Larry Kamerman introduced me to cinema. His own films have been an inspiration and few are better teachers of the craft. To

Matt McGuire, Sunil Garg, Nathaniel Deutsch, Ethan Michaeli, David Sussman, Baron Pineda, and Daniel Brown, I'm eternally grateful for your friendship. To Robert and Judy Millner, thank you for opening up your hearts and your home. I couldn't have studied sex work in New York without the support of the Urban Justice Center. They work tirelessly on behalf of sex workers and they remain a beacon for those with nowhere else to turn. Maxine Doogan taught me more than anyone about the daily struggles of the sex work community—and she spoke up for me on countless occasions when the arrows came my way. Thank you, Maxine.

More than anyone else, my father helped me survive elite education; he taught me to remain confident when waters were unsettled. Little did I know he was also teaching me how to be a father to my own son. From my mother, I learned the value of giving voice to those less fortunate. My sister, Urmila, is that compassionate and loving person you can't live without.

My wife, Amanda, is the loveliest person I know. Thank you for Theodore.

AUTHOR'S NOTE

I began researching New York City's underground economy in 1997. Commuting from Massachusetts made an extended study impractical, though I did manage to develop contacts with several black marketers. In 1999, after joining Columbia University, I was awarded a grant to gather oral histories of black Americans in New York and Chicago who worked in the city's illegal trades. That body of work culminated in a monograph on the underground economy of one Chicago neighborhood.

For New York, the experience catalyzed my interest in economies that transcended a single neighborhood. I worked with the Sex Worker Project at the Urban Justice Center (UJC) on their study of indoor sex work. My students and I collaborated with UJC staff to interview sex workers living and working in all five boroughs of New York City, as well as northern New Jersey. We completed interviews, which were given to the UJC, and we kept field notes on our own about our experiences speaking with people in the sex trade. That material was featured in a UJC report and an academic publication.

After my work with the UJC was completed, I began gathering material for a documentary film. I also launched a formal study of the middle- and upper-class segments of New York's sex trade, which ended in 2009; material from that study is currently being prepared for academic publication.

This book is a memoir of these experiences. As such, the bulk of this book is not appropriate for mainstream academic social science publications. Only the formal research findings have appeared in academic publications. Some parts of the book are based on field notes, others on personal diaries and journals, and the rest is based on memory.

In an effort to conceal the identities of some people and organizations, for the sake of protecting their privacy in some cases and to maintain academic protocol in others, I have adopted pseudonyms—although all the people and organizations portrayed are real, and no composites have been created. I have also altered dates to ensure that the incidents reported could not be traced back to the actual persons who were involved.

INDEX